IMAGES
of America

MARYVILLE

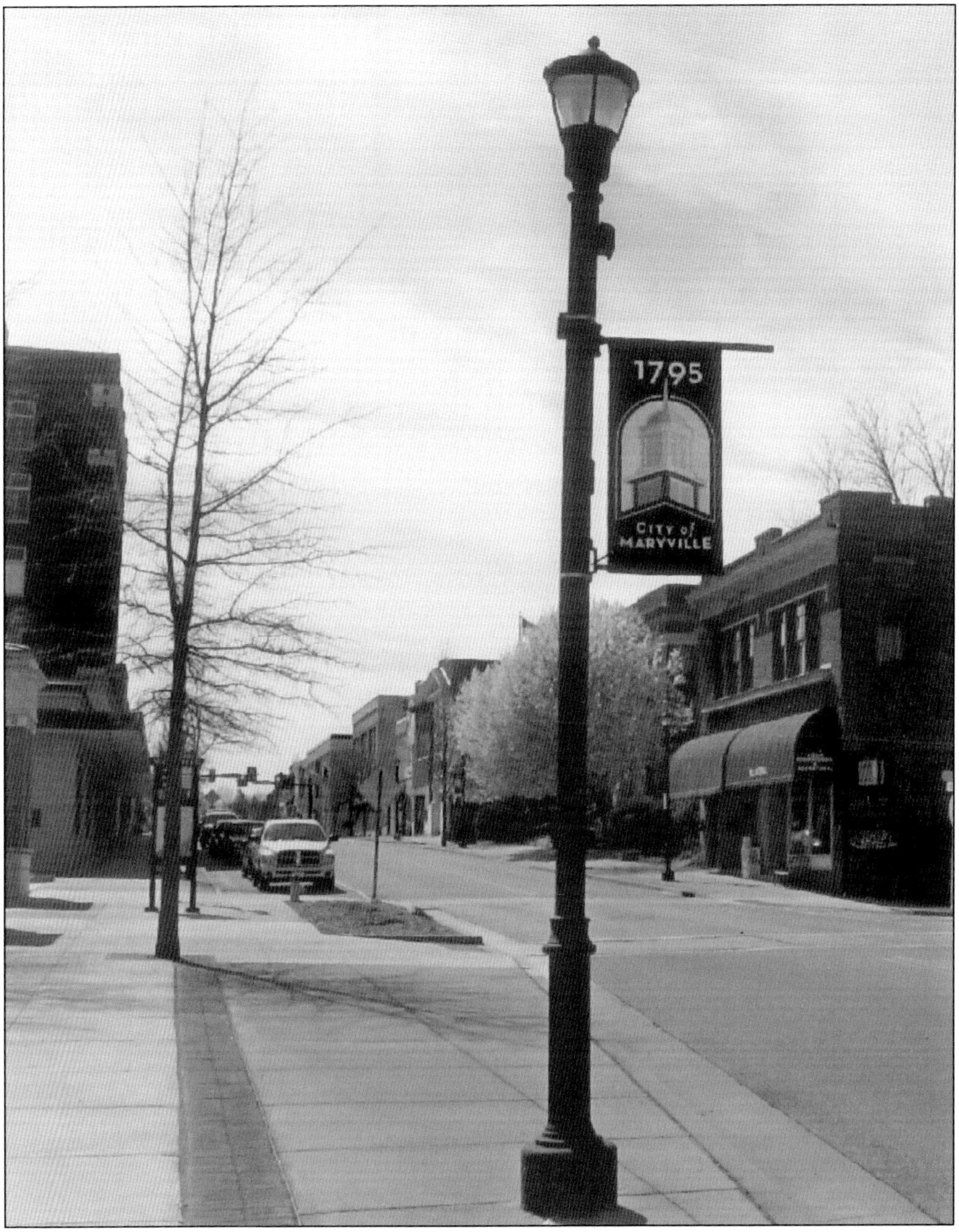

Through the years, businesses along Main Street, now Broadway, have come and gone. What was once the lifeblood of local commerce has been replaced by supermarkets and shopping malls far from the downtown area. Broadway remains, however, a testament to Maryville's rich history, as do many of its buildings—monuments to a former way of life. This photograph was taken in March 2012, looking west from Founders Park. (Courtesy of Linda Braden Albert.)

ON THE COVER: This scene looks east on Main Street, now Broadway Avenue, around the 1930s. On the right can be seen the five-story First National Bank Building, completed in 1921, which would become Blount National Bank in 1934. (Courtesy of the *Daily Times*.)

IMAGES
of America

MARYVILLE

Linda Braden Albert
and David R. Duggan

ARCADIA
PUBLISHING

ISBN 978-0-7385-9072-1

Published by Arcadia Publishing
Charleston, South Carolina

Printed in the United States of America

Library of Congress Control Number: 2012943200

For all general information, please contact Arcadia Publishing:
Telephone 843-853-2070
Fax 843-853-0044
E-mail sales@arcadiapublishing.com
For customer service and orders:
Toll-Free 1-888-313-2665

Visit us on the Internet at www.arcadiapublishing.com

To my children, Adam Albert and Emily and Jordan Effler, and my grandchildren, Ellie and Seth Effler.

To my father, Kenneth Reed Duggan.

Contents

Acknowledgments

The authors wish to thank all the groups and individuals who so generously shared their photographs and memories of Maryville to be preserved for future generations to enjoy. Without the assistance of all contributors, in particular the city of Maryville, Maryville Schools, Maryville College, Blount Memorial Hospital, the Blount County Public Library, the Blount County Genealogical and Historical Society, and Larry Aldridge, executive editor at the *Daily Times*, this book would not have been possible. Special thanks go to Maryville Historian Sarah B. McNiell, Blount County Historian Lorene Smith, and historians Becky Blankenship Darrell and B. Kenneth Cornett for their invaluable assistance, and to Kari L. Duggan, wife of the coauthor, for her support and encouragement.

INTRODUCTION

The city of Maryville, Tennessee, has long been a desirable place for families, businesses, schools, and houses of faith. Even before the single act by the General Assembly of the Territory South of the Ohio River on July 11, 1795, formed both Blount County and Maryville, the county seat, settlers were drawn to this area that now is a gateway to one of the most popular tourist destinations in the United States, Great Smoky Mountains National Park. Territorial governor William Blount, for whom the county is named, in 1795 appointed a seven-man commission—including Joseph Black, David Craig, Samuel Glass, Samuel Henry, Alexander Kelley, John Trimble, and William Wallace—to obtain a site for the county seat and erect the necessary governmental buildings. The commission was also instructed to lay out the town—named in honor of Mary Grainger Blount, wife of the territorial governor—to sell and make deeds for all lots, and to apply the money so raised toward building a courthouse, prison, and stocks for the county.

The commission chose a 50-acre site adjoining Capt. John Craig's fort, located on Pistol Creek near the site of the present-day Blount County Chamber of Commerce on Washington Avenue. Fort Craig was the first settlement in the area that is now the city of Maryville. The fort was built in 1785 to protect settlers from Indian attacks and was located near an abundance of springs for a water supply.

Almost a year after the formation of Maryville and Blount County, on June 1, 1796, the state of Tennessee became the 16th state in the Union. The Tennessee Act of 1796 decreed that Maryville was to continue as a town and that the citizens of Blount County were permitted to have a fair in the town on the last Wednesday of March and October for the purpose of selling all kinds of goods and wares free of tax.

Craig contributed the 50 acres from the 243 acres he had bought from Stockley Donelson, who had acquired a grant of 100,000 acres from what was then North Carolina in exchange for his Revolutionary War service. However, it was not until Craig left Maryville to settle in Mississippi in 1809 that he made a deed to the Maryville Commission for the land comprising the town of Maryville.

Maryville was divided into 120 lots, containing one-fourth-acre each. These lots took up 30 acres while the remaining 20 acres contained the necessary streets and alleys. At that time, New Providence Presbyterian Church, founded in 1786, was outside the town limits. It was located near present-day Broadway and Cates Streets.

A legislative act of 1807 established a board of commissioners for Maryville. This act authorized the commissioners to have the lots surveyed and to have corners set according to the original plan. They were also to keep the streets in repair, tax the property, prevent damage by fire, collect fines, and "suppress horse running." The commission was restrained from selling the Cedar Springs, with its waters being reserved for the use of the town. Today, a minipark is located at this historic spring, now called Hannum Spring, at the intersection of Louisville Road and McGhee Avenue near the Blount County Department of Health, former location of the Blount County Public Library.

In 1813, a relatively unknown Sam Houston began his journey into the history of this country by enlisting in the US Army. The legendary Houston, in addition to his military career, served as governor of Tennessee, congressman from Tennessee, Indian agent, commander-in-chief of an army, president of the Republic of Texas, governor of the state of Texas, and US senator. A marker commemorating his enlistment is on Broadway Avenue at the First Tennessee Bank Building.

In 1819, Southern and Western Theological Seminary, founded by Dr. Isaac Anderson, was opened. The name was changed to Maryville College in 1842. This institution of higher learning remains a vital part of the city today, so vital that an entire chapter of this book is dedicated to its long and distinguished history.

By 1834, Maryville had grown to 600 inhabitants, including four preachers and lawyers, three hatters, tailors, and saddle makers, and two silversmiths. There were three churches and two taverns. The town was incorporated in 1837. In January 1850, however, the Tennessee General Assembly authorized any village, town, or city in the state to form a corporation, providing for the annual election of seven aldermen, who would, in turn, elect the mayor. The same legislature repealed all laws and parts of laws previously incorporating Maryville.

Blount County Court minutes show that on May 6, 1850, a petition seeking incorporation of Maryville was granted. Aldermen elected were Samuel T. Bicknell, a lawyer, planter, and politician; Reuben L. Cates, a saddle maker; Julius Caesar Fagg, who had served as an army captain in the Mexican War and was a merchant and a farmer; Andrew McClain, a tanner; William McTeer, a tailor and innkeeper; and John E. Toole, a lawyer. Dr. Samuel Pride, whose three-story brick home was located at the site of the present Maryville Municipal Center, became the first mayor.

During the Civil War, much of Maryville was damaged by fire and artillery. In one instance, troops commanded by Confederate general Joe Wheeler set fire to the houses on the west side of Main Street, now Broadway, between Love and Cusick Streets in an attempt to smoke a small contingent of Union soldiers commanded by Capt. James Dorton from the courthouse. When the blaze reached its objective, however, it jumped the street and burned the other side, leaving the courthouse unscathed.

Maryville's first commission after the Civil War was made up of four black men and three white men. William B. Scott, the first and only black mayor of Maryville, served in that capacity from 1869 to 1870. Scott was also the founder of one of the first black schools in East Tennessee, the Freedman's Normal Institute, which operated for 30 years.

The first railroad was built into Maryville in 1868, the Knoxville and Charleston. In the late 1870s, Maryville acquired and opened its first public school.

In 1879, the temperance people of Maryville declared war on whiskey saloons in the town. They urged Maryvillians to vote to dissolve the corporation of the town because the sale of liquor could not be controlled under a law passed two years earlier. The law prohibited the sale of intoxicants within four miles of a school, but exempted incorporated towns. The incorporation was abolished on March 24, 1879, with the law to take effect 25 days after passage. At that time, Maryville was described as a neat and thriving town of 1,200 to 1,500 residents. The town was again incorporated in 1907.

The *Maryville Times* was founded in Maryville in 1883 by A.J. Neff. The newspaper has operated continuously since then; today, the Maryville *Daily Times* is Blount County's newspaper of record, with more than 21,000 subscribers. The paper has been instrumental in providing photographs and information for this book.

The face of Maryville has changed throughout the years, but unlike many other downtowns, dozens of its historic buildings remain and are in use today. Photographs used in this book reflect that pride in history, preserved so others will be connected to the town's roots far into the future.

One

Early Days

Maryville has changed substantially since its formation on July 11, 1795, in a frontier area where Native Americans and a few hardy settlers had once resided. We are fortunate to have maps from those early days showing the layout of the town on 50 acres donated by Capt. John Craig, 120 lots covering 30 acres complete with 20 acres of the necessary roads.

We are also fortunate to have images of some of the homes, churches, businesses, schools, and individuals from the 1800s and early 1900s that show snippets of our past.

For example, the Thompson-Brown House is one of the oldest two-story, two-pen log buildings in East Tennessee, believed to have been constructed in the first quarter of the 19th century; it is now home to the Blount County Historic Trust and the Cades Cove Museum. Pride Mansion, built by Dr. Samuel Pride before 1830, served as the headquarters for Gen. William T. Sherman in December 1863 and later as a school. The Maryville Municipal Center now occupies that site. The present-day Blount County Courthouse occupies the site of Sunny Hill, built by Confederate veteran Dr. John Cates.

Mount Gilead Methodist Episcopal Church was organized sometime after 1804, and by 1819, a small wooden structure was built on "Methodist Hill," near the site of what is now Olympia Townhouses. The second-oldest cemetery in Maryville remains on that tract of land.

Images of the Maryville College campus in 1871, the Freedmen's Institute near the turn of the 20th century, the Jackson House in 1900, soldiers going to World War I in 1918—these and additional photographs capture only a small part of the early days of Maryville.

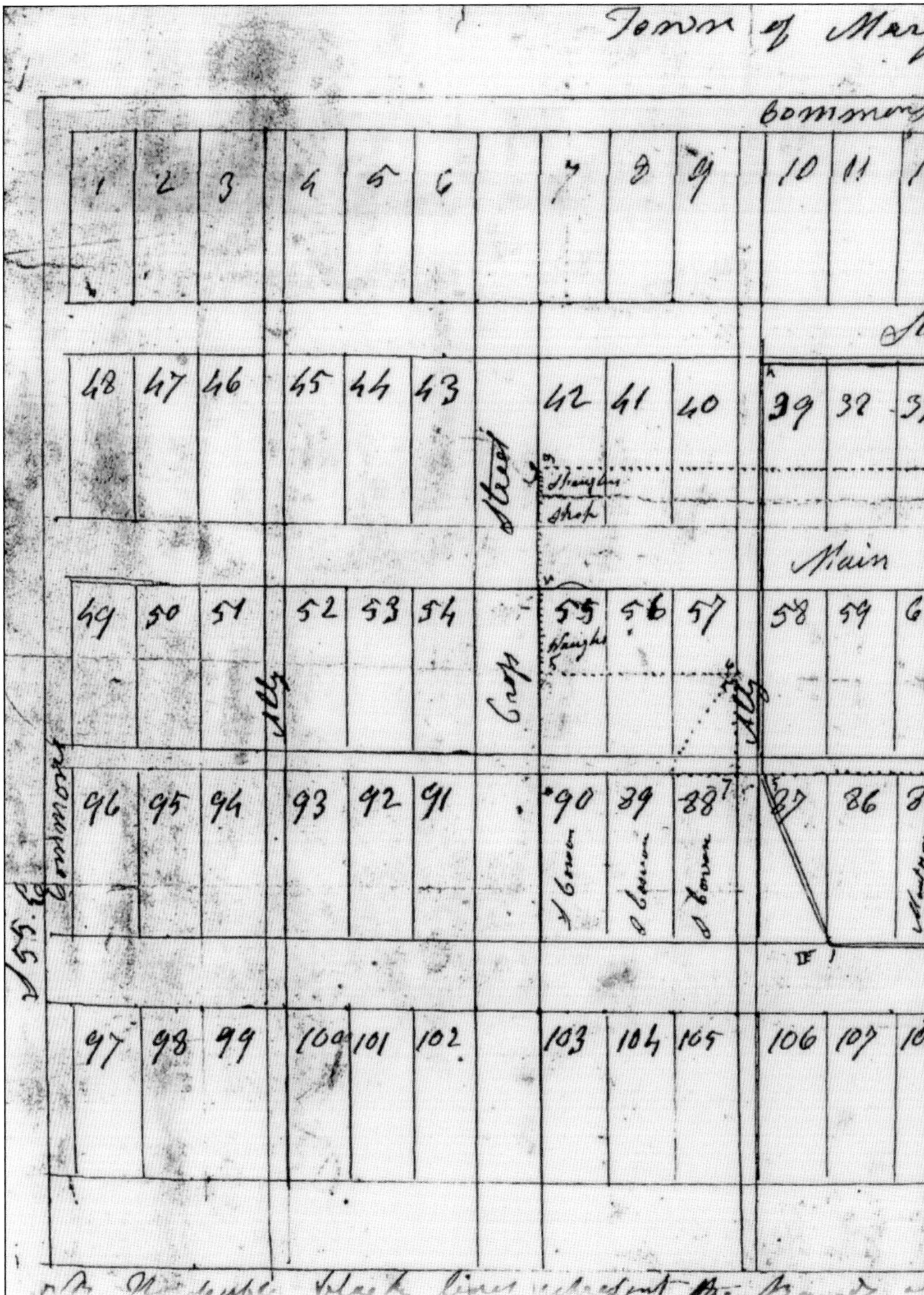

A legislative act of July 11, 1795, formed both Blount County and Maryville, the county seat. The Maryville map drawn in 1821 shows 120 lots, each a quarter of an acre in size, taking up 30 acres while the remaining 20 acres allotted to the town contained the necessary streets and alleys. "The

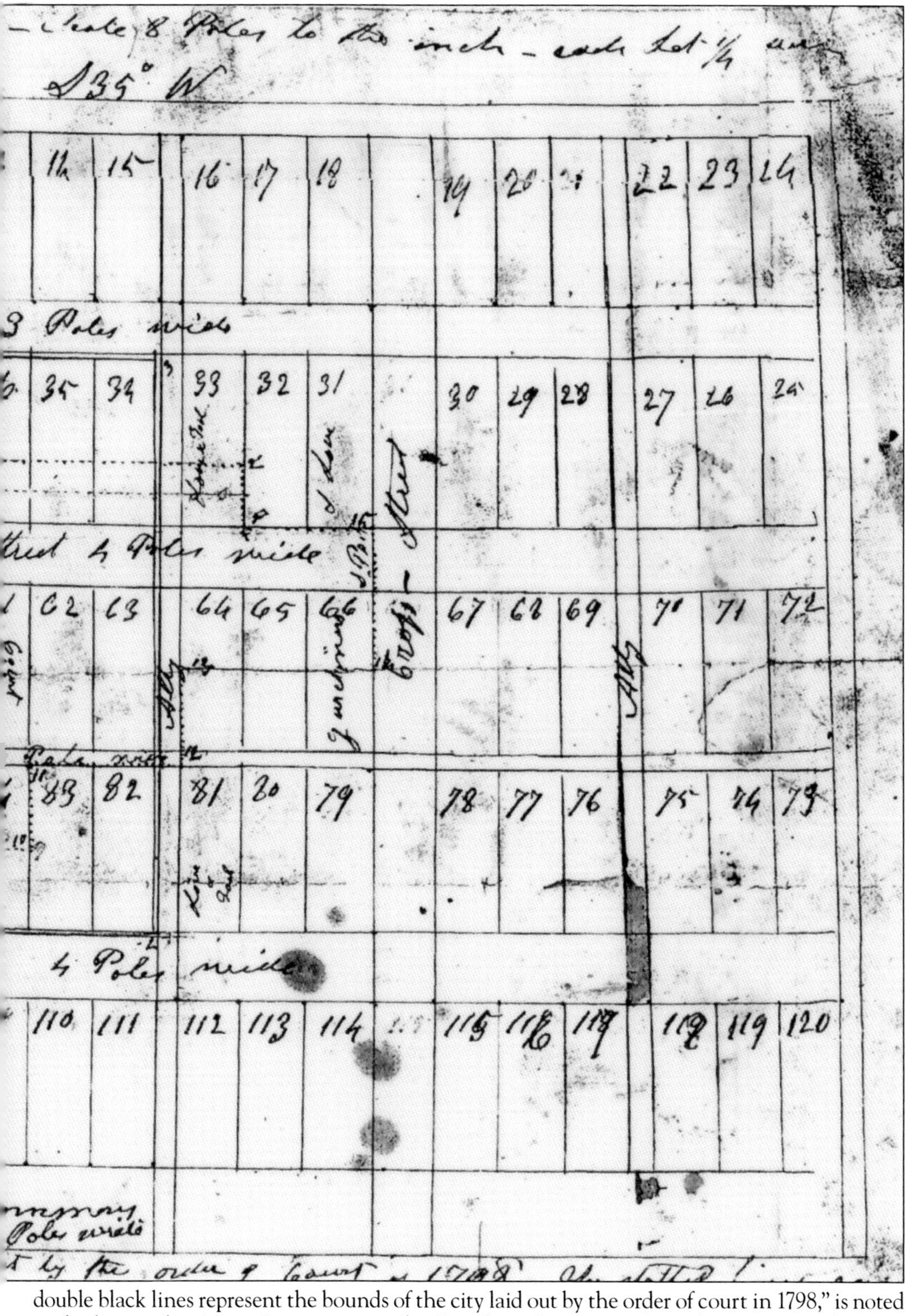

double black lines represent the bounds of the city laid out by the order of court in 1798," is noted at the lower edge. Main Street, present-day Broadway Avenue, is the only street named on the map. The others are designated as either cross streets or alleys. (Courtesy of City of Maryville.)

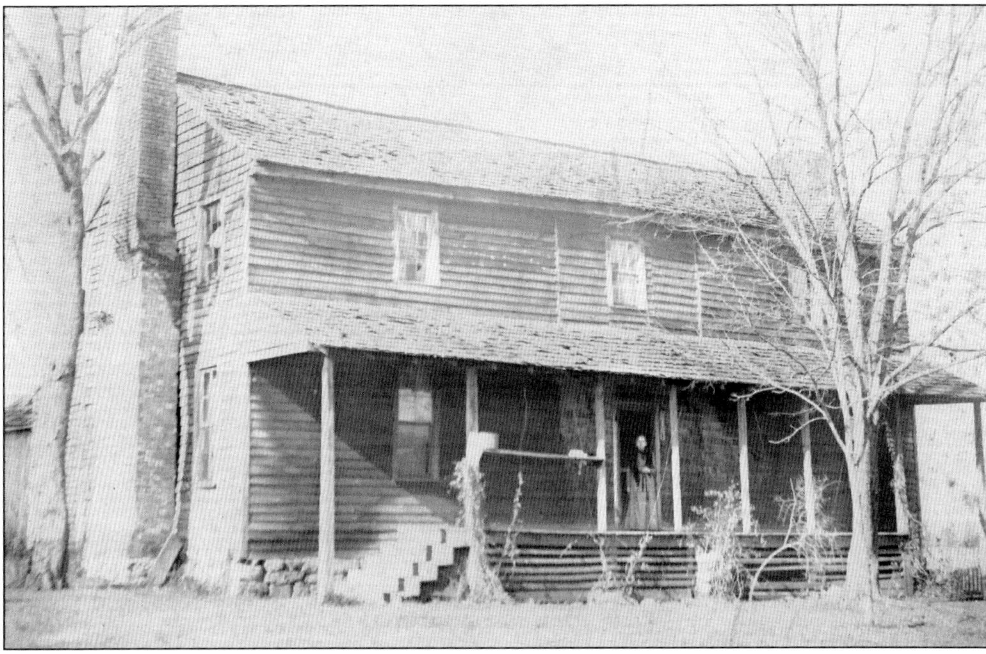

The Thompson-Brown House, pictured above prior to 1919, is believed to have been built in the first quarter of the 19th century, one of the oldest two-story, two-pen log buildings in East Tennessee. William Thompson, a substantial landowner, farmer, and land trader, is believed to be the builder. Thompson family history tells of the birth of a daughter in the house in 1823. The Reverend William Beard Brown purchased the home in 1867. His wife, Mary Elizabeth Bicknell Brown, is standing on the porch. Pictured below is the home in 1929. In 1919, owner John Brown rebuilt the porch to make it wider, moved the steps to the center, and extended the porch the full length of the house for the double wedding of his daughters, Margaret Brown Gibson and Olivia Brown Henry. (Both, courtesy of Sarah Brown McNiell.)

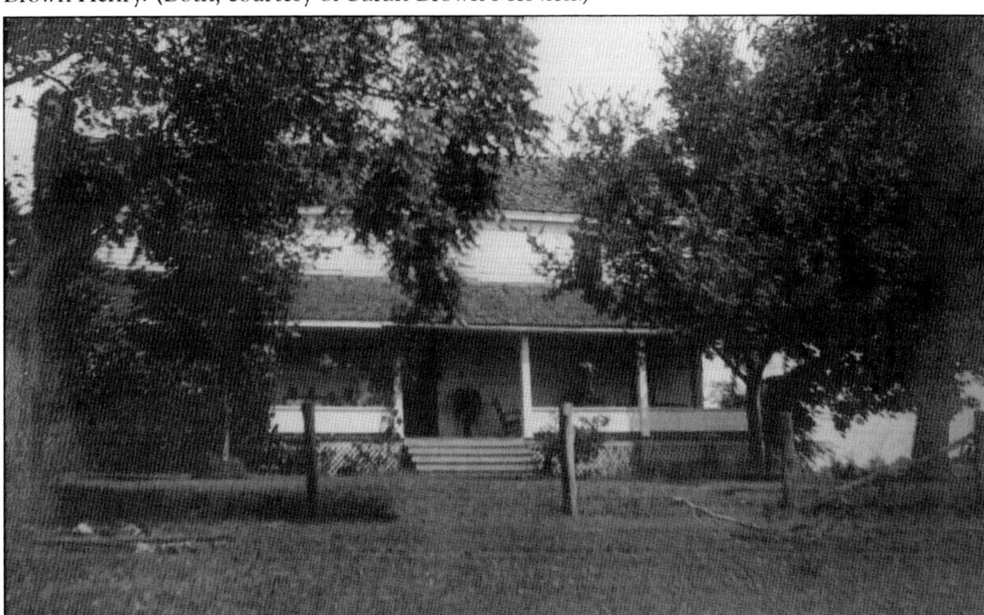

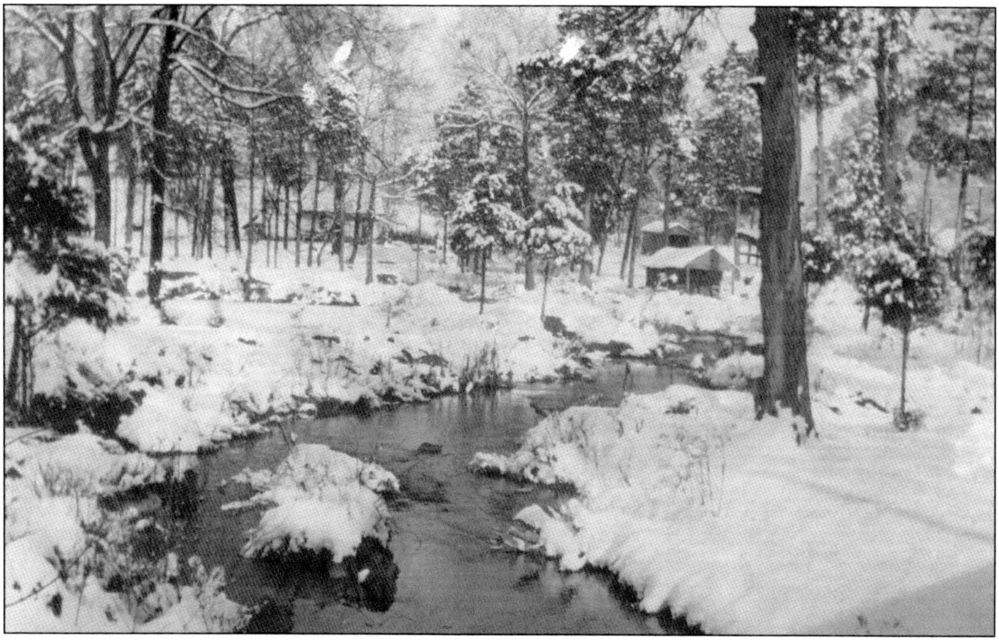

The Grove at the Brown Farm owned by William Beard Brown was a popular gathering place for young people in Maryville. The Brown's Creek Springhouse is at the right, while the cottage built by Brown after the Civil War for his mother-in-law, Barbara Moore Bicknell Pritchard, her son Union veteran George Bicknell, and daughter Phoebe Bicknell, is at the left. The family relocated from Morganton to Maryville so George could attend nearby Maryville College. He later had a career in ministry and education. (Courtesy of Sarah Brown McNiell.)

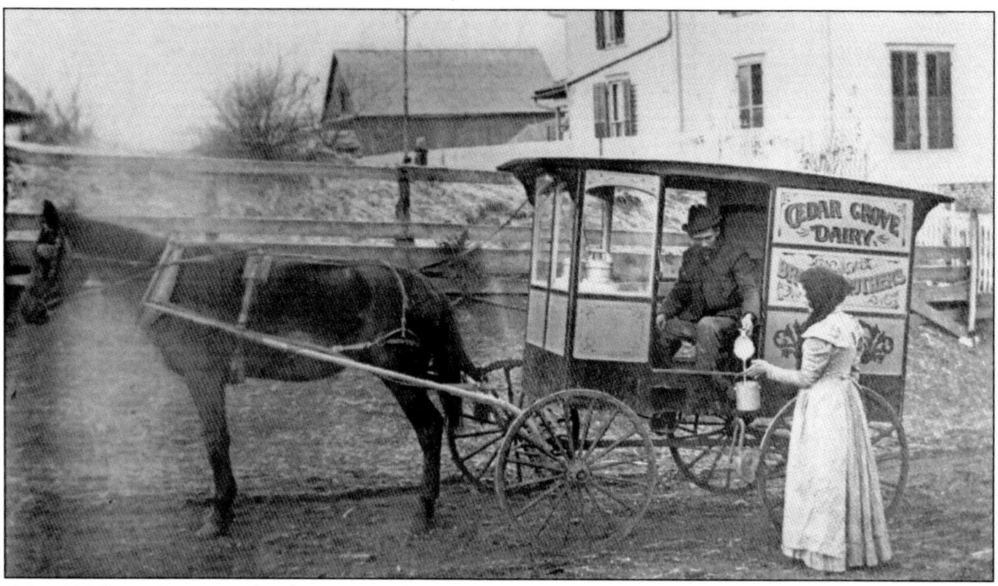

After William Brown's death in 1879, his widow, Mary Elizabeth Bicknell Brown, and son John Fielding Brown continued to operate the family farm. At the turn of the 20th century, they established Brown Brothers Cedar Grove Dairy, the first in Maryville to deliver milk house to house. The property was sold to Maryville College in 1934. In this photograph, John Brown, left, pours milk for Emily Webb on Lamar Street in Maryville. (Courtesy of Sarah Brown McNiell.)

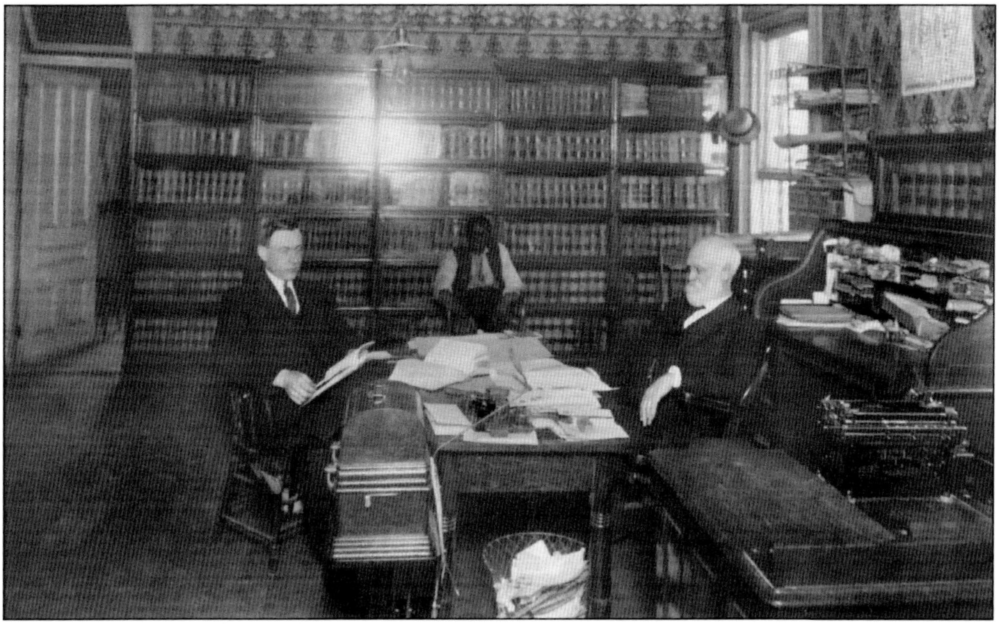

R.R. Kramer (left) and Maj. Will McTeer (right) are pictured inside their new law office in 1913 in Maryville when they formed their partnership. The gentleman in the center is unidentified. Kramer moved his practice to Knoxville in 1934, and his son R. Arnold Kramer joined him there. The present firm of Kramer Rayson is the successor firm. (Courtesy of Wayne Kramer.)

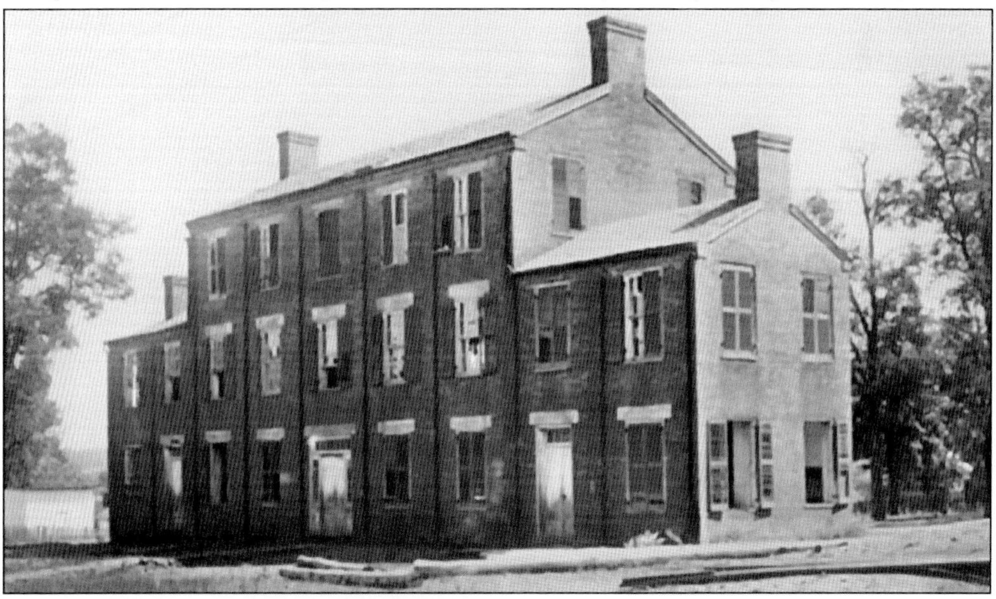

The East Tennessee Masonic Female Institute, shown here in 1899, was built by New Providence Lodge No. 128 about 1850 to care for the education of female orphans of indigent Masons. The building was damaged extensively during the Civil War, but in 1868, the lodge renovated the building and opened a school. In 1878, the deed was transferred to the city of Maryville and became the site of Blount County's first public school. The institute, removed in 1905, stood where McCammon-Ammons-Click Funeral Home is today at Broadway Avenue and Cates Street. (Courtesy of City of Maryville.)

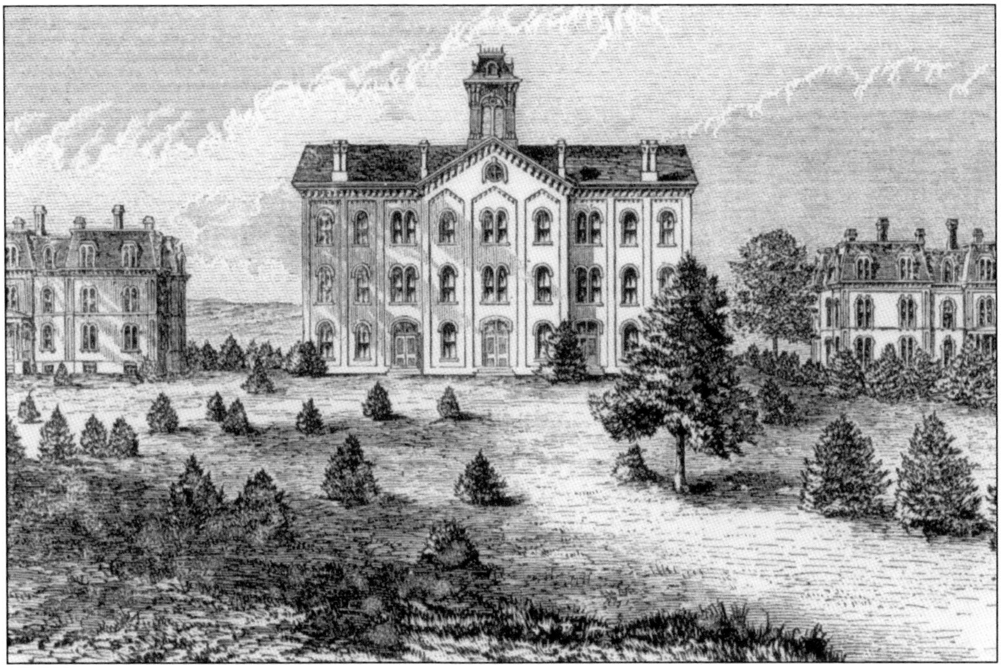

Maryville College began in 1819 as Southern and Western Theological Seminary, established by Dr. Isaac Anderson on Maryville's Main Street. In 1842, the name was changed to Maryville College. The college closed on April 22, 1861, because of the Civil War and reopened in 1866. Soon after, Maryville College moved to its present location on East Lamar Alexander Parkway. The campus in 1871 included, from left to right, Baldwin, Anderson, and Memorial Halls. (Courtesy of Maryville College.)

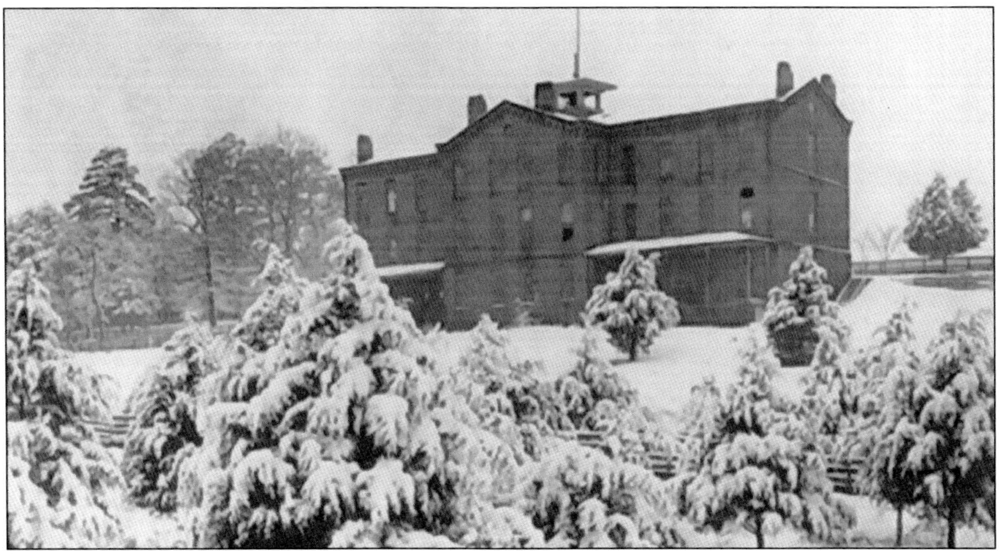

Freedman's Normal Institute, one of the first black schools in East Tennessee, began in a log building in 1867 at the present site of St. Paul AME Zion Church on Main Street to train black men and women as teachers for the African American population. A three-story brick building was begun in 1872 at what is now Maryville High School. It closed in 1901. (Courtesy of City of Maryville.)

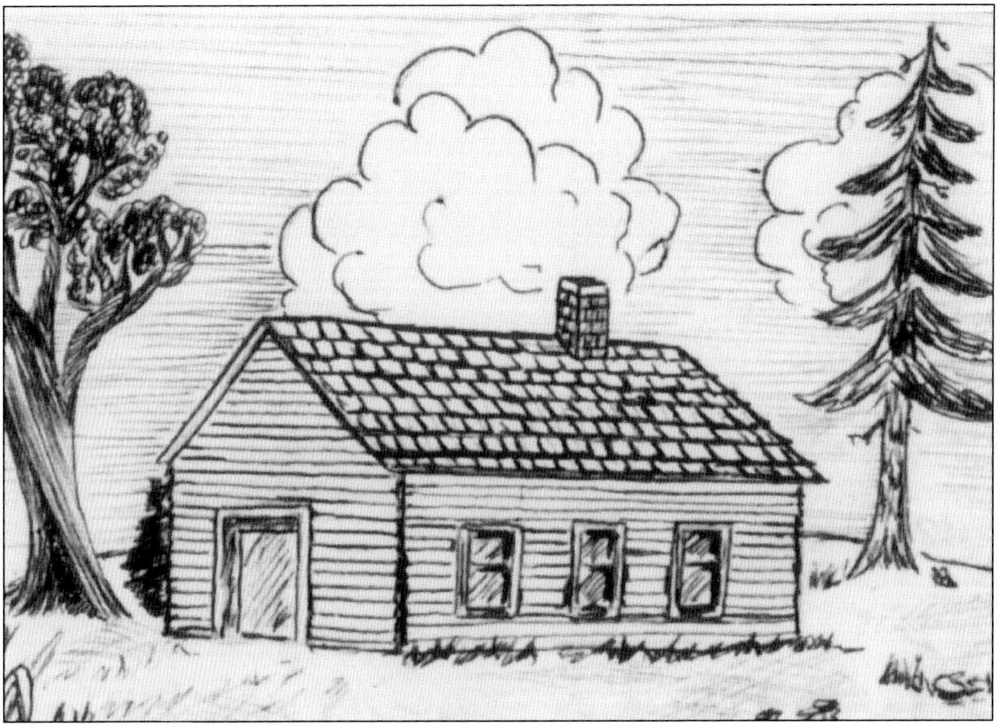

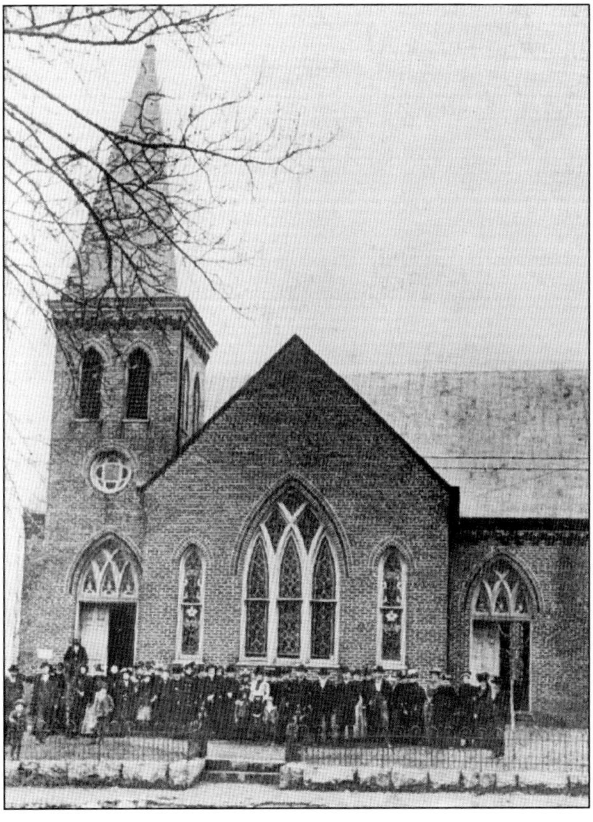

Mount Gilead Methodist Episcopal Church was organized sometime after 1804, and by 1819, a small wooden structure was built on "Methodist Hill," near the site of what is now Olympia Townhouses. The drawing above shows the building in 1820. By 1860, a larger structure was built at the corner of Church and Norwood Streets in Maryville. The church split during the Civil War into the Methodist Episcopal Church South and Methodist Episcopal Church North, forerunners of Broadway United Methodist and Maryville First United Methodist, respectively. At left, members of First Church, formed in 1865, stand in front of the first Main Street church in 1891. In 1922, this structure was torn down and the second Main Street church was erected where Citizens Bank now stands. First UMC moved to its current location on Montvale Station Road in 1967. (Courtesy of A.B. Goddard.)

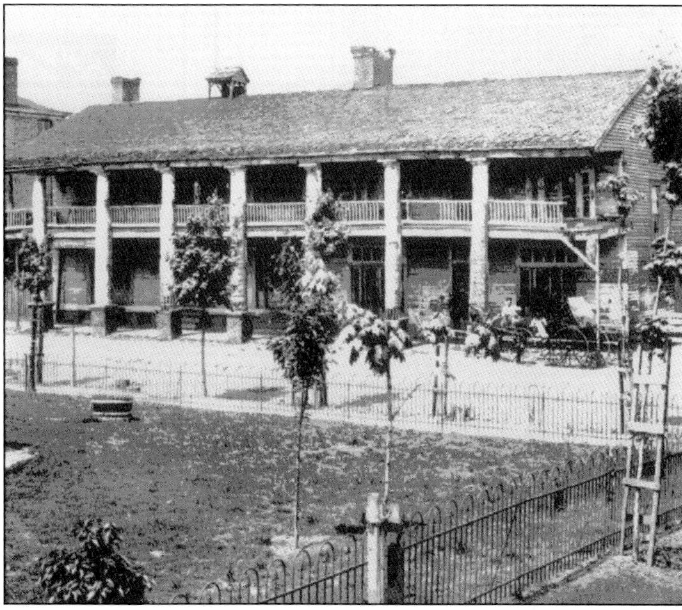

Broadway United Methodist Church was constructed in 1899 on the site of a hotel that had its beginning in 1842 when William McTeer built what was known at first as the College Inn, then the Citizen's Hotel. In 1852, after a porch with massive white pillars was built over the sidewalk, the name was changed to the Verandah Hotel, shown here. The property was known as the McKenzie House from 1860 to about 1880, then Austin House. (Courtesy of City of Maryville.)

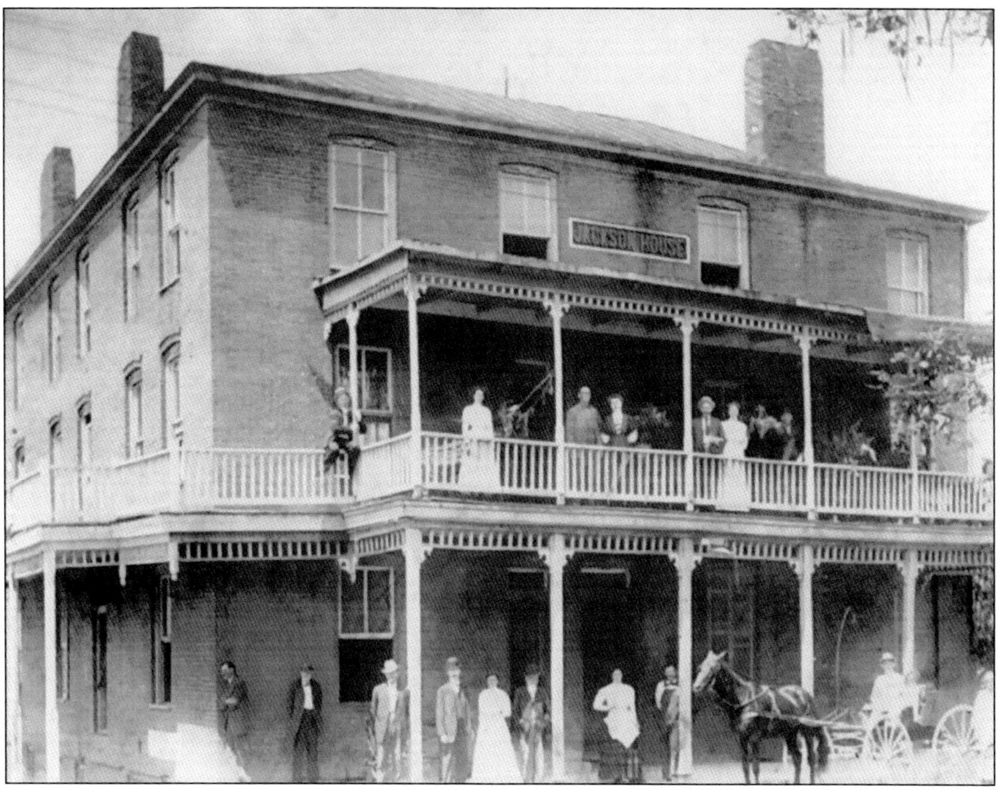

In 1886, George C. Jackson bought the lot at the corner of College and Broadway from Alexander Henry and built a three-story brick hotel operated as the Jackson House, shown here in 1900. It operated as such until 1914. The property changed hands several times from 1914 to 1919, when Dr. A.M. Gamble became the owner and changed the name to Blount Hotel. (Courtesy of City of Maryville.)

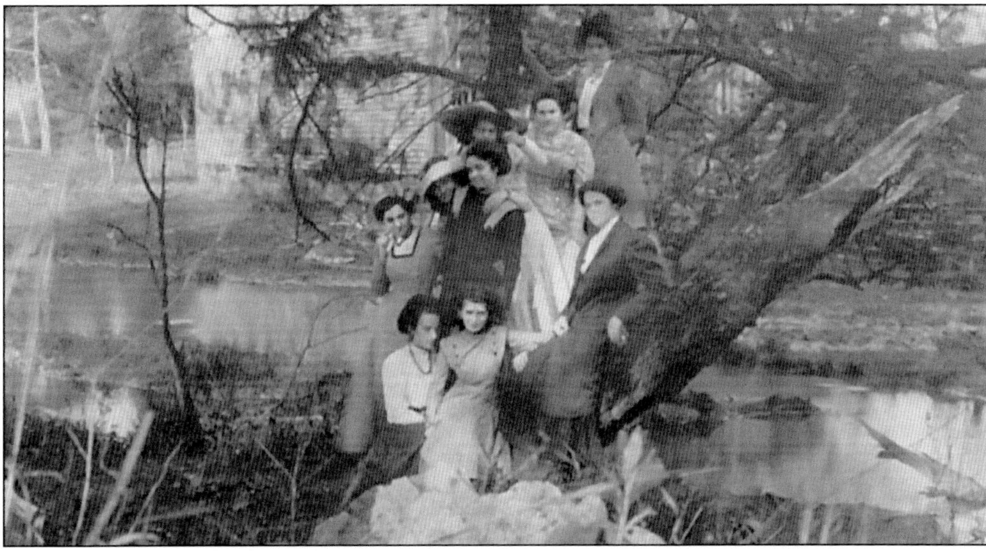

These unidentified ladies are shown in 1895 at "the old knitting mill," possibly Anchor Woolen Mills on Sanborn Street, where East Main ran into Pistol Creek. Drivers forded the creek to drive up to Washington Avenue before the Church Street viaduct was completed. The mill may instead be Maryville Woolen Mills, began in 1873 and bought by W.T. Parham in 1877, located near the present site of Maryville's Bicentennial Park on the Greenway. (Courtesy of City of Maryville.)

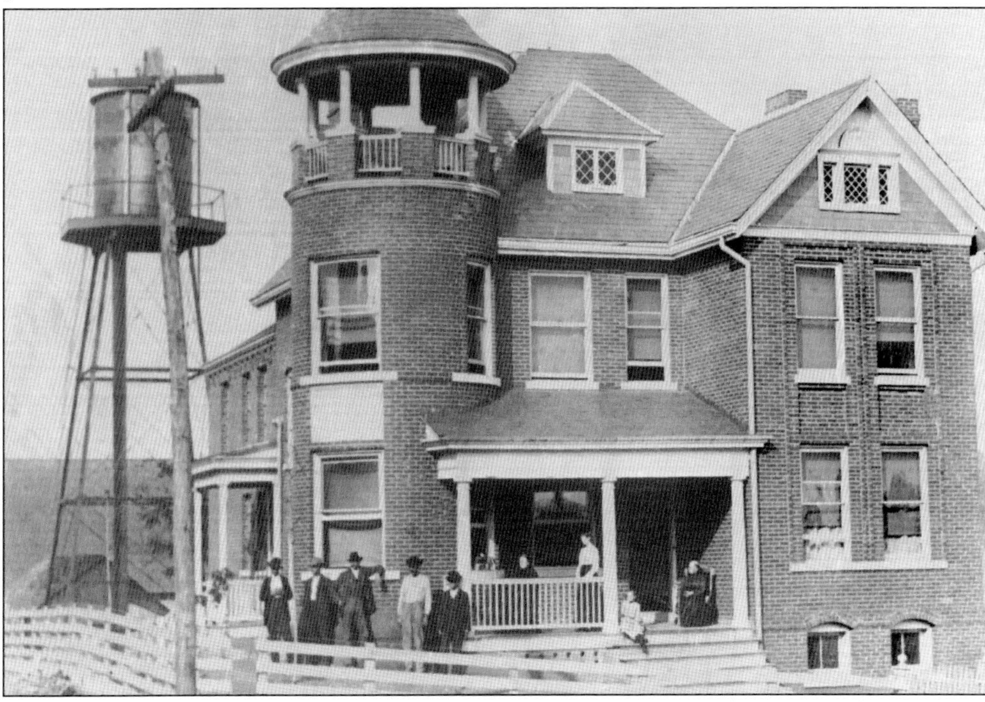

The Blount County Jail, shown in 1902, was completed in 1900 at the corner of Harper and Cusick, now a parking lot. From left to right are Jessie Hutton, deputy; John McMurray, jailor; Sam Greer, deputy; Oliver Pickens, brother of Sheriff John H. Pickens; Sheriff Pickens; Jane Boyd (Mrs. John) Pickens; Minnie Pickens (Hutton); Belle Pickens (Goddard); and Mrs. Robert Pickens, mother of the sheriff. (Courtesy of A.B. Goddard.)

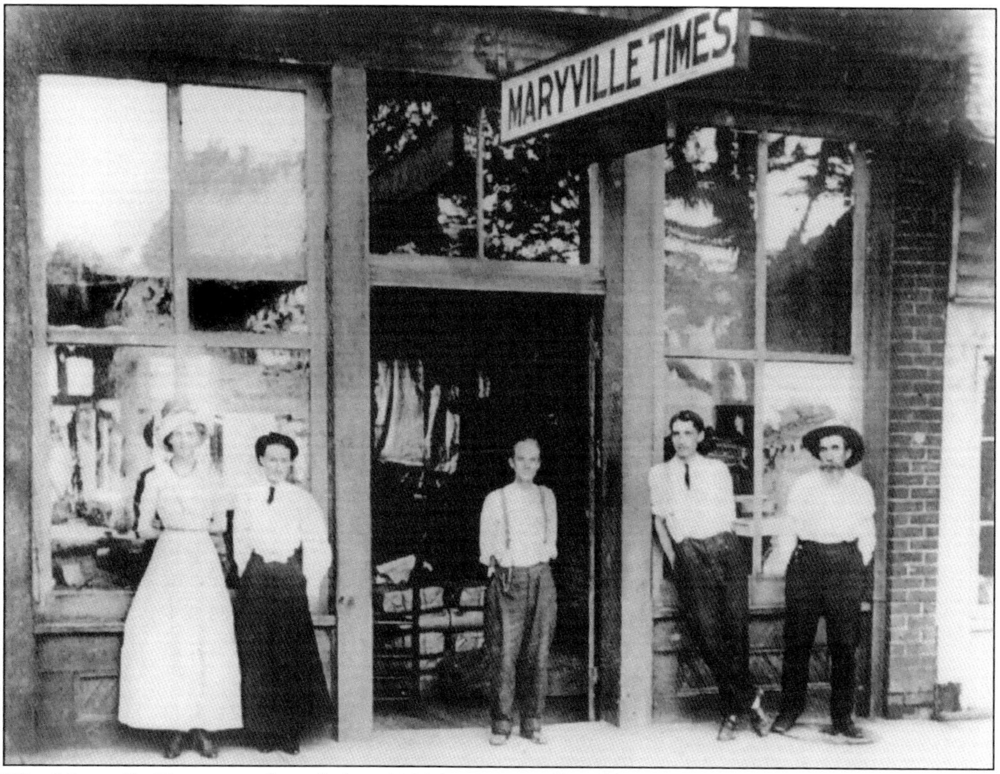

The *Maryville Times* was founded in 1883 by A.J. Neff and his son, George Neff. The newspaper office was located in the Poland Building on Broadway Avenue, across from present-day Broadway Towers. The above photograph shows the entrance to the newspaper office around 1913 with editor Clyde Goddard, center, and Blanche Bayless Bailey, second from left, who was employed by the *Times* for 59 years. The others are unidentified. The newspaper moved in July 1919 to the basement of Proffitt's Department Store at the northeast corner of North Cusick Street and East Broadway. In 1942, the *Times* moved into a new building at its present location, 307 East Harper Avenue. This building, pictured below in 1958, has been expanded at least seven times. The *Daily Times*, Blount County's newspaper of record, is currently owned by Jones Media, based in Greeneville, Tennessee. (Courtesy of the *Daily Times*.)

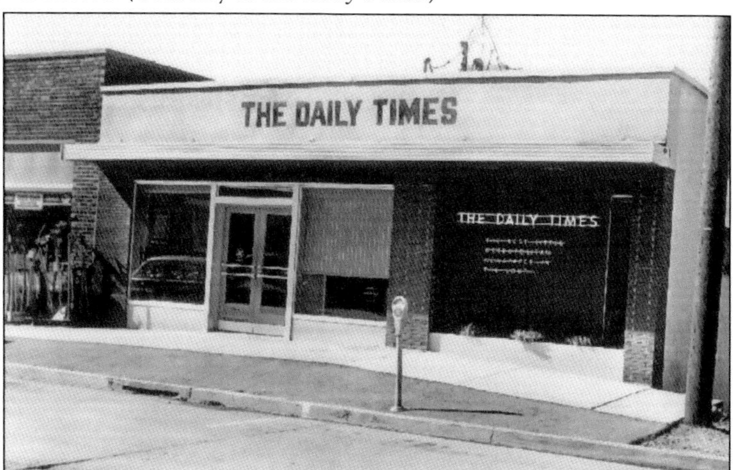

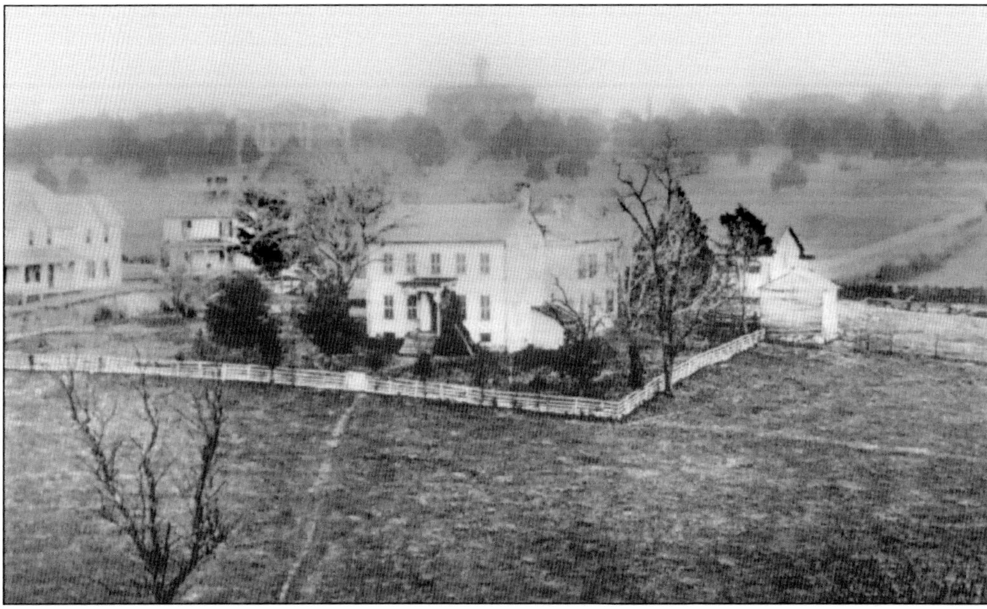

Sunny Hill, the home of Dr. John W. Cates, was sold in 1905 and is the site of the Blount County Courthouse. Cates, a graduate of Maryville College and Vanderbilt Medical School, started practice before the Civil War with Dr. Samuel Pride. He served as a physician in the Confederate army during the war. Cates died in 1916. (Courtesy of the Blount County Genealogical and Historical Society, photograph donated by Ben C. Clark, Jr.)

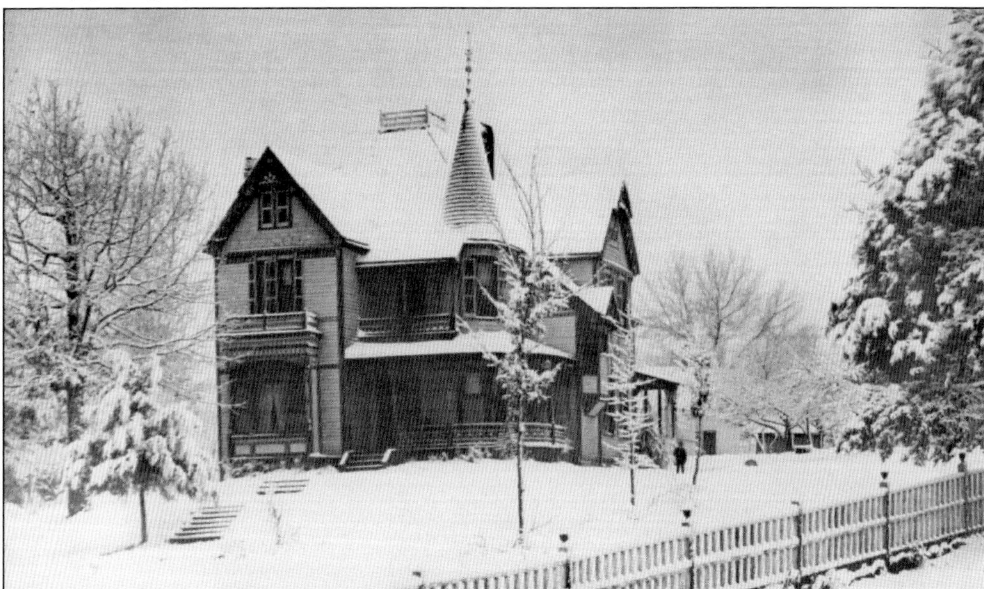

The home of Jo Burger, shown here in 1895, stood at what is now the intersection of Broadway Avenue and Lamar Alexander Parkway near the Maryville Municipal Building. Burger was one of the founders of the Bank of Maryville. He was cashier from 1885 to 1914 and president from 1915 to 1927. Born in 1849, Burger, whose signature was always written as "Jo," died in 1935. (Courtesy of the Blount County Public Library, W.O. Garner Collection.)

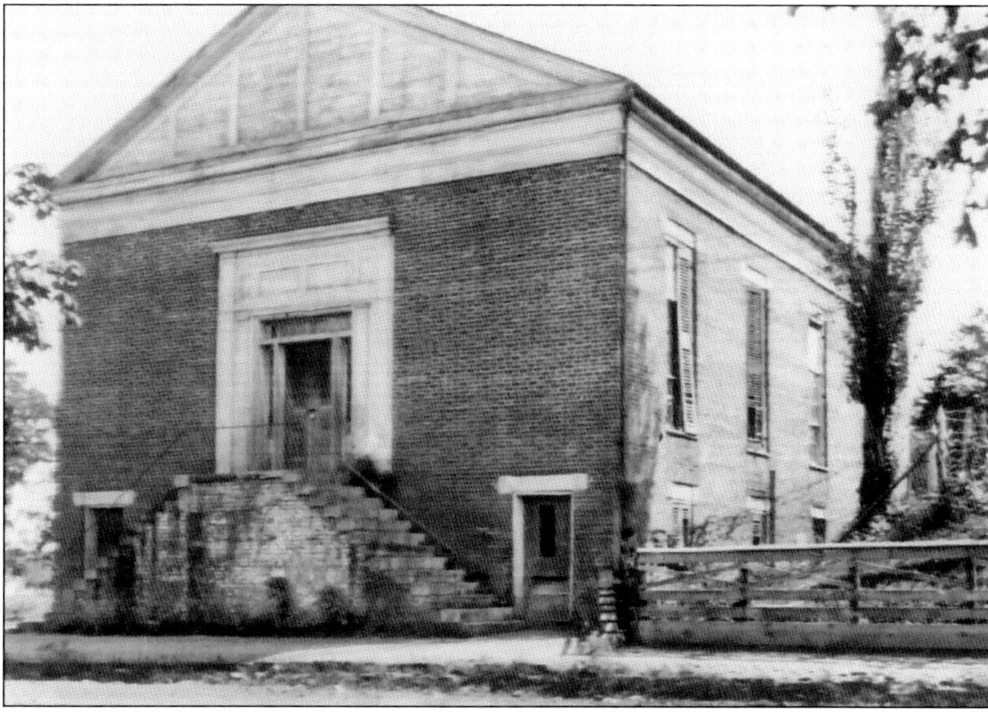

The building above, known as Columbian Hall, was built about 1852 at the corner of Main and Cates Streets. It served as the third church building for New Providence Presbyterian Church until about 1892, when it became a community gathering place and was the site of many special events such as Christmas gatherings, cultural programs, debates, and speakers. It was torn down about 1911. (Courtesy of the Blount County Public Library, W.O. Garner Collection.)

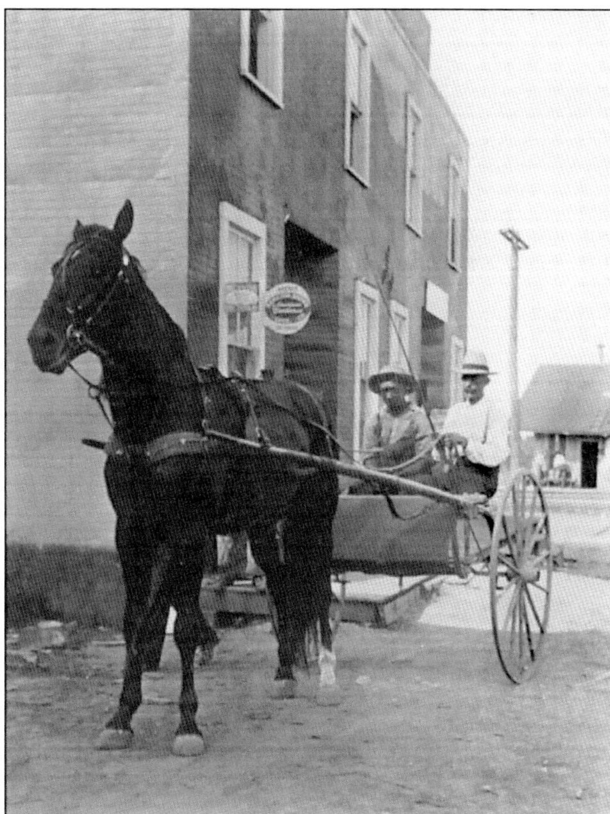

Horses and buggies, such as the one pictured to the right in 1915 in front of the Hamilton Brown Shoe Company, were common on the streets of downtown Maryville. Note the unpaved roads. (Courtesy of City of Maryville.)

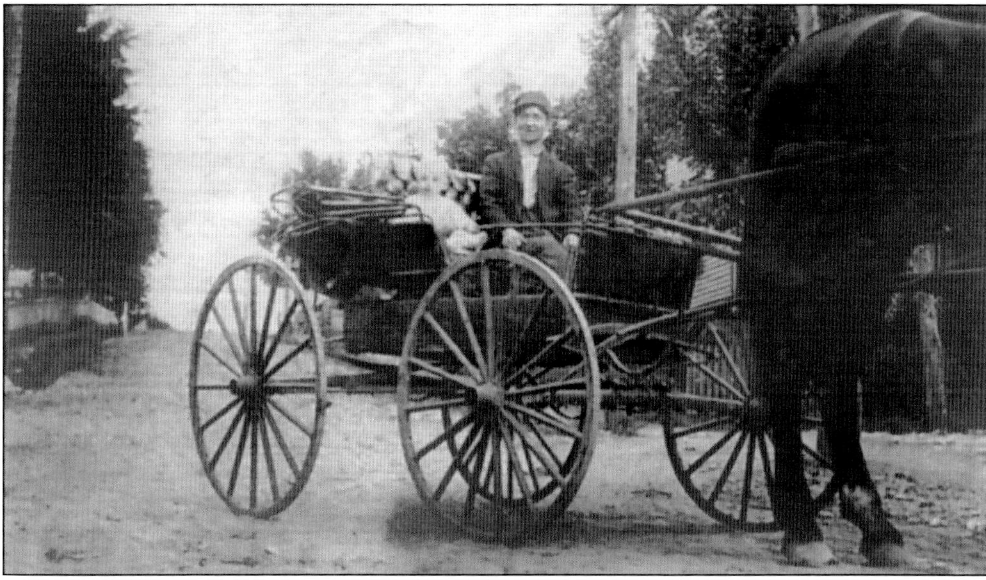

Max McCulloch, left, and Walt Stevens take a buggy ride down Main Street around 1907. Stevens was the driver for Dr. J.A. McCulloch, the little boy's father. In the 1926 Maryville-Alcoa Directory, John A. McCulloch is listed as a physician at 105 South Cusick Street. He resided at 817 West Main Street with his wife, Grace. Max is listed as an employee of J.C. Gillespie Insurance Office, residing at the same address as Dr. McCulloch. (Courtesy of Kathryn McCulloch Peery.)

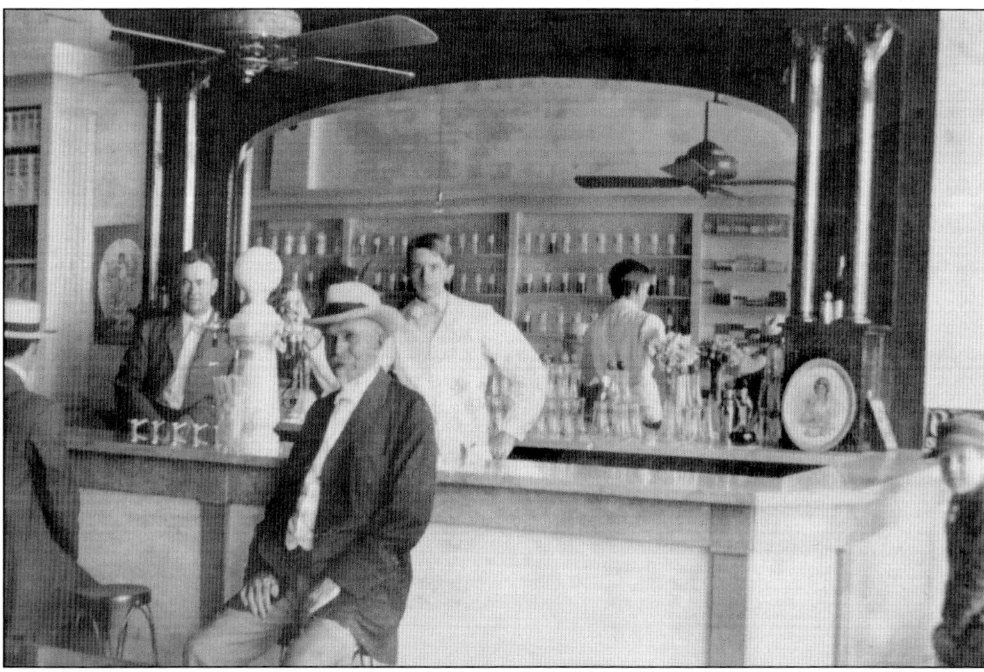

Dr. John P. Blankenship is seated at the soda fountain at City Drugs around 1904; Charlie Taylor Blankenship, his son, is the soda jerk. Eula Gray Goddard, wife of long-time Maryville attorney A.B. Goddard, remembers the soda fountain from her youth. She said that she and a friend would stop in on their way home from the library, and for 10¢ each they could purchase a chicken salad sandwich to split and two Coca-Colas. (Courtesy of Becky Blankenship Darrell.)

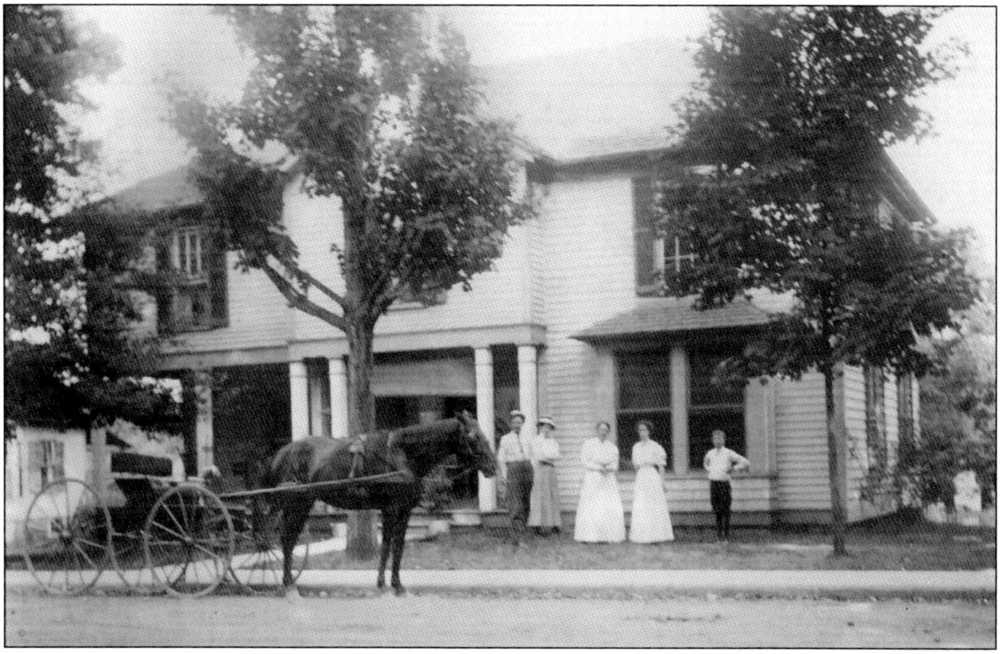

The home of John H. and Lillian Webb at 140 High Street in Maryville is shown here in the early 1900s. Adeline Murphy, who was the mother of Louise Berry, is shown second from right. The others are unidentified. (Courtesy of Louise Crawford Berry.)

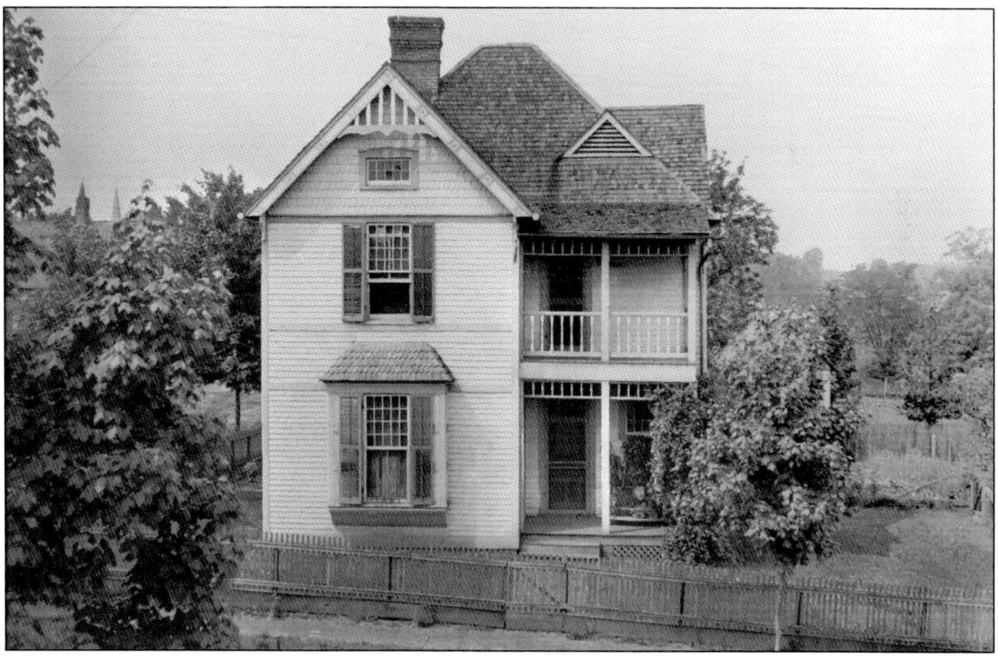

The pastor at First Methodist Church lived in this parsonage at 208 Washington Avenue from 1904 to 1924. In the 1926 Maryville-Alcoa Directory, Sam H. Dunn, listed as an attorney with Dunn & Jackson, lived in the home with his wife, Mary. Dunn and Jackson Law Office, S.H. Dunn and Charles C. Jackson, was at 309 First National Bank Building, Main Street. (Courtesy of the Blount County Public Library, Adele McKenzie Collection.)

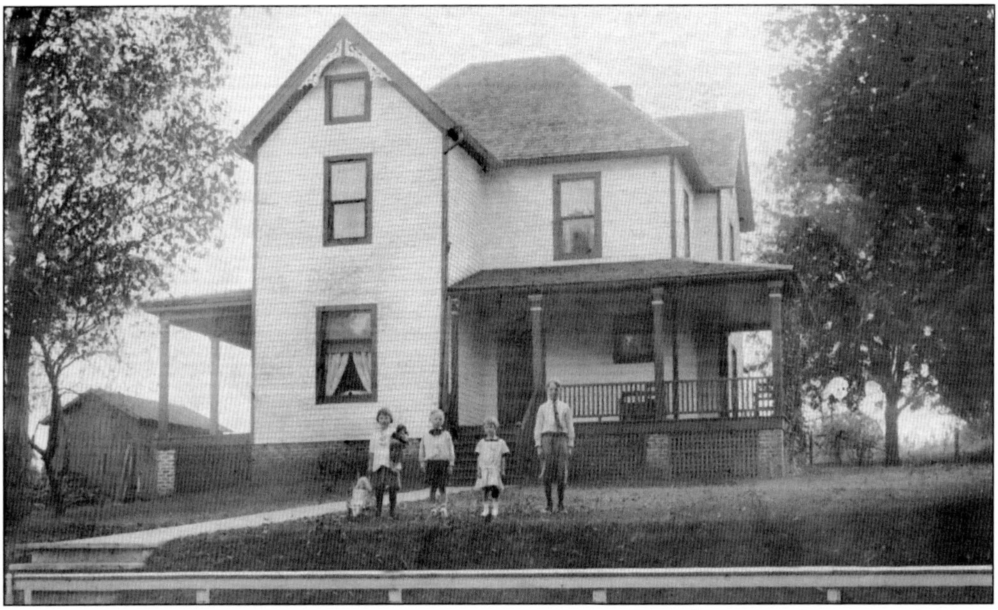

The J.E. Rowan home at 315 Cunningham Street is pictured in the early 1900s. The Rowan children, from left to right, are Margaret, Ray, Aleen, and Victor. (Courtesy of Marion Rowan Brink.)

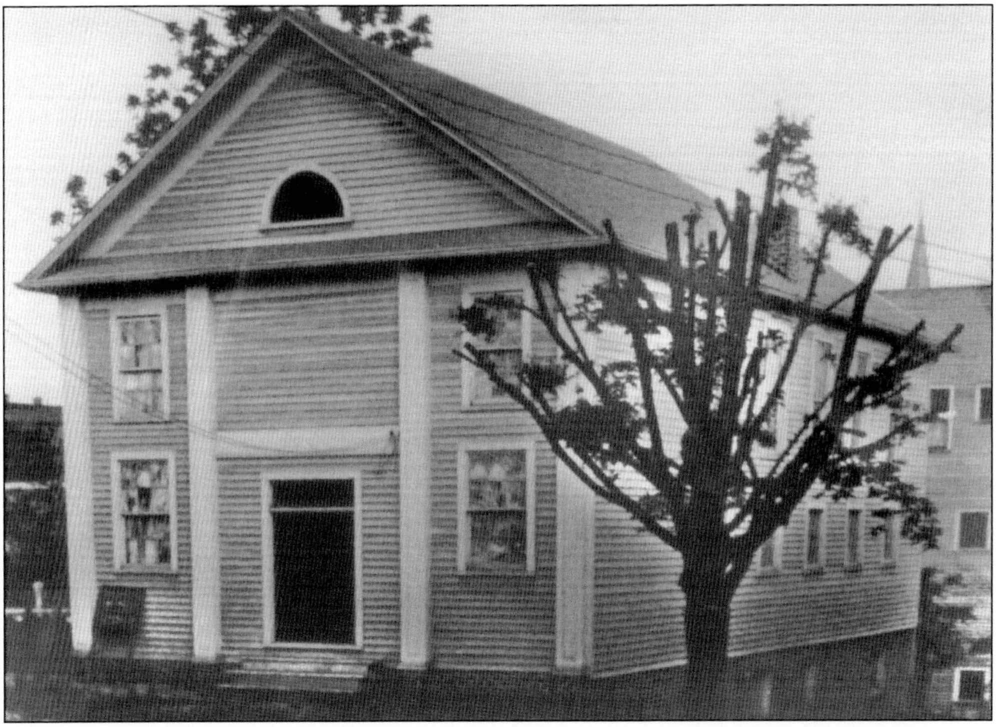

First Christian Church was organized on Jan. 18, 1912, with 25 charter members who met in this building on the corner of Ellis Avenue and College Street. The Sullinger property on Court Street was purchased in 1949, and in 1950, ground was broken for the brick building that stands today. The church was in use by 1952 and was dedicated on June 16, 1957, when the debt was paid in full. (Courtesy of First Christian Church.)

Two

Downtown

Maryville's Broadway, known as Main Street until the 1940s, was once the commercial center of Blount County. Until the 1960s, Broadway was lined with retail establishments, theaters, banks, professional offices, churches, and restaurants.

Department stores included Moser's, J.C. Penney, Young's, Badgett's, Parks-Belk, MacArthur's, S.S. Kresge, Eagle's, and the original Proffitt's Department Store. Proffitt's expanded across the United States before it was purchased by Belk.

Broadway was also the financial and governmental center of the county. Banking institutions included the Bank of Blount County, which later merged with the Bank of Maryville, and First National Bank, later known as Blount National Bank.

Telephone and electric utility offices, and Maryville's municipal offices, were located on or near Main Street, as was the post office, located in the beautiful Federal Building constructed in 1916.

The corner of Cusick Street and Broadway was also once known as Courthouse Square. Between 1805 and 1906, four Blount County courthouses were located there, the last destroyed by fire. Two log structures located on Harper Street behind this corner lot also served as courthouses. The courthouse built in 1842 was attacked by Confederate general Joseph Wheeler's cavalry during the Civil War, and it was during the battle that a slave, Polly Toole, rescued county records from a fire while under rifle fire. A statue honoring her stands in the present courthouse.

It was also on Broadway that Sam Houston, later president of the Republic of Texas, "took a dollar from the drum" and thus enlisted in the US Army on March 24, 1813. He later commanded the Army of Texas. Houston served as Tennessee's governor before going to Texas, and later as Texas governor, thus becoming the only person in American history to serve as governor of two states.

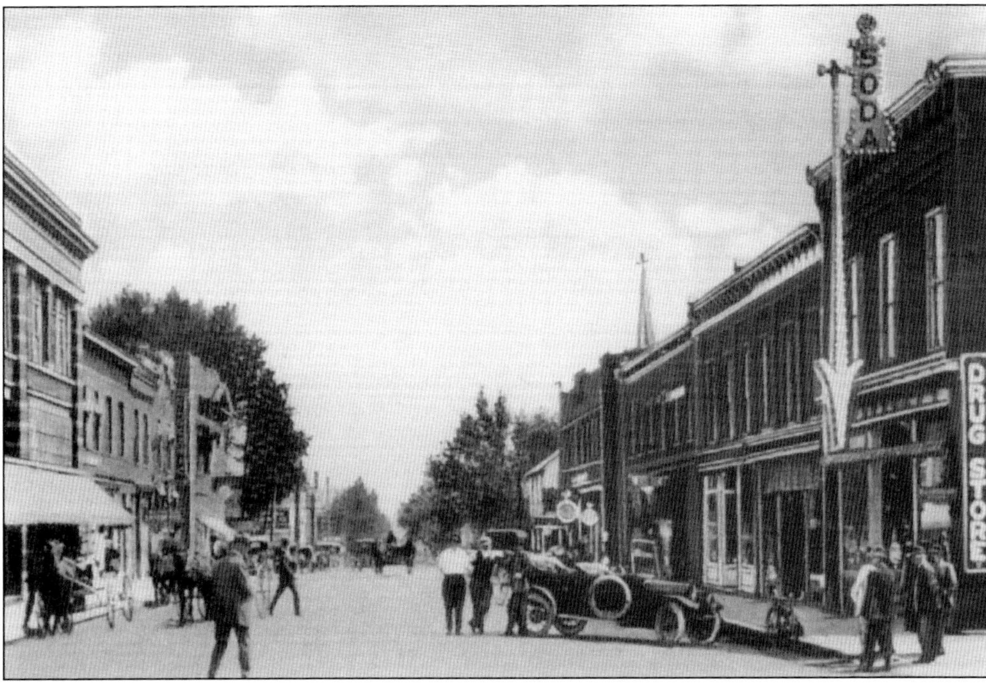

The view above looks eastward down Main Street, later Broadway, from Cusick Street, around 1917. The first building on the left is the Badgett's Department Store building. In 1919, Proffitt's Department Store would locate there. The first two buildings on the right were constructed between 1897 and 1902 on Parham Corner. The New Providence Presbyterian Church steeple can be seen on the right. (Courtesy of Ken Cornett.)

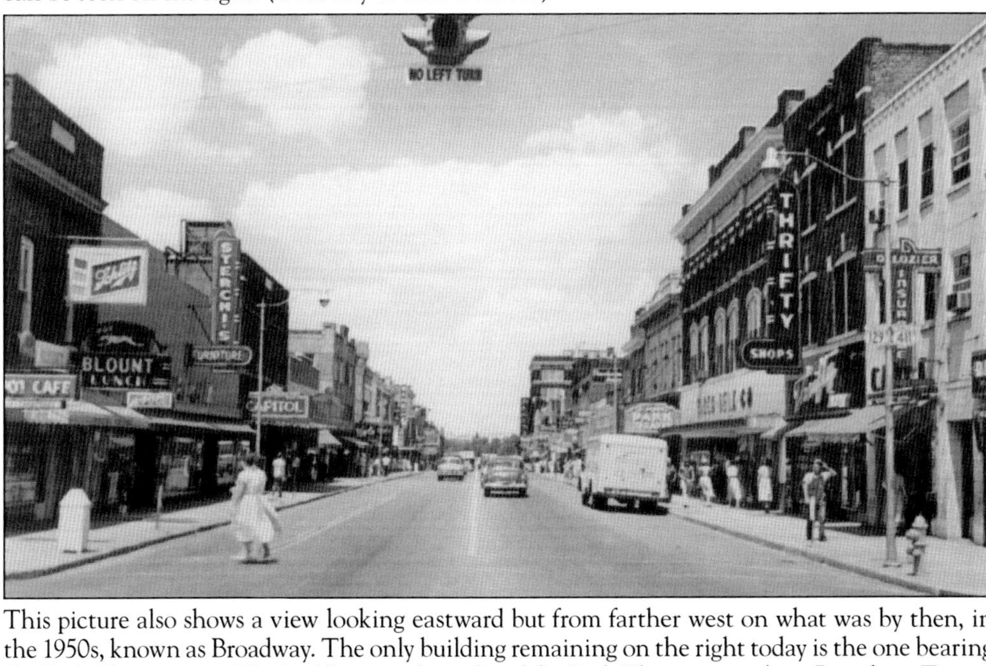

This picture also shows a view looking eastward but from farther west on what was by then, in the 1950s, known as Broadway. The only building remaining on the right today is the one bearing the Park Theatre sign. The buildings to the right of the Park Theatre are where Broadway Towers now stands. (Courtesy of Louise Crawford Berry and Tom Crawford.)

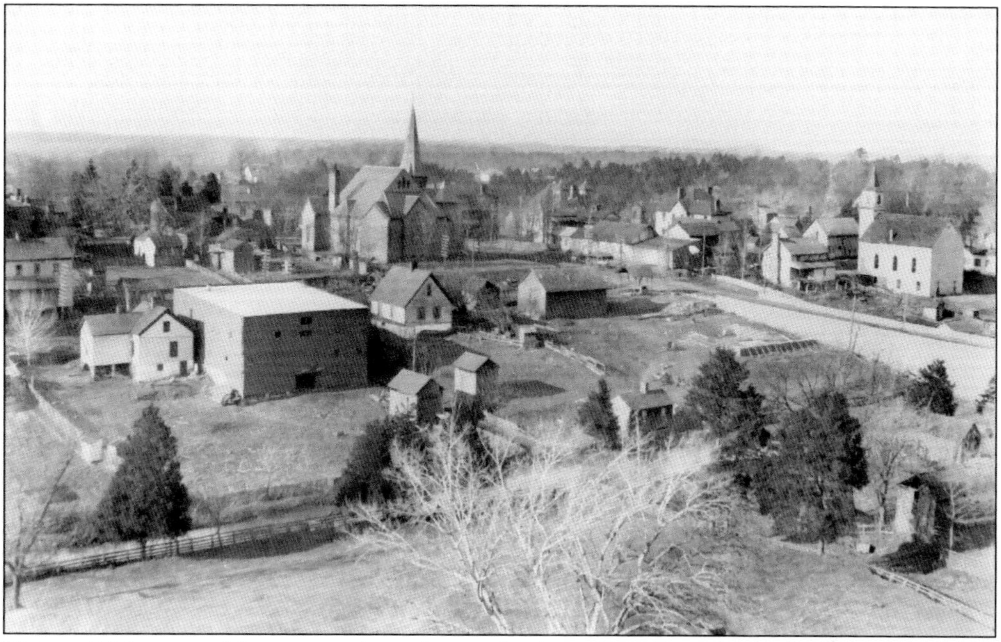

This c. 1920s view of downtown, from the south, shows New Providence Presbyterian Church located between what are now Broadway and Church Avenues. The former First National/Blount National Bank Building, now Preservation Plaza, presently stands on the site. To the right is Second Presbyterian Church, an African American congregation. Pistol Creek can be seen in the foreground. (Courtesy of Blount County Public Library.)

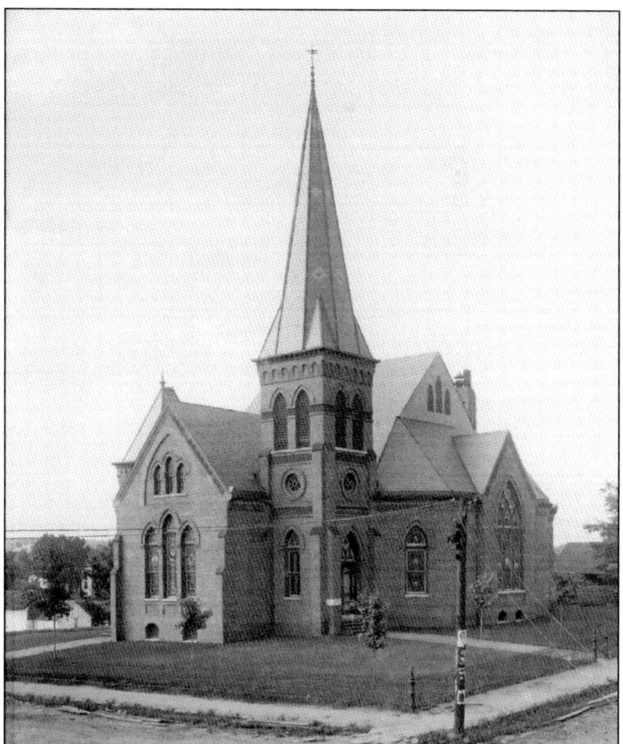

The New Providence Presbyterian Church building, facing Broadway, was built in 1895. The church was founded in 1786. The Southern and Western Theological Seminary was located on this site in 1819. In 1842, it would become known as Maryville College. (Photograph by W.O. Garner; courtesy of Blount County Public Library.)

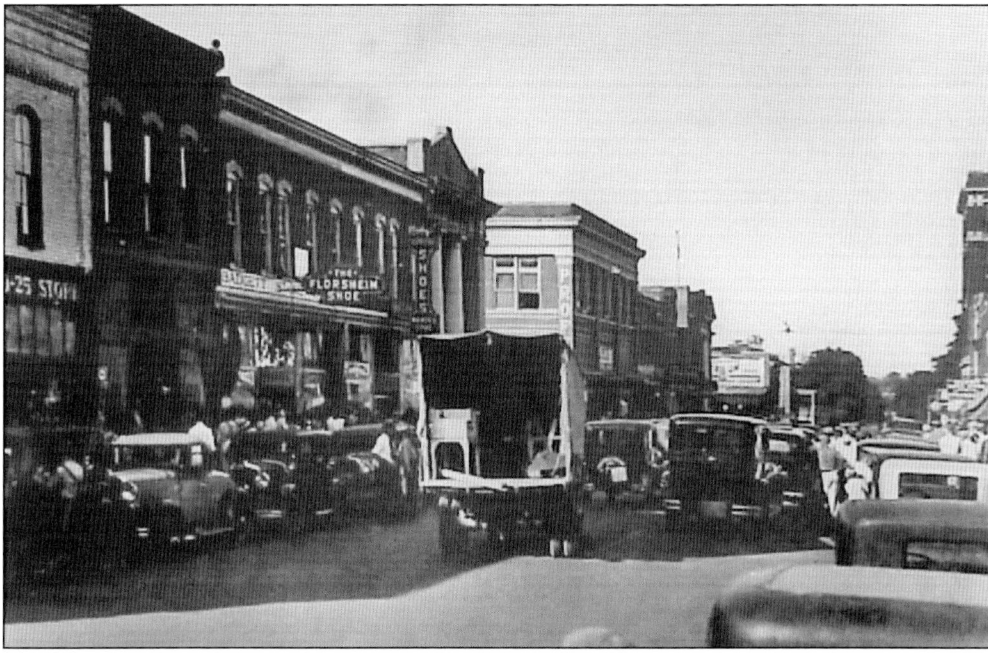

This c. 1920s picture shows, toward the left center with two columns, the Bank of Blount County Building constructed in 1915 at the corner of Cusick and Main Streets. In 1932, this bank merged with the Bank of Maryville, now First Tennessee Bank. The second building from the left was built in 1885 and was once home to, among other businesses, Stanberry Grocery Company. (Courtesy of City of Maryville.)

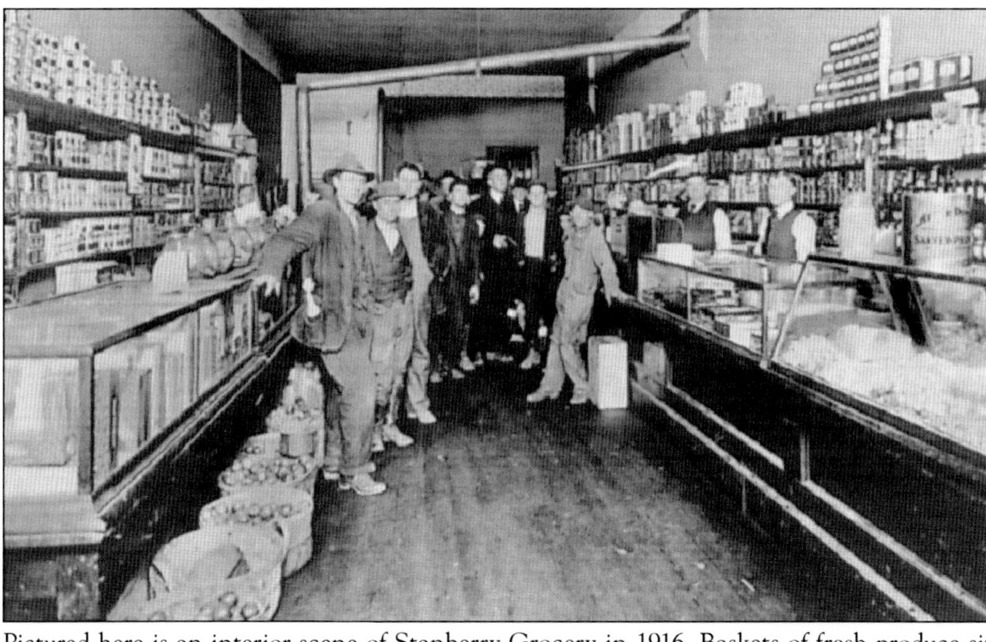

Pictured here is an interior scene of Stanberry Grocery in 1916. Baskets of fresh produce sit on the floor to the left. In this period, grocery products were generally kept behind the display cases and counters, and grocers would assist customers by obtaining for them their desired items. (Courtesy of City of Maryville.)

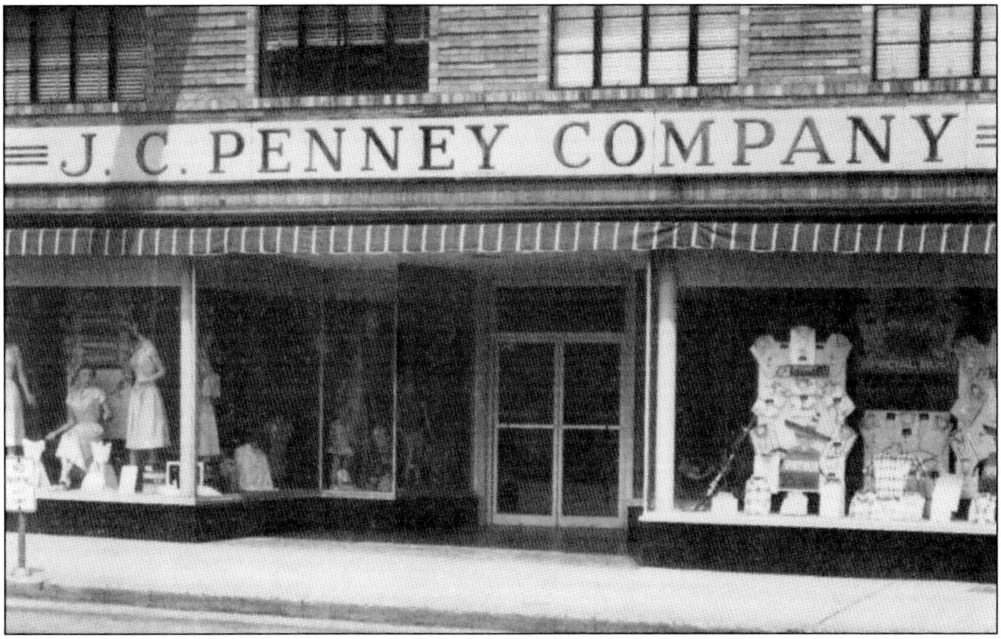

The J.T. Trotter Building, constructed in 1935, once was home to the J.C. Penney Company. Sullivan's Restaurant is now located there. To the left of the building, Cedar Spring Alley separated Moser's Department Store and the Trotter building. (Courtesy of Sandra Lee Stevens.)

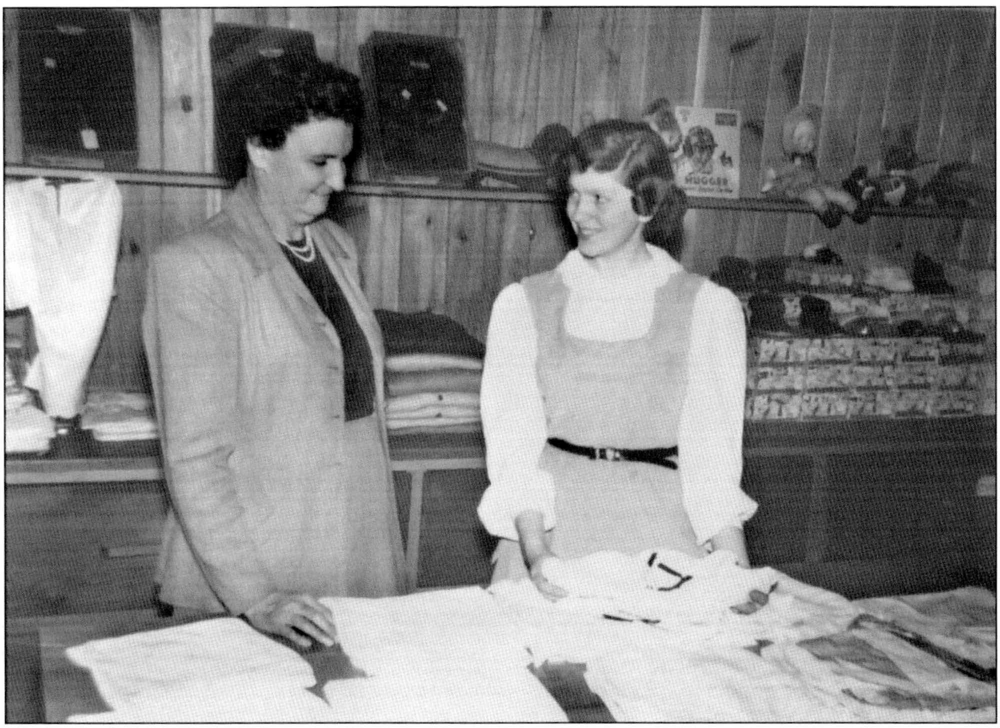

Pictured is an interior scene of Moser's Department Store in 1950. Jeanne Hancox (right) at the time was working there as a member of the Maryville High School Distributors Club. The clerk to the left is unidentified. (Courtesy of Maryville City Schools.)

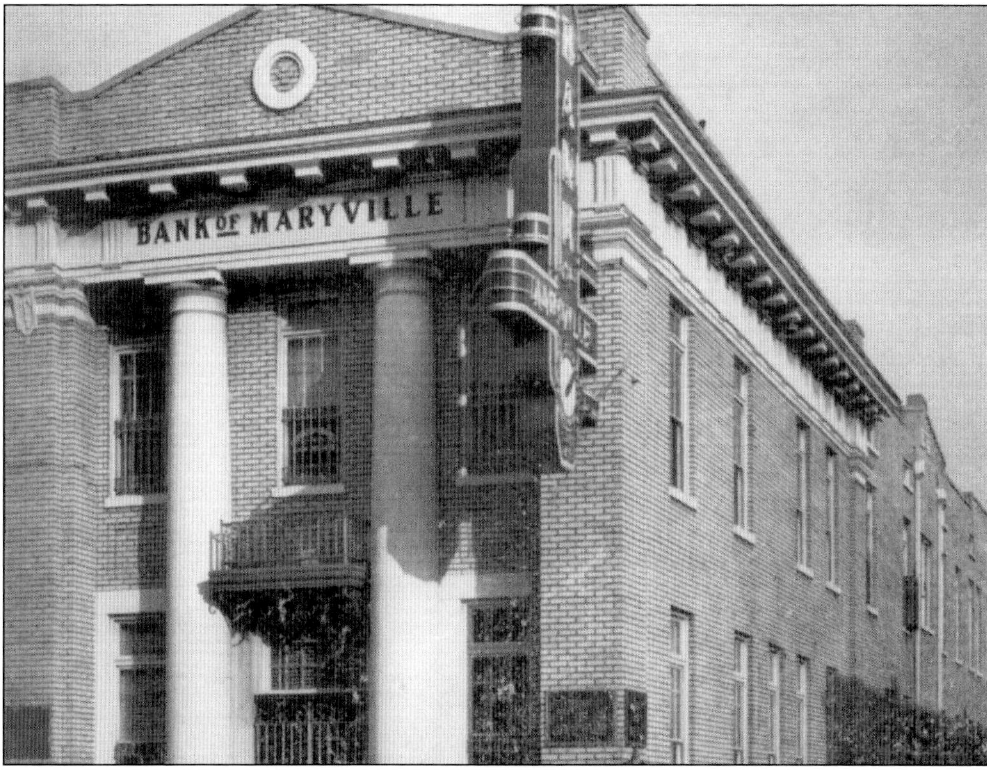

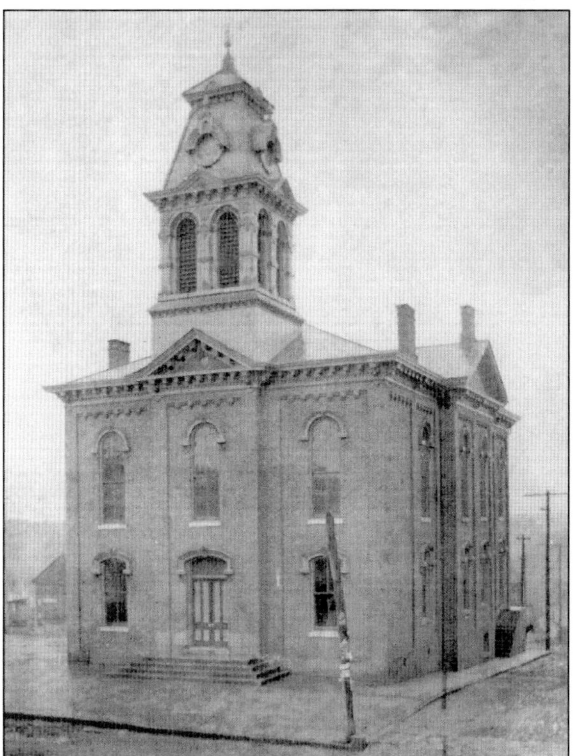

Pictured above is the Bank of Maryville building. A historical marker on the side of the building commemorates the spot where Sam Houston joined the US Army in 1813. Previously, this corner lot was known as Courthouse Square, for it was here that four prior courthouses stood, including the one shown at left built in 1879 and destroyed by fire in 1906. The courthouse located on the site before the one shown was attacked by Confederate general Joe Wheeler's cavalry during the Civil War. It was during the battle that Polly Toole, a slave, rescued county records from an ensuing fire. (Above, courtesy of Sandra Lee Stevens; left, courtesy of City of Maryville.)

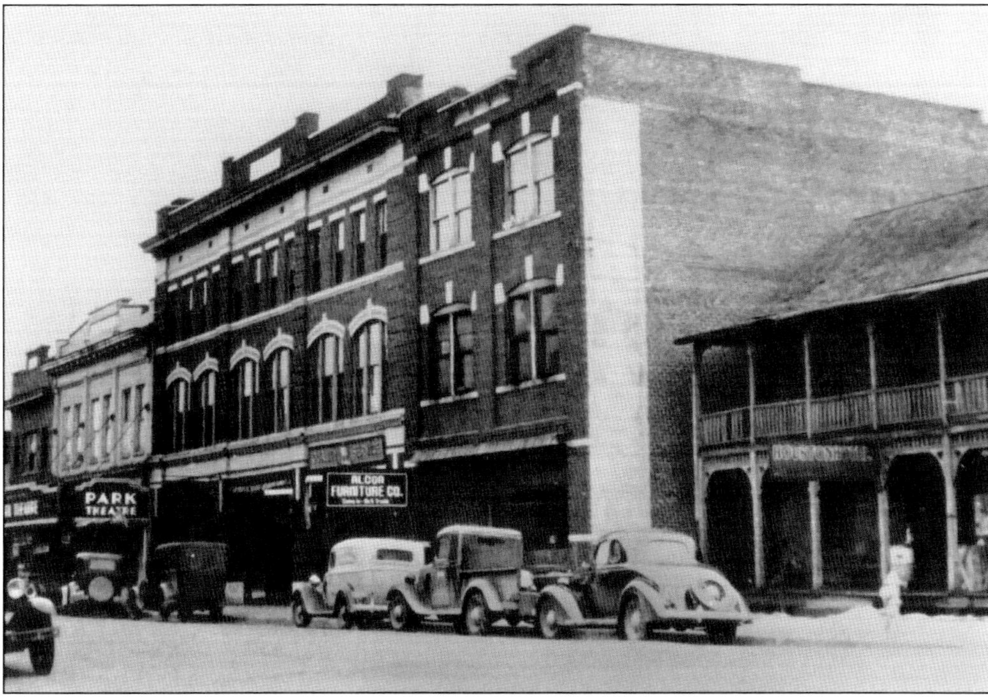

Shown above around the 1930s are the westernmost buildings on this block of Main Street. To the right is the Houston Hotel, formerly known as the Sam Houston Inn. It was replaced with the Gamble Building, constructed in 1939, shown to the right in the picture at right. The Gamble Building was home to Royal Jewelers for many years. The fourth building from the left shown above is the Herman Reuter building constructed in 1912. It was the first home of Palace Theatre and then for many years the home of Park Theatre. This building, most recently home to Roy's Record Shop, is the only building left standing. Broadway Towers now stands on the site of the three buildings shown to the right in the picture above. (Above, courtesy of the *Daily Times*; right, courtesy of City of Maryville.)

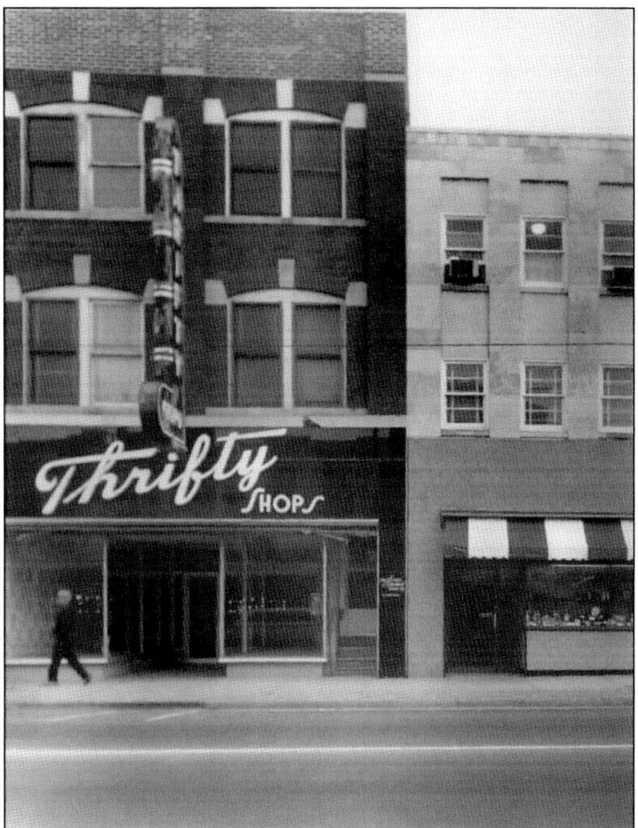

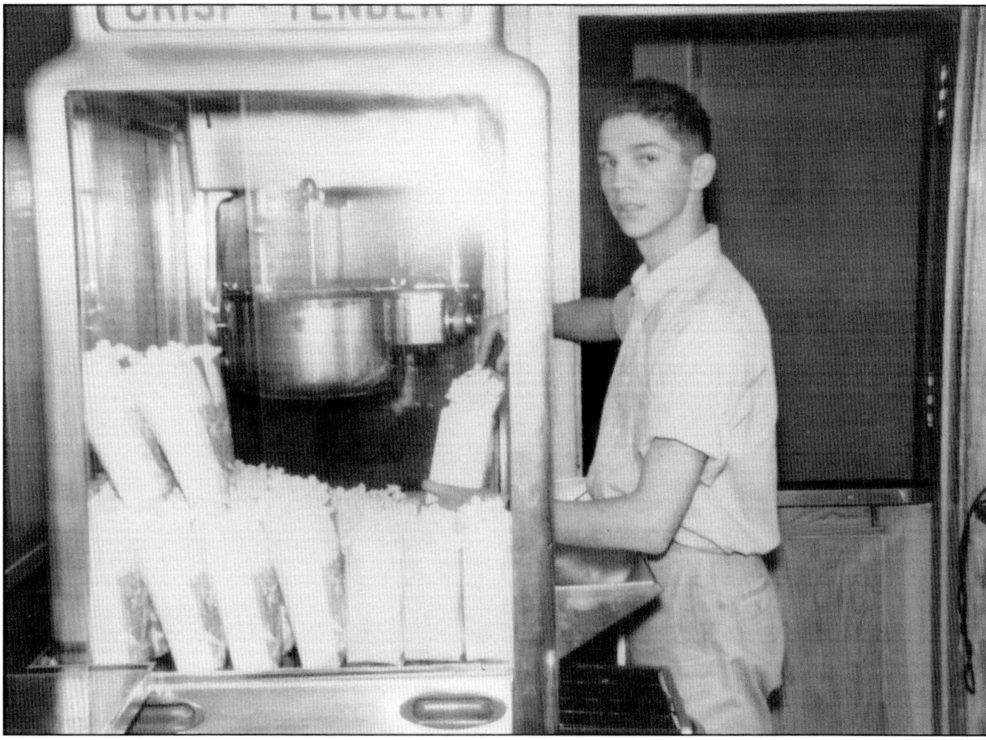

Charles Belcher is shown bagging popcorn in the Park Theatre in 1950. At one time, three different theaters were located on Main Street within a short distance of each other. The Candy Kitchen and Luke's Billiards were also located in the Reuter Building. (Courtesy of Maryville City Schools.)

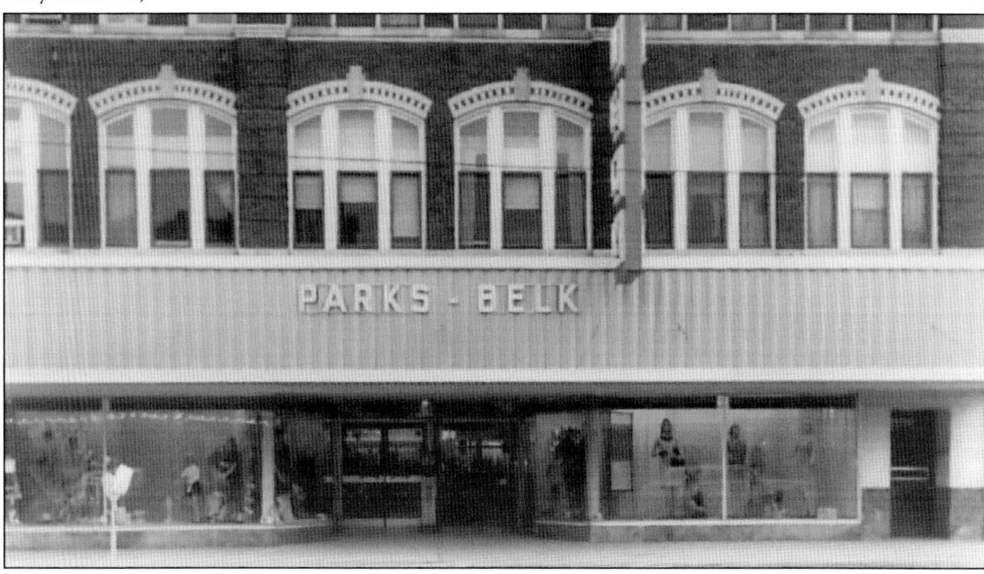

This building once stood to the right of the Reuter Building, and was home to many businesses and professional offices, including Peoples Telephone & Telegraph Company. Parks-Belk Department Store was one of many department stores to call Main Street, then Broadway, home. (Courtesy of City of Maryville.)

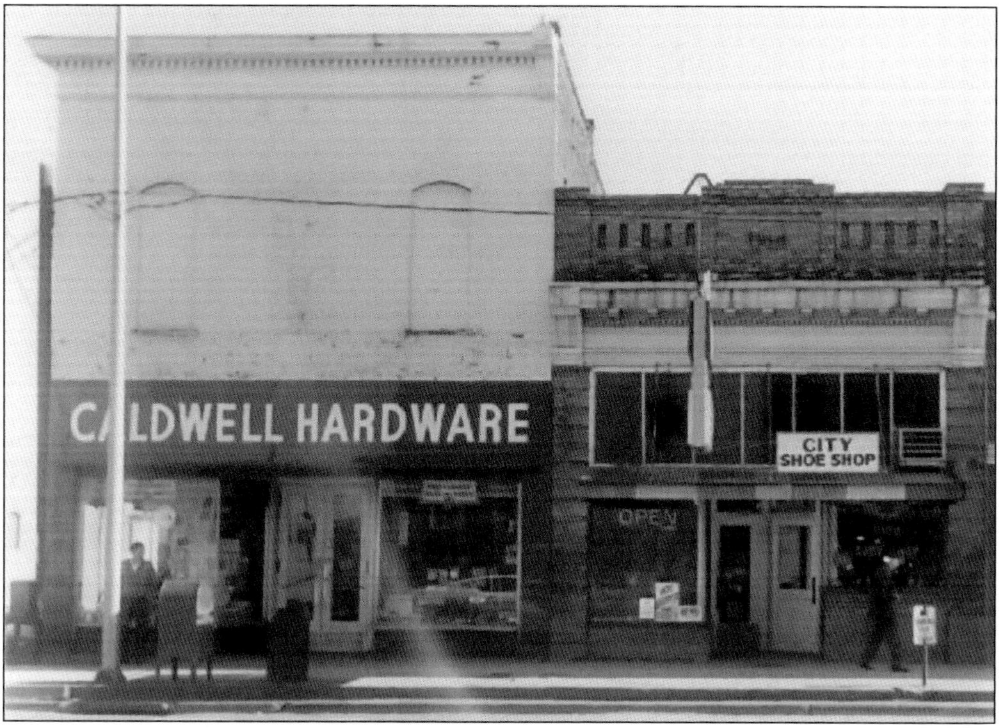

Shown above, at left, is the Elmer B. Waller Building, erected in 1910, and at right, a building constructed in 1908 that was home to First National Bank from 1914–1921. For many years, Crawford and Caldwell Hardware, then Norton Hardware, was located in the Waller Building on the corner of Cusick and Main Streets. In more recent years, the Down Yonder Saloon was located in the basement. Crawford and Caldwell had telephone number 1. Shown below is an interior scene of Crawford and Caldwell around 1910. (Above, courtesy of City of Maryville; below, courtesy of Louise Crawford Berry.)

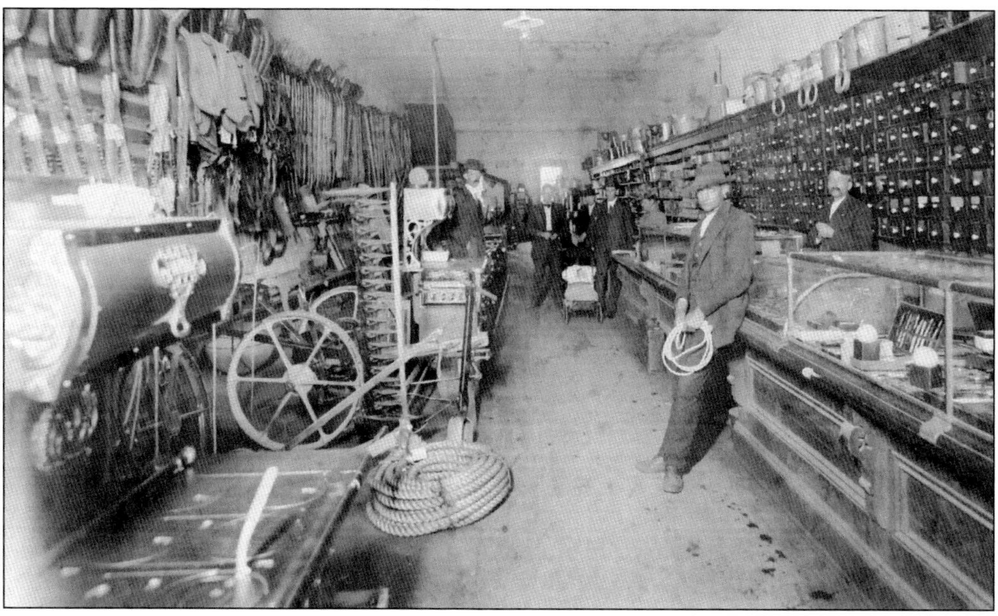

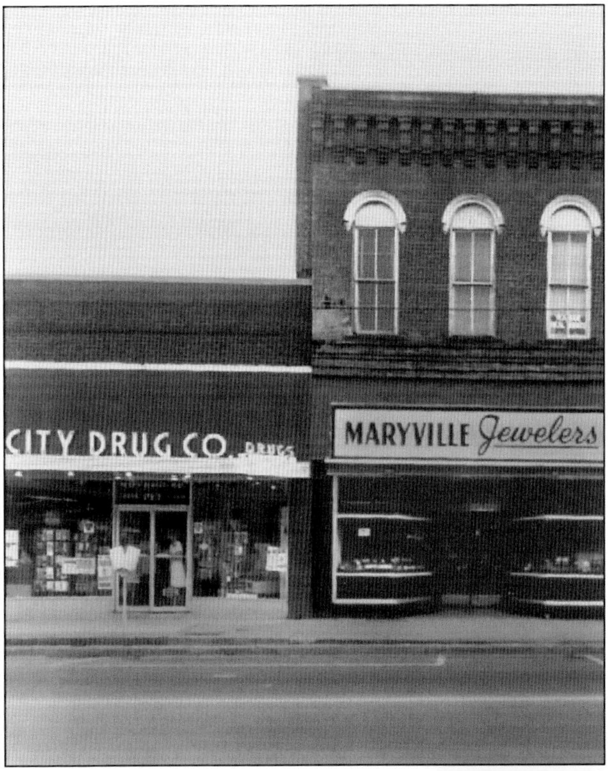

Shown in the photograph to the left, on the left, is the Bank of Blount County Building, erected in 1908, and on the right, a portion of a building constructed around 1870 on three lots owned by J.M. Greer, Will Henry, and Charles Pflanze. This building was the first large building constructed on Main Street after the Civil War, and was also previously home to the Bank of Blount County, seen below. Also located in the building on the right was the Maryville Telephone Exchange. Shown below is the Bank of Blount County when it was located in the building to the right in the image at left, around 1900. In the center of the entryway is Tom F. Cooper, first executive officer (cashier). With the umbrella is Joe Lamon. The other persons are unidentified. (Left, courtesy of City of Maryville; below, courtesy of A.B. Goddard.)

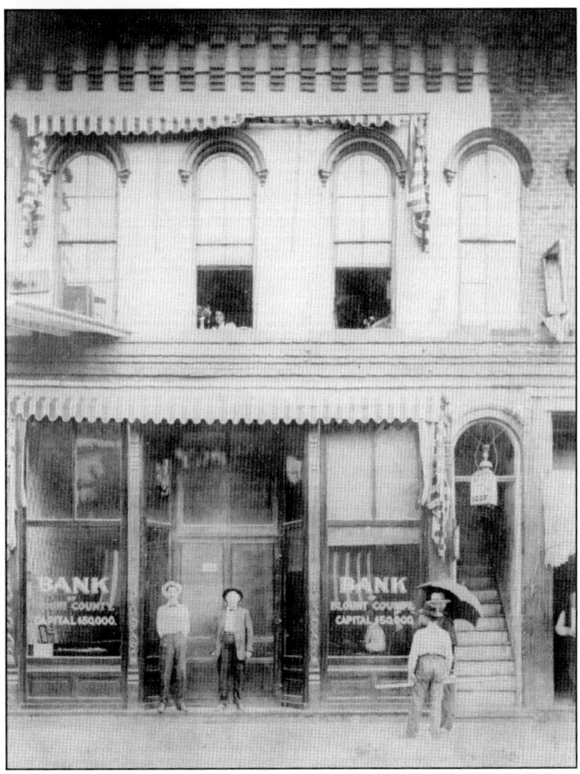

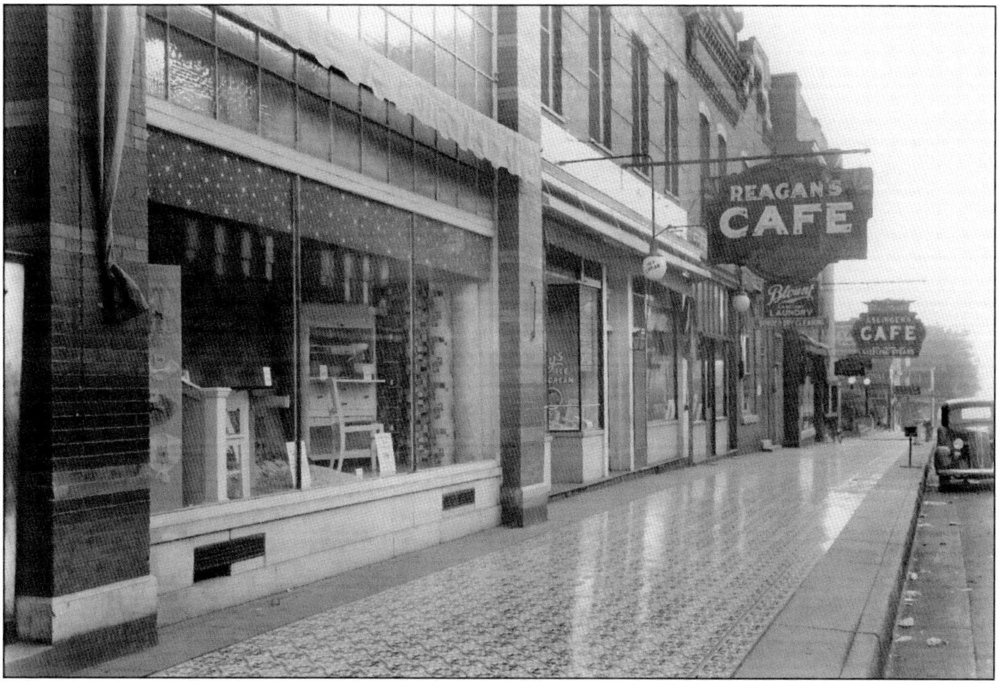

Proffitt's Department Store was once located in the building on the left. The store was founded in 1919 by David Wilson "D.W." Proffitt. As shown in this picture taken in the 1930s, Proffitt marketed linoleum by spreading it along the Main Street sidewalk. Most recently, National School Products was located in the Proffitt's building. (Courtesy of the Daily Times.)

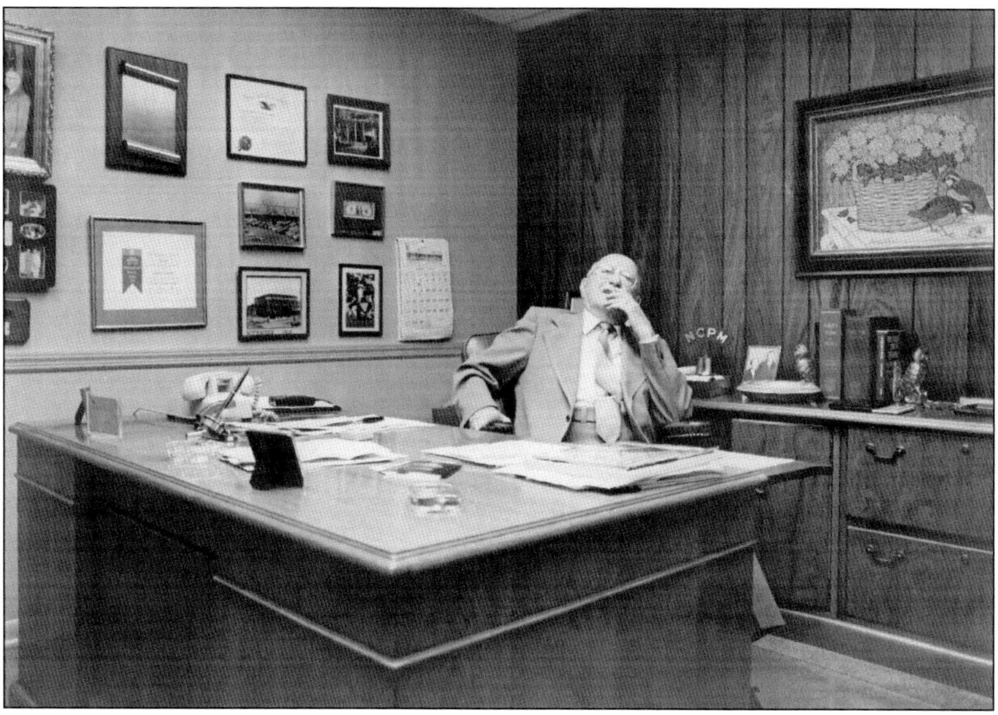

D.W. Proffitt is pictured in his office in later years. (Courtesy of the *Daily Times*.)

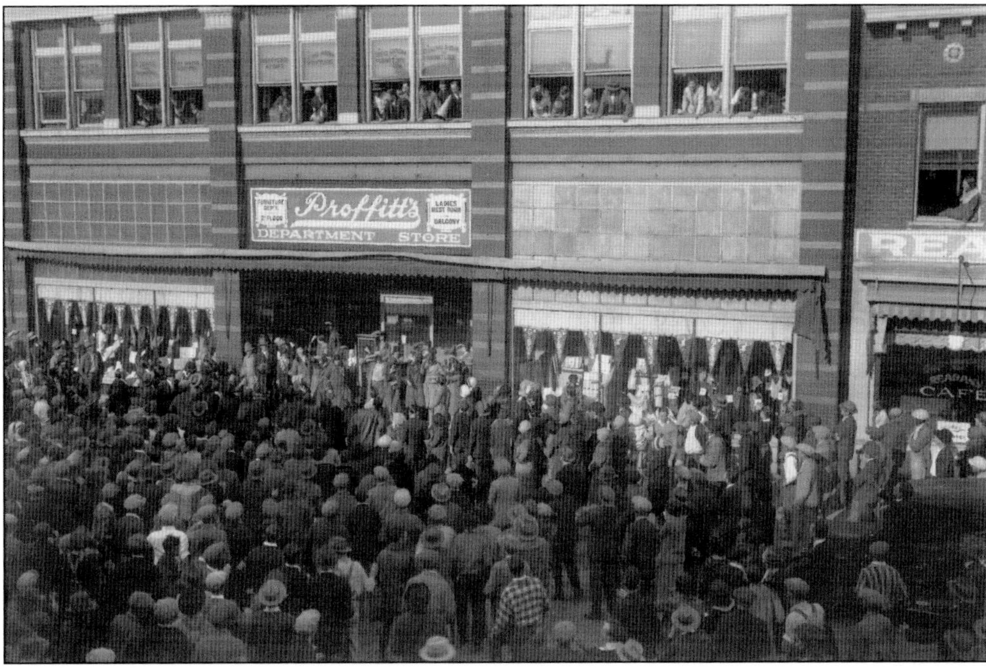

The Badgett Department Store Building was constructed in 1907 after the A.K. Harper Building was destroyed by the same fire that engulfed the courthouse. After Proffitt's opened and during the Great Depression, D.W. Proffitt established a promotion, shown above, of tossing fowl to the crowd below for Thanksgiving dinners. (Courtesy of the *Daily Times*.)

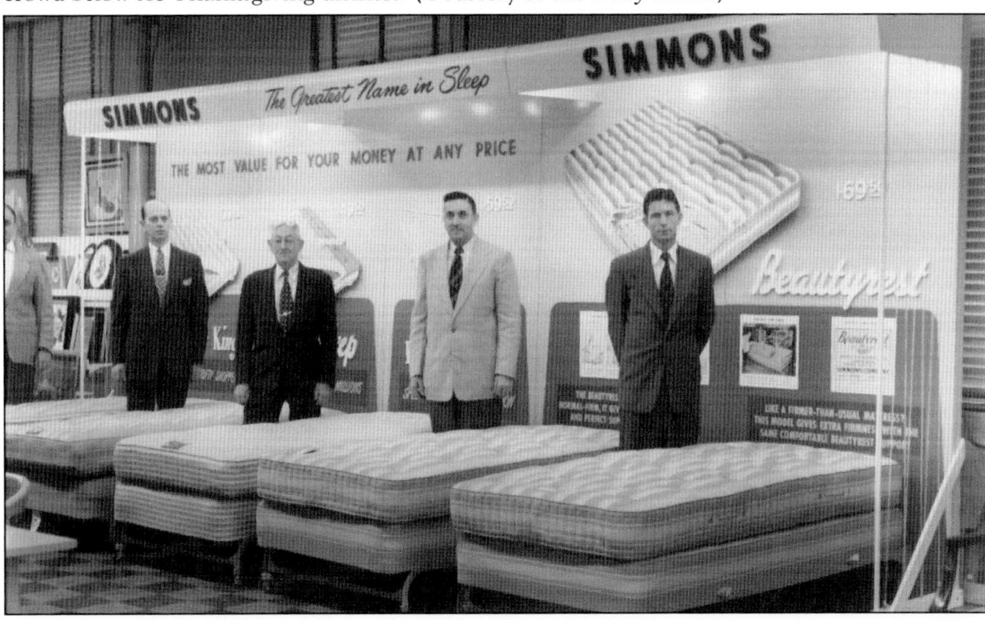

Pictured on the floor above the mezzanine inside Proffitt's Department Store are, from left to right, John Harrison (partially obscured), Charlie Stapp, Ben Cunningham, John Blackburn, and Raymond Snider. When Proffitt's stopped carrying large appliances, it was the oldest General Electric dealer in America. (Courtesy of Blount County Genealogical and Historical Society, Ned Sherer Collection.)

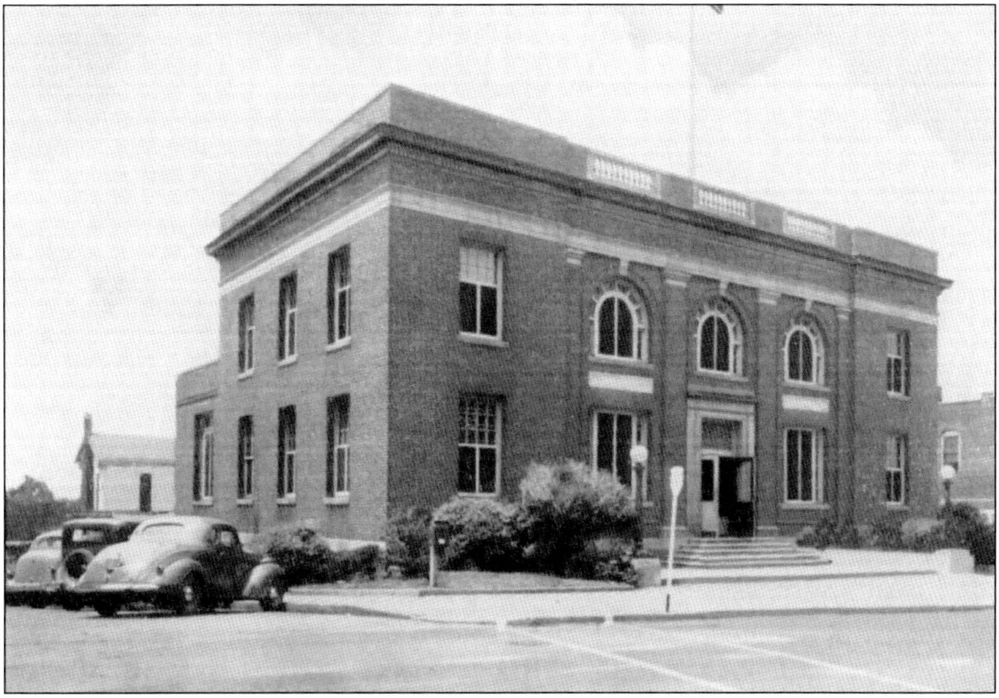

The Federal Building was erected in 1916. It was once home to the Maryville Post Office. A cornerstone commemorates the construction of the building, which was listed in the National Register of Historic Places in 1989. (Courtesy of Ken Cornett.)

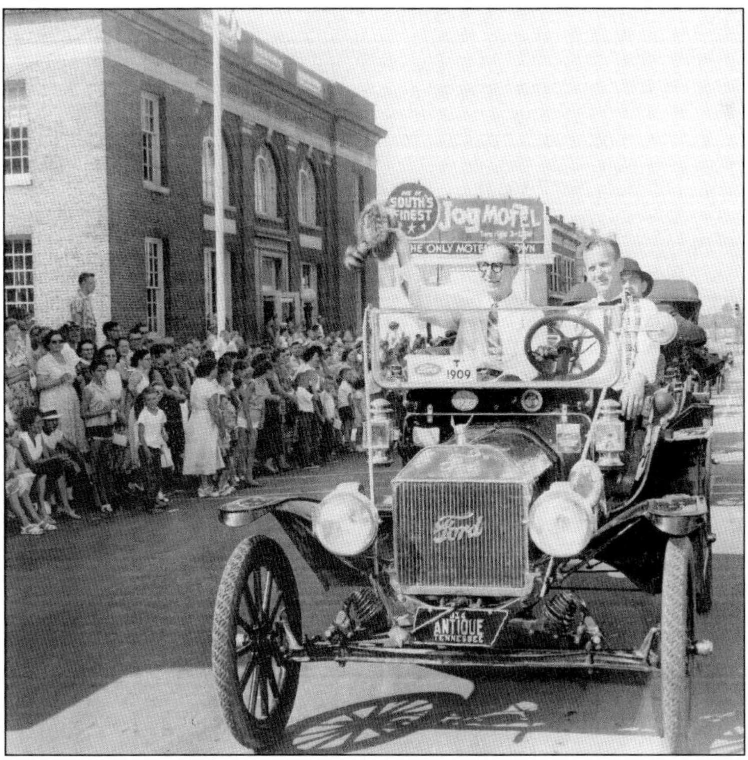

In this 1950s photograph, Kenneth Coulter drives Sen. Estes Kefauver in a parade along Broadway. Kefauver, the 1956 Democratic candidate for vice president, is waving his trademark coonskin cap. In the left background can be seen the Joy Motel sign that stood atop the Elder's Cash and Carry Grocery Store building. For many years, the sign also advertised the J & K Super Stores. (Courtesy of the *Daily Times*.)

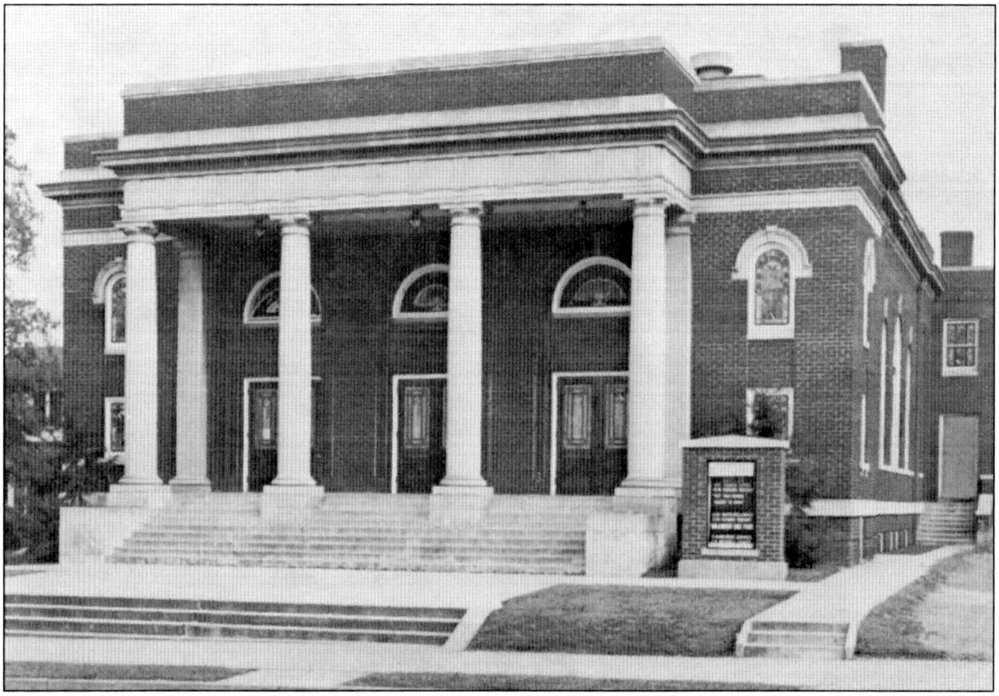

The Maryville First United Methodist Church building, constructed in 1923, once stood on the corner of Norwood Street and Broadway facing Broadway. The CBBC Bank building is now located there. Two earlier buildings housing this Methodist congregation had previously stood on the site. (Courtesy of A.B. Goddard.)

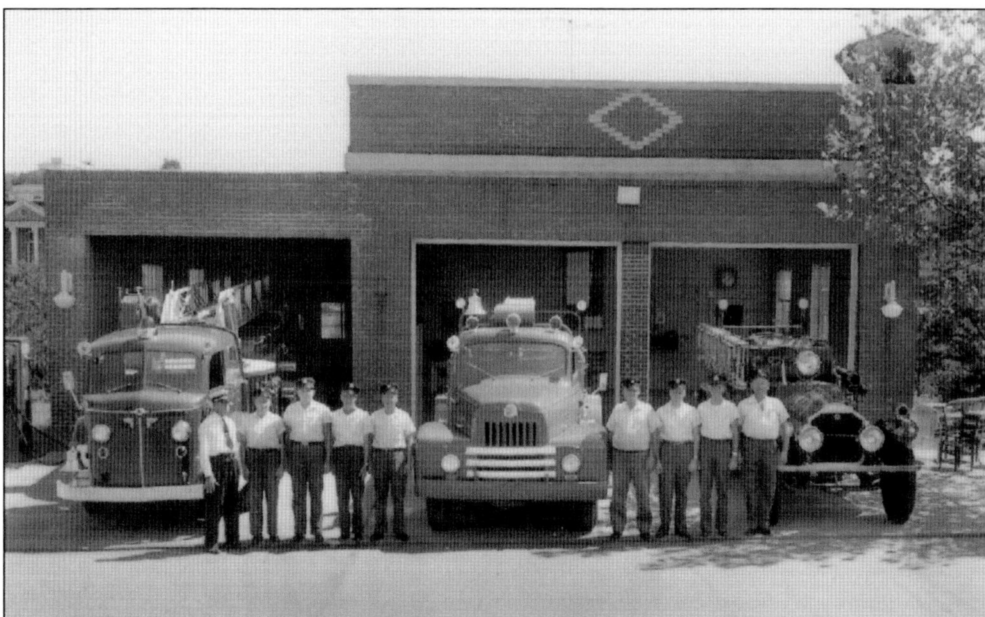

The Maryville Fire Hall, shown here in the 1950s, was built in 1927 on Church Avenue. It was Maryville's only fire station until the municipal building was constructed in 1956. The municipal building was razed and replaced by the present building in 2005. (Courtesy of the *Daily Times*.)

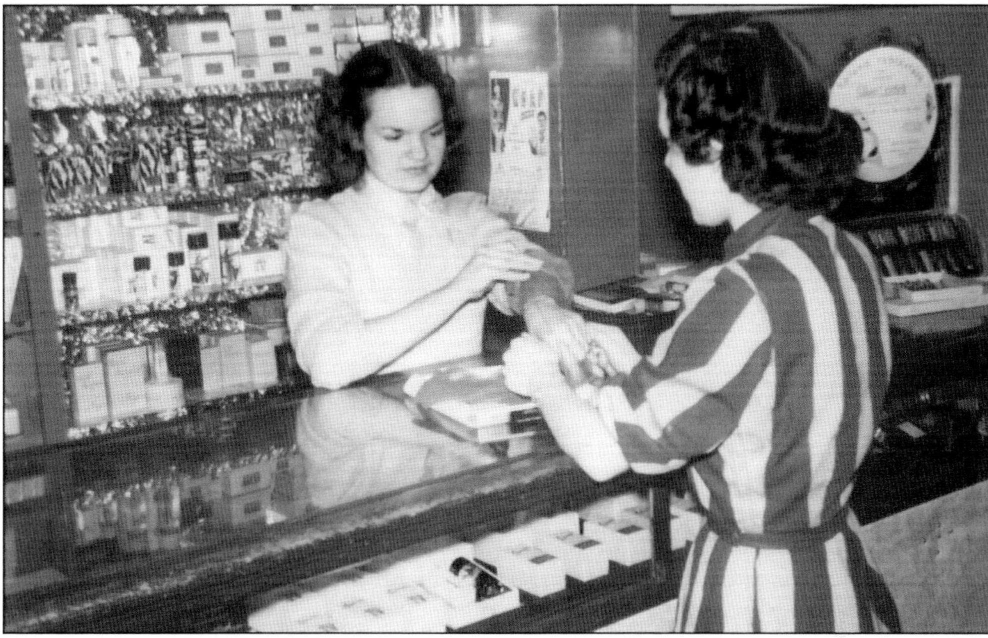

Shown in 1950 assisting a MacArthur's Department Store customer is Annalee Jones. Byrne's Drug Store would later locate in this building. (Courtesy of Maryville City Schools.)

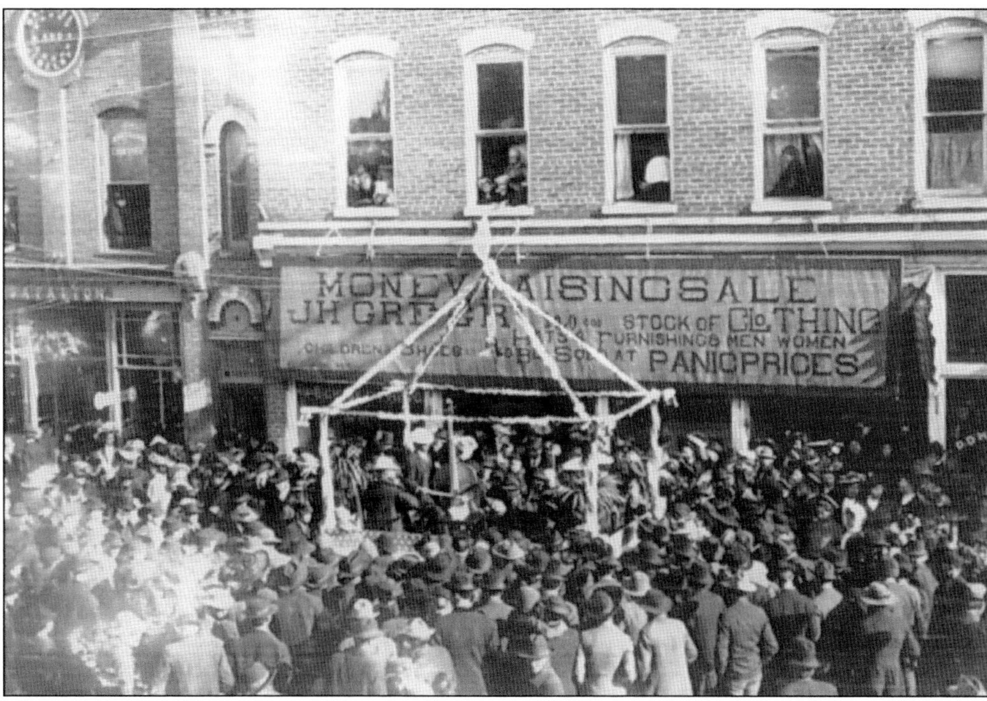

The Samuel A. Patton Building, left, was constructed in 1879. Patton operated a jewelry store there. To the right are the 1878 Andrew Gamble buildings, once home to the Maryville Library. When this picture was taken in 1908, the J.H. Greer Clothing Store was located in the Gamble Buildings, and the marriage of Austria Bright to Millard Cupp was being celebrated. (Courtesy of City of Maryville.)

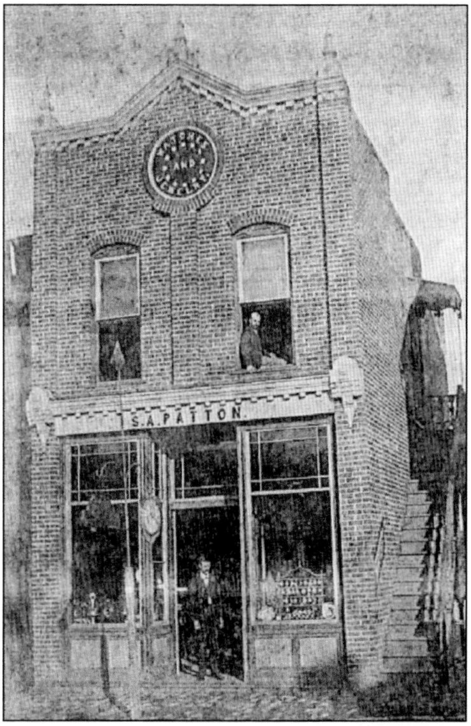

The Patton Building is shown again here. The letters "S.A. Patton," and the reference to watches and jewelry can be seen today. Hope Brothers Jewelry would later locate there, and their inlaid tiles can still be seen at the entrance to the building, which was listed in the National Register of Historic Places in 1989. (Courtesy of City of Maryville.)

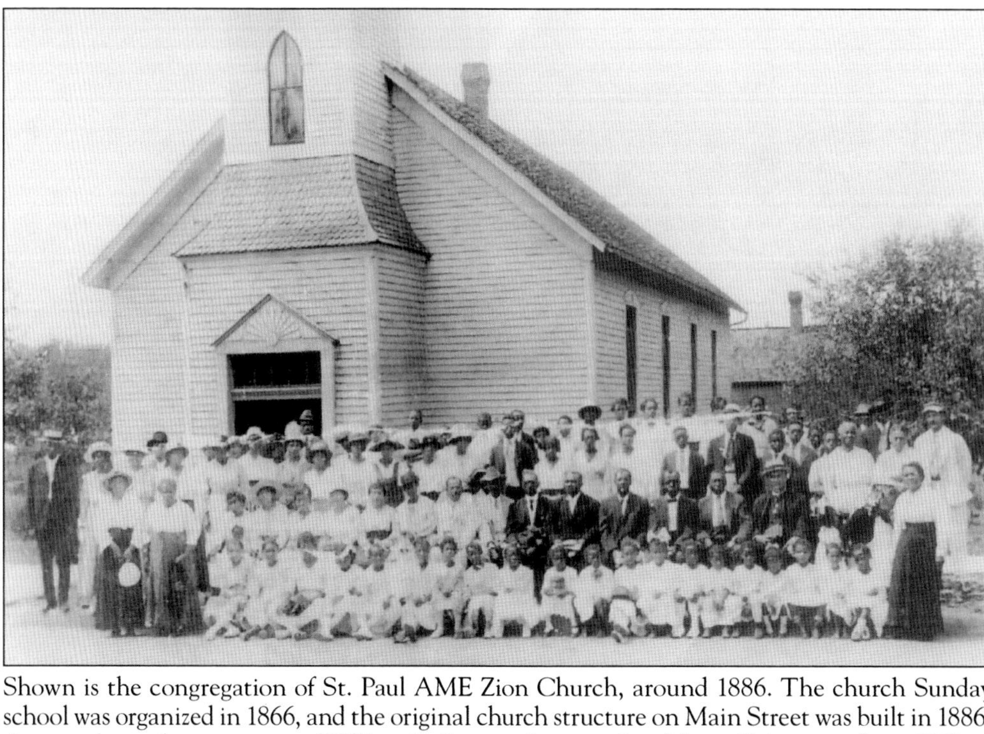

Shown is the congregation of St. Paul AME Zion Church, around 1886. The church Sunday school was organized in 1866, and the original church structure on Main Street was built in 1886. Among the early trustees was William B. Scott, who served as Maryville's mayor from 1869 to 1870. Scott was also Tennessee's first African American newspaper publisher. (Courtesy of St. Paul AME Zion Church.)

New Providence Presbyterian Church was one of the first two churches organized in Blount County in 1786 when it was located near Craig's Fort. This photograph shows the church as it appeared around 1915 at the intersection of College Street and East Church Avenue, presently Preservation Plaza. Its pastors included Isaac Anderson, who founded Maryville College. The cornerstone for the present New Providence building was laid in 1952 on West Broadway. (Courtesy of the Blount County Public Library.)

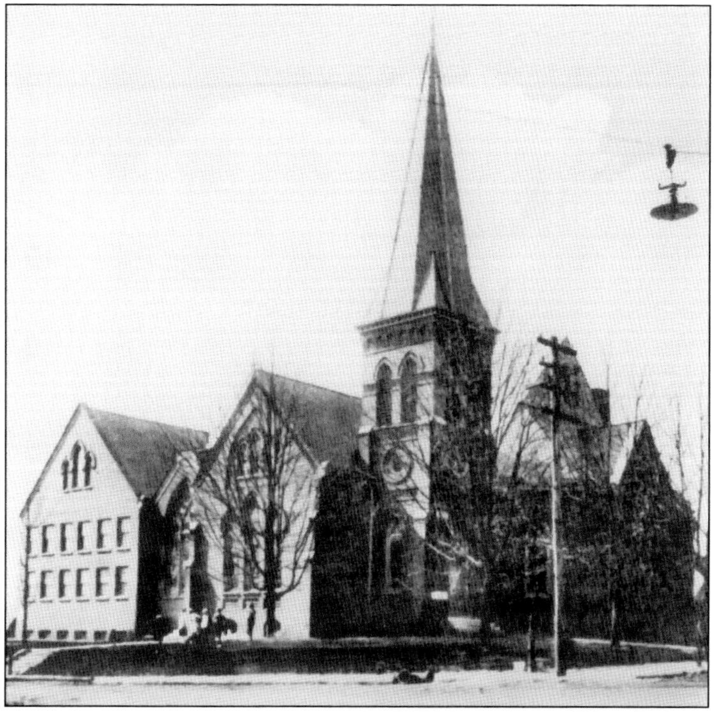

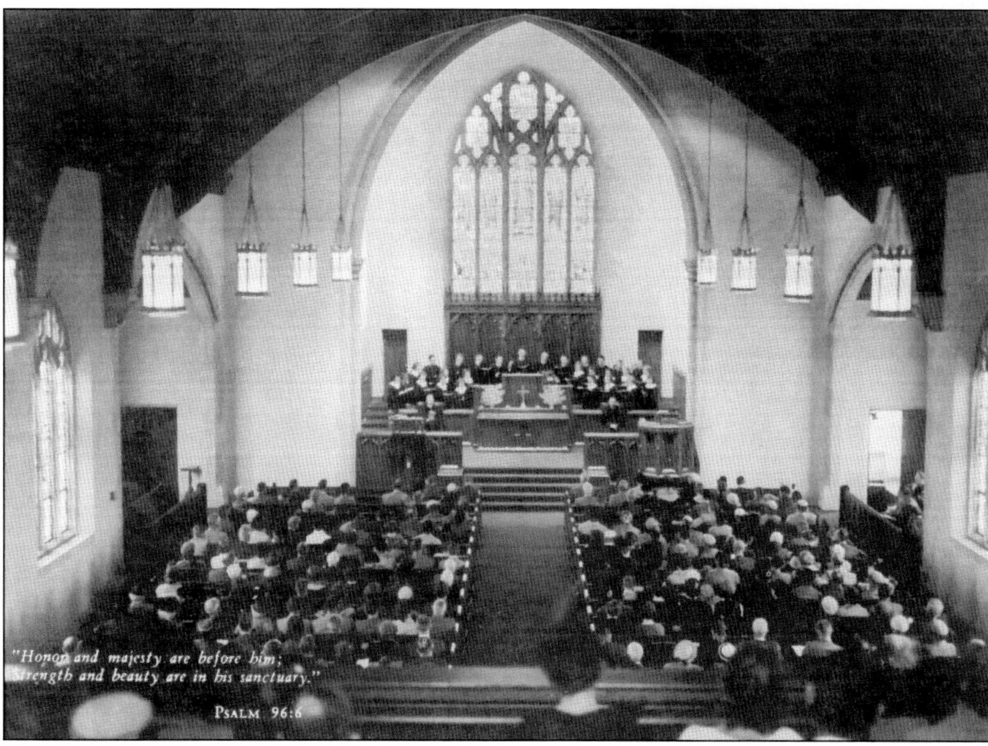

Shown in this photograph is one of the early services inside New Providence's new sanctuary in 1953. Sen. Lamar Alexander was a member of the congregation when he was growing up in Maryville. (Courtesy of Ann Talley Hitch.)

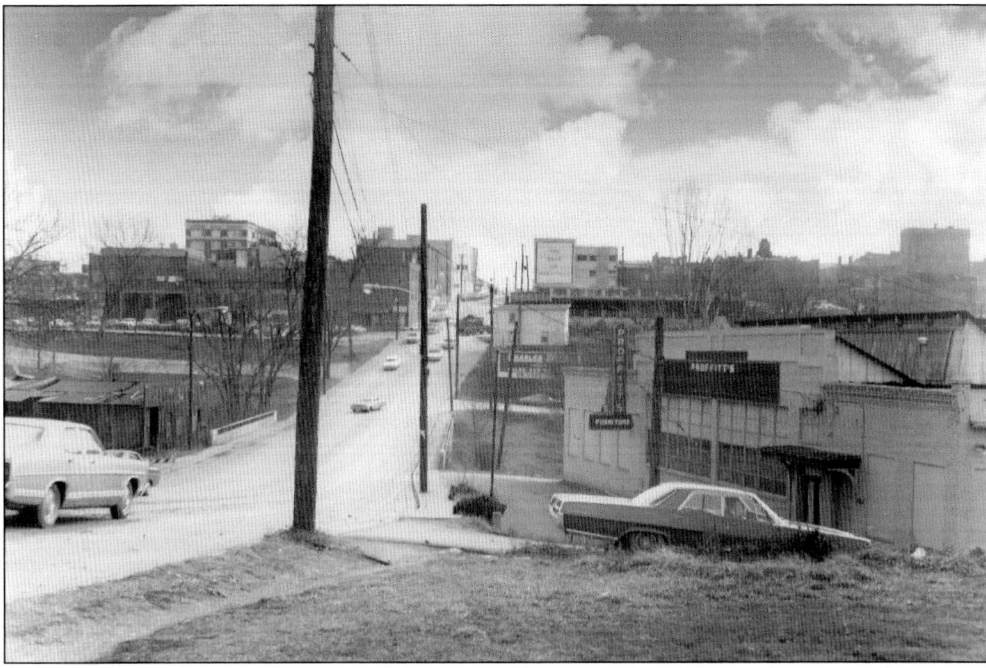

Pictured above is the Cusick Street bridge. Proffitt's Warehouse is on the right. The picture below was taken from the same general area, but looking north toward Alcoa and Midland Shopping Center. The road to the right in the picture below is the approximate entrance today to the Blount County Public Library. The road then led to Parham Hill where the library, Regal Towers, Olympia Athletic Club, and other businesses are presently located. (Above, courtesy of *Daily Times*; below, courtesy of City of Maryville.)

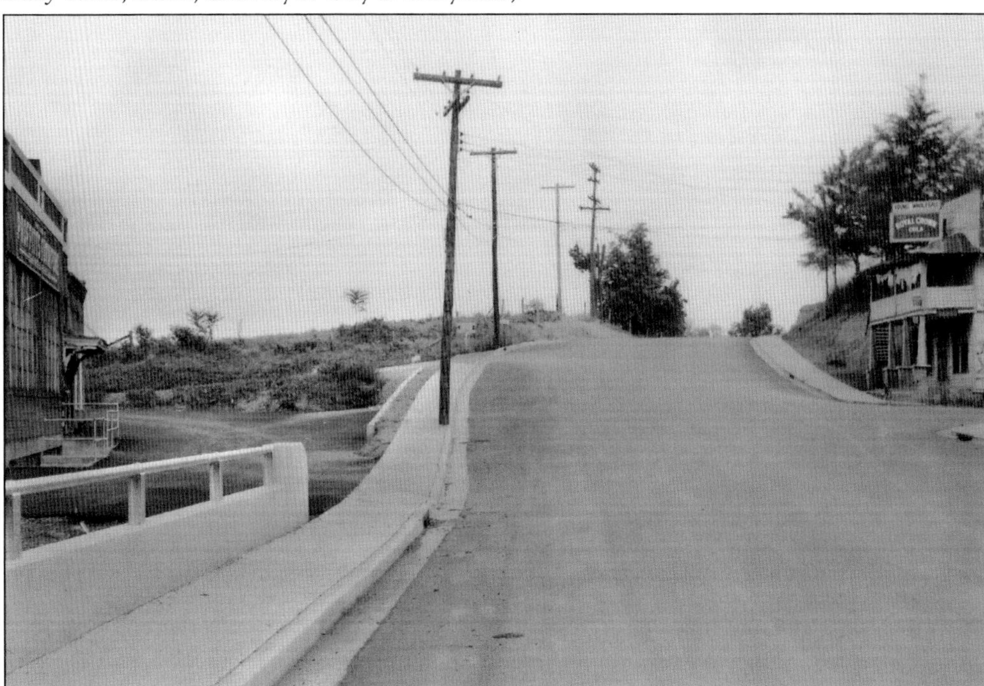

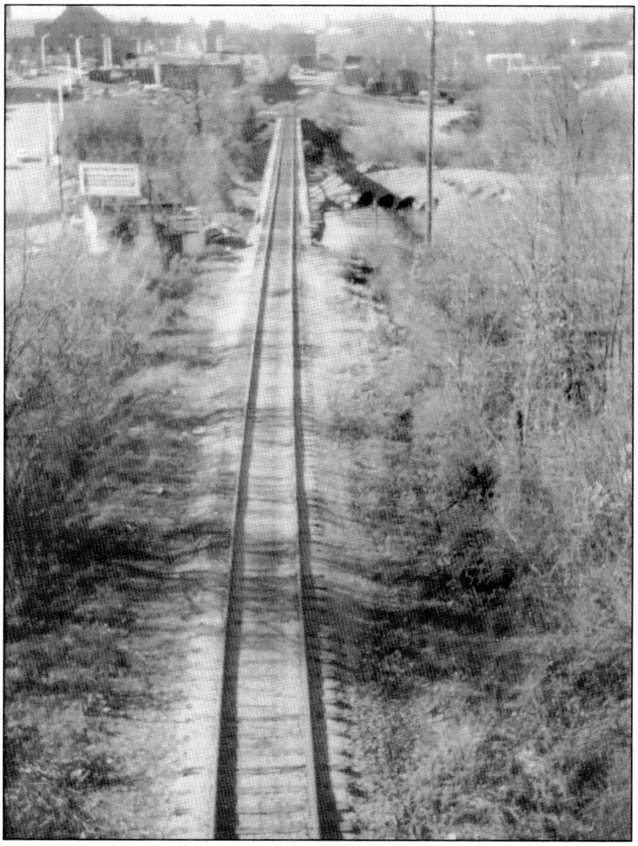

The L&N Railroad tracks once ran parallel to Harper Street north of Broadway. An L&N branch line was first built in to Maryville in 1906. The L&N tracks in this area included a 516-foot trestle across Pistol and Brown Creeks. The scene below looks north from the L&N tracks toward Parham Hill. The Fred Morton and Son Food Market can be seen atop the hill to the right. The hill was named for William Thomas Parham and William Edmund Parham. (Right, photograph by Hyldard Stinnett, courtesy of Becky Blankenship Darrell; below, courtesy of City of Maryville.)

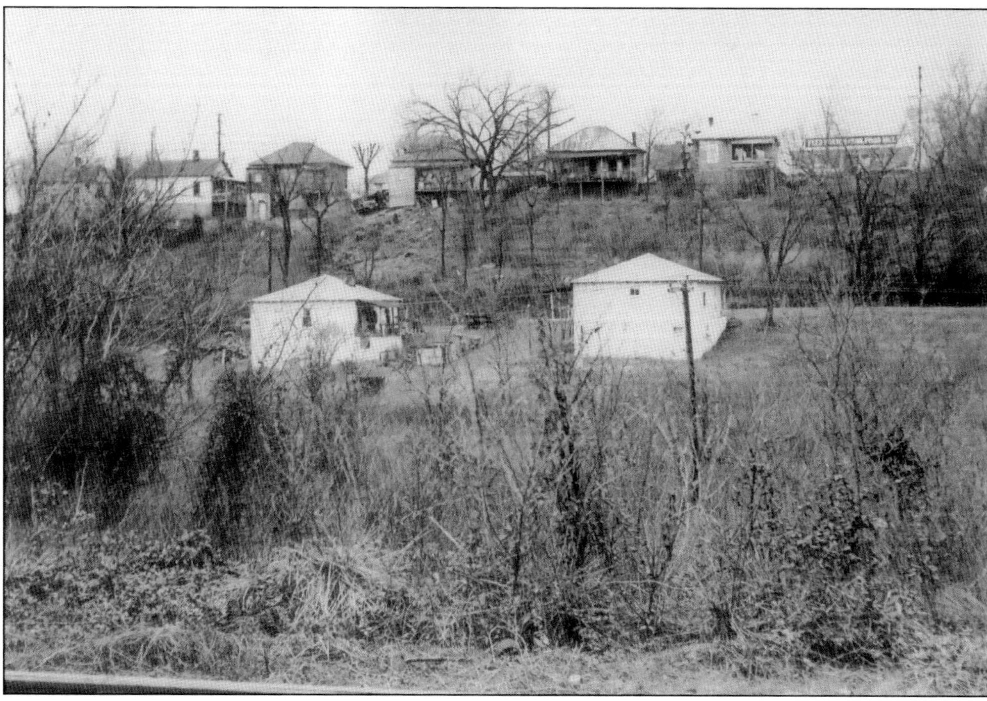

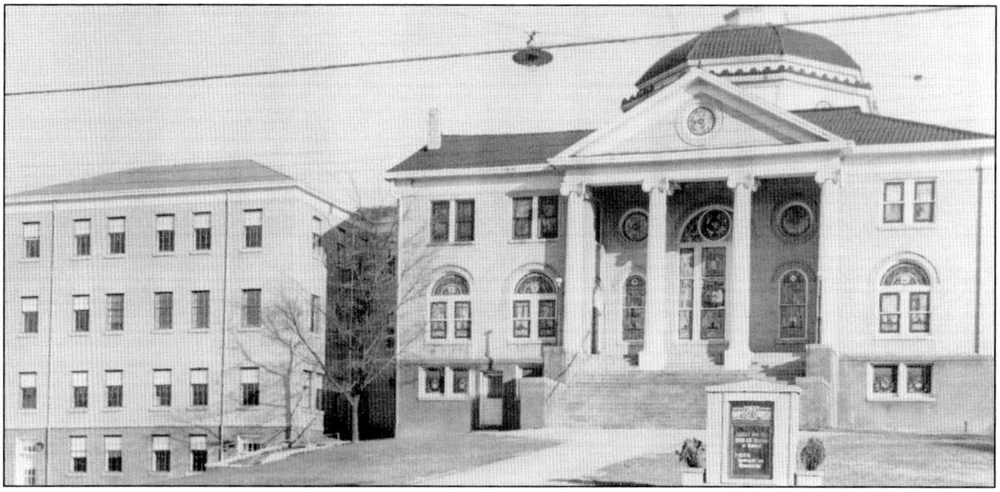

The original First Baptist Church of Maryville, located on Ellis Avenue, was constructed in 1914. The educational building to the left was constructed in 1949. The first church building, constructed in 1876, stood on the same lot but fronted on High Street. The church moved to its present location in 1957, and the building shown here became home to Second Baptist Church. (Courtesy of *Daily Times*.)

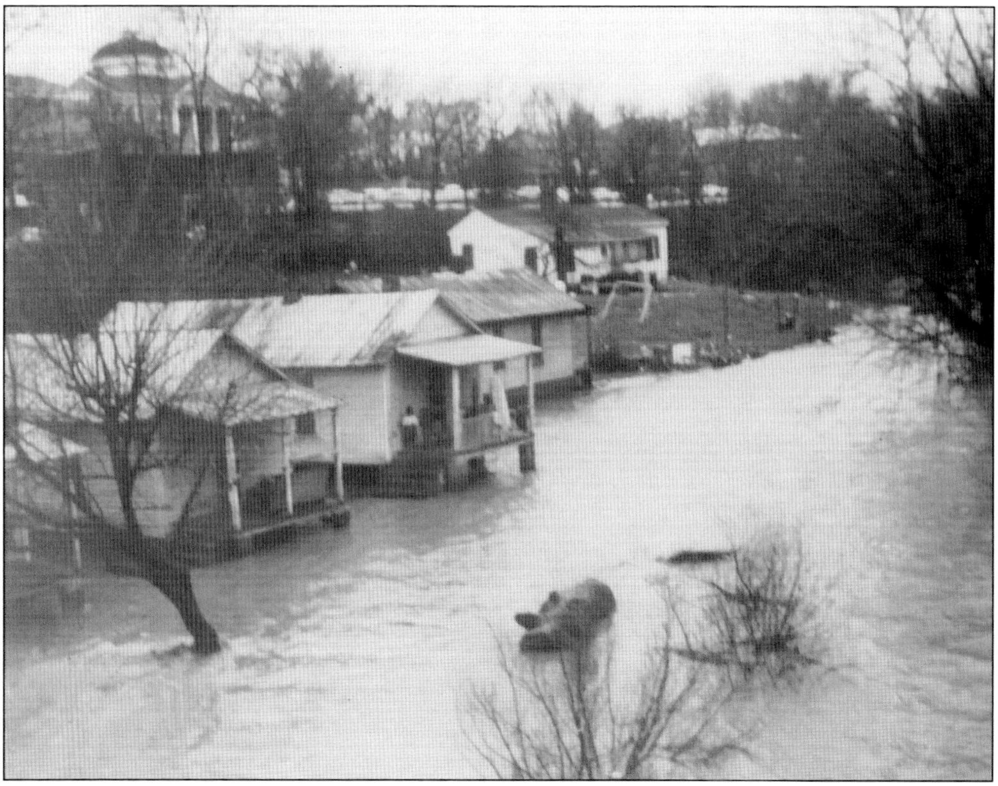

Through the years, Pistol Creek has sometimes flooded. First Baptist Church can be seen in the left background. In an effort to make room for parking for the church, the lots across Ellis Avenue were filled with tons of dirt and stone in 1952 to make a large parking area. The development necessitated the diversion of Pistol Creek. (Courtesy of City of Maryville.)

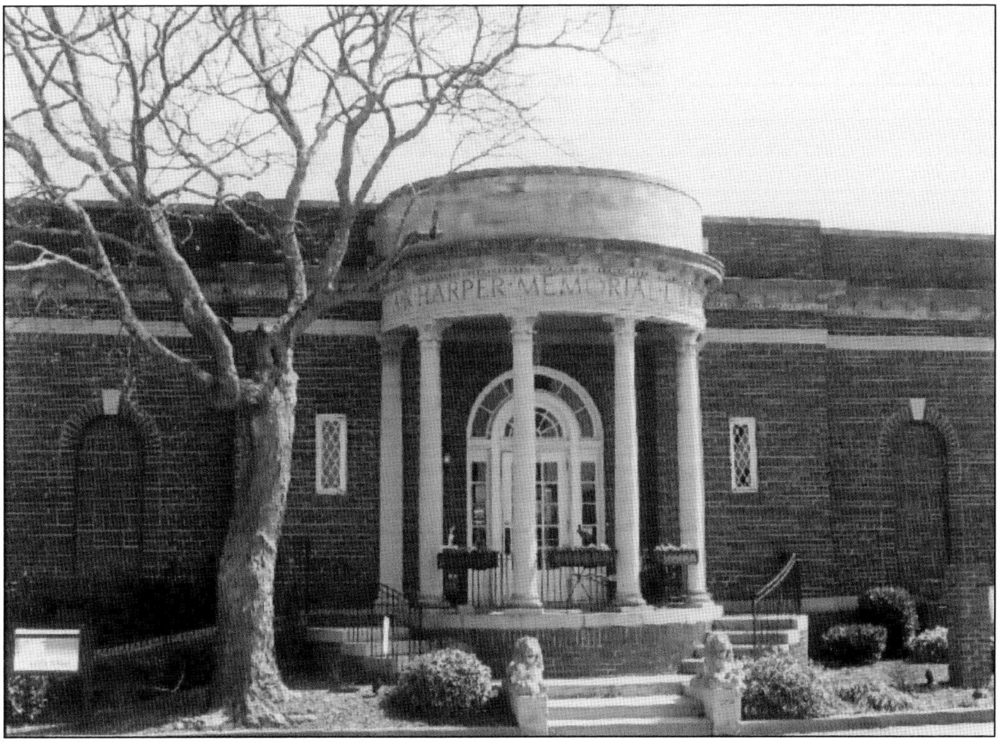

The A.K. Harper Memorial Library Building, shown here in 2012, was constructed in 1931 and served as the public library until the early 1980s. Mrs. A.K. Harper donated the funds to construct this building as a memorial to her late husband, a former Maryville mayor and prominent businessman. Harper Avenue was named for their son Milton, who was killed in World War I. The building now houses Dandy Lions Gift Shop. (Courtesy of Linda Braden Albert.)

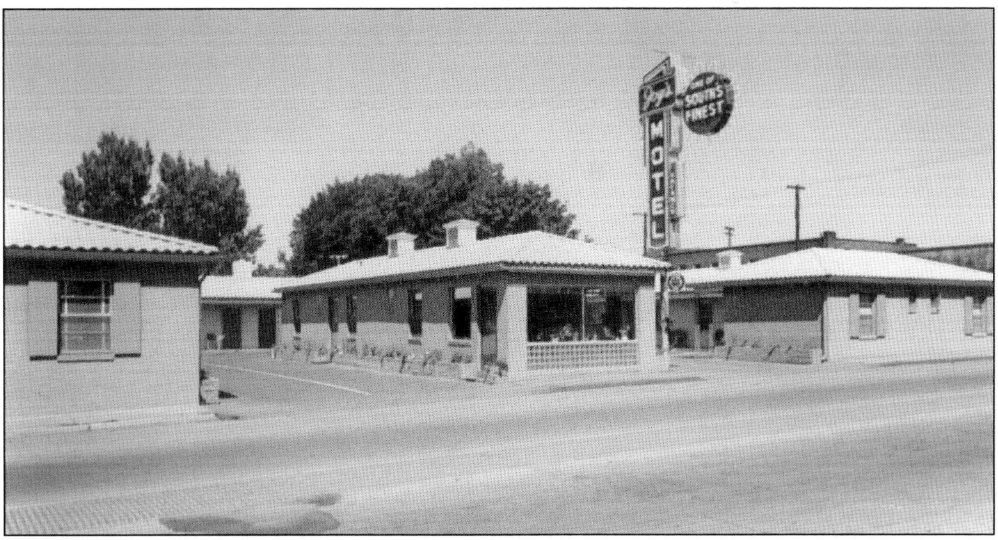

Pictured here is the Joy Motel, located on Washington Street. It once billed itself as "One of the South's Finest," and "The Only Hotel in Town." In those days, hotels and other businesses proudly advertised if they had air conditioning and color television available to patrons. (Courtesy of Ken Cornett.)

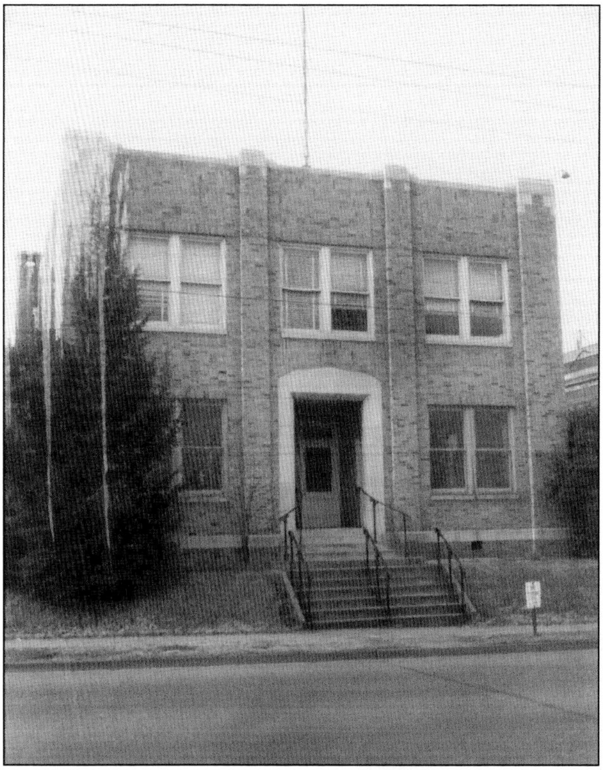

The Southern Bell Telephone Company Building was constructed in 1929. It stood on Church Avenue where a parking lot now separates CBBC Bank from Preservation Plaza. People's Telephone Company merged with Southern Bell just before the new building was constructed. The old Maryville Fire Department was located across the street. (Courtesy of City of Maryville.)

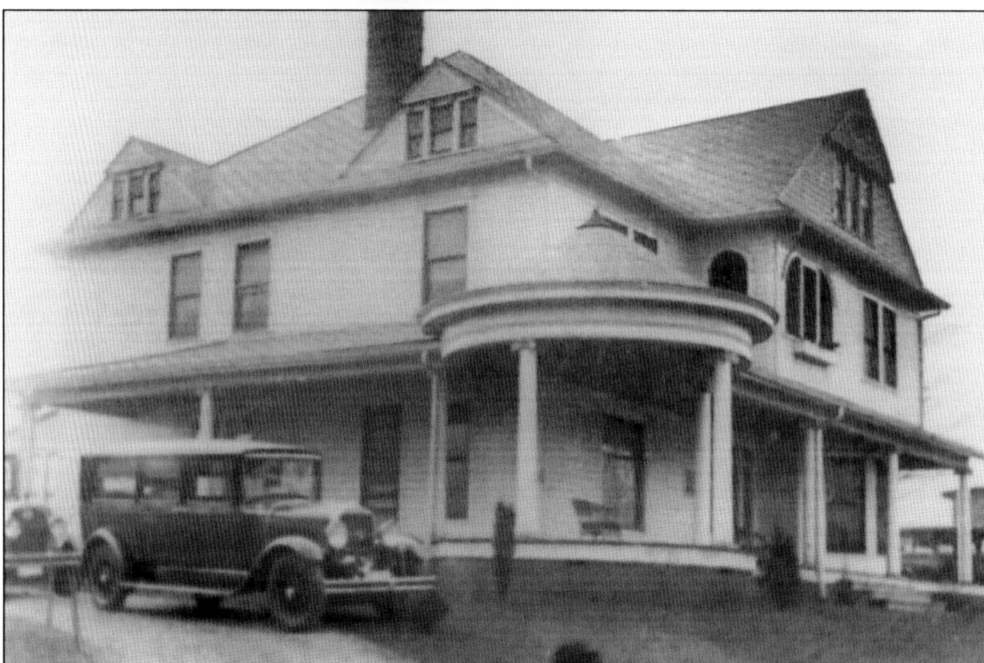

McCammon-Ammons Funeral Home is pictured in 1930. The business also provided ambulance service. The ambulance pictured had just been acquired from the Stanley Bird Motor Company, a Studebaker dealer. (Courtesy of Tom Click, McCammon-Ammons-Click Funeral Home.)

Three

Maryville College

Maryville College, founded in 1819, is the 12th oldest institution of higher learning in the South and maintains an affiliation with the Presbyterian Church (USA).

Dr. Isaac Anderson, who was also the pastor of New Providence Presbyterian Church in Maryville, presented a proposal to the Presbyterian Church's Synod of Tennessee to establish a seminary modeled on Princeton and Andover. On October 19, 1819, the Synod approved the plan for the Southern and Western Theological Seminary. Anderson was appointed president and the only faculty member.

Seminary students were required to produce a diploma from a college or pass an examination by the professors on a course of literature. None of Anderson's first class of five met those qualifications. In response, provision was made for instruction on three levels: preparatory, a four-year college, and three-year seminary. In 1842, the institution, on Maryville's Main Street, was officially named Maryville College.

Maryville College was primarily attended by white men but Native American and black students were enrolled as early as the 1820s, making Maryville the first college in Tennessee to admit minorities. In 1875, graduate Mary Wilson became the first woman to receive a bachelor's degree from a Tennessee college.

The college closed on April 22, 1861, because of "armed hostilities"—the Civil War. It was reopened in 1866 with 13 students. Soon after, Maryville College moved to its present location on land purchased from the Fagg family. Today, the beautiful Maryville College campus encompasses 350 acres with 21 major buildings, 14 of which are listed in the National Register of Historic Places. Total enrollment for the fall 2011 semester was 1,078.

Maryville College, in addition to its rigorous academics, has a proud athletic heritage. John Stone, captain of the 1927 baseball team, was an outfielder with the Detroit Tigers from 1928 to 1933, and with the Washington Senators from 1934 to 1938. He had a .310 career batting average. The Scots played the University of Tennessee in football until the 1920s, tying the Volunteers 14-14 in 1923. The 1946 football team was undefeated in regular season play before losing to Catawba in the Tangerine Bowl, finishing the season at 9-1.

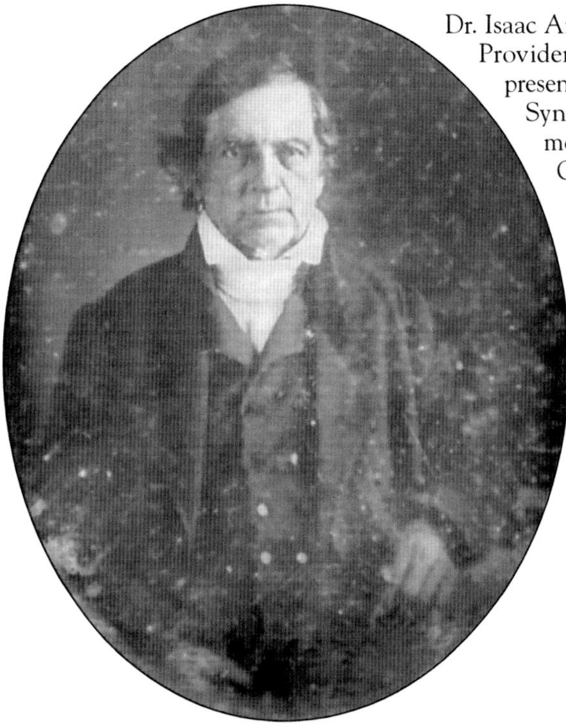

Dr. Isaac Anderson, who was also the pastor of New Providence Presbyterian Church in Maryville, presented a proposal to the Presbyterian Church's Synod of Tennessee to establish a seminary modeled on Princeton and Andover. On October 19, 1819, the Synod approved the plan for the Southern and Western Theological Seminary. Anderson was appointed president and the only faculty member. (Courtesy of Maryville College.)

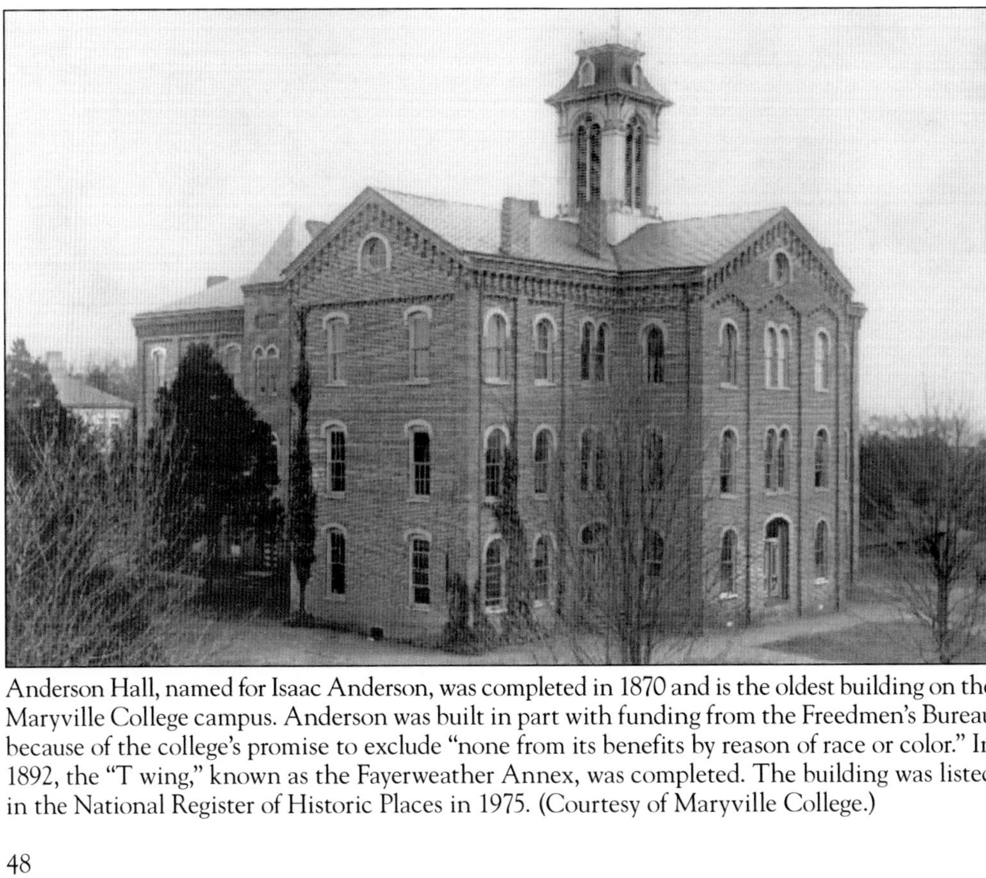

Anderson Hall, named for Isaac Anderson, was completed in 1870 and is the oldest building on the Maryville College campus. Anderson was built in part with funding from the Freedmen's Bureau because of the college's promise to exclude "none from its benefits by reason of race or color." In 1892, the "T wing," known as the Fayerweather Annex, was completed. The building was listed in the National Register of Historic Places in 1975. (Courtesy of Maryville College.)

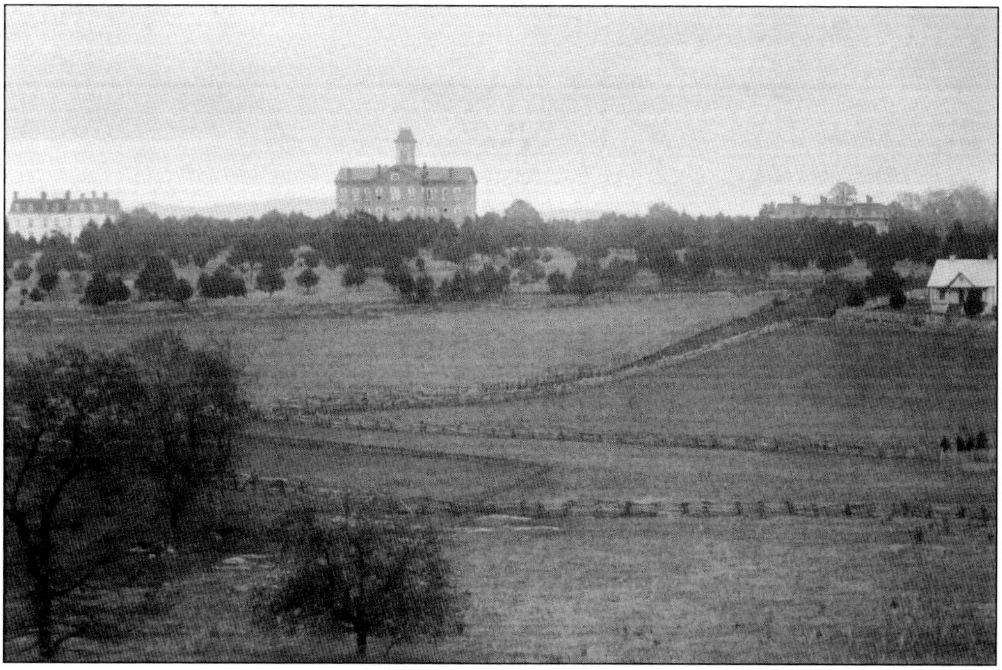

This view of the Maryville College campus from around 1880 shows, from left to right, Baldwin, Anderson, and Memorial Halls. Anderson was completed in 1870; Memorial, the men's dormitory, was completed in 1871; and Baldwin, the women's dormitory, also in 1871. Baldwin was removed in 1968 to make way for the Sutton Science Center. (Courtesy of Maryville College.)

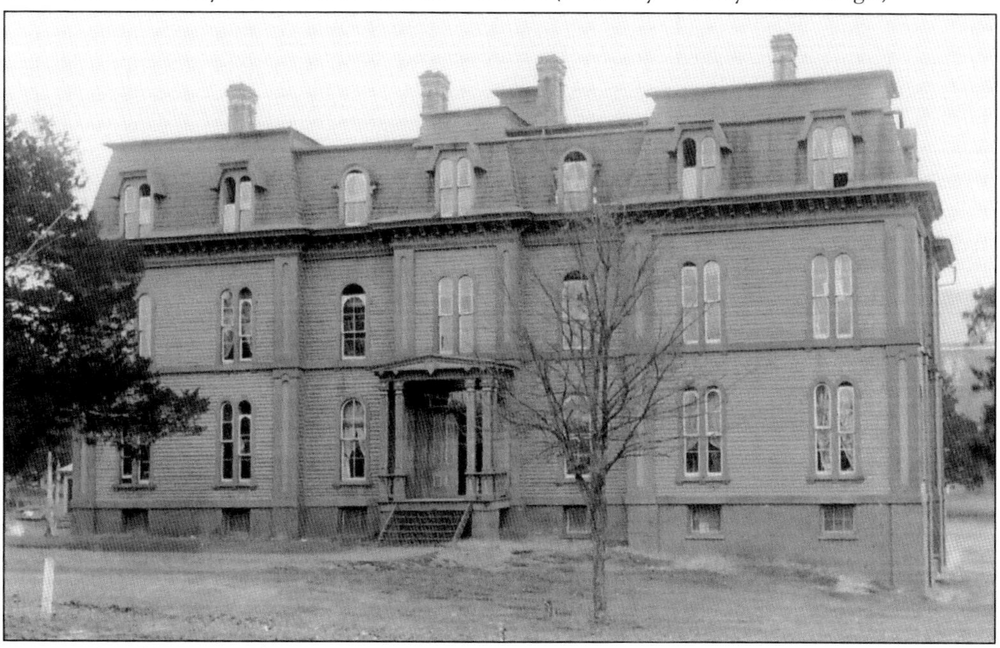

Memorial Hall, pictured here in 1900, was completed in 1871. The frame building served as the men's dormitory at Maryville College and as a boarding hall, where meals were served. Each room was heated by a woodstove, and the male students chopped the wood. The building was torn down in 1975. (Courtesy of Maryville College.)

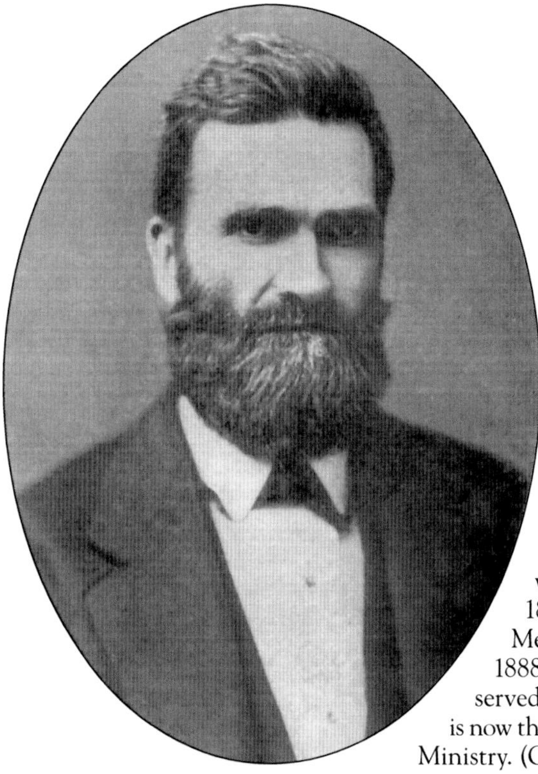

Prof. Thomas Jefferson Lamar, pictured at left, is known as "the second founder" of Maryville College because he was the driving force behind the reopening of the college after the Civil War. In 1865, Lamar recommended to the Synod of Tennessee that the college, which had suffered the ravages of war, neglect, and loss of funds, be reopened. The Synod agreed and on September 5, 1866, Lamar conducted the first chapel service and the first classes in the Brick College building on Main Street with 13 male students present. Lamar died in 1887 after 30 years as a professor. The Lamar Memorial Library, pictured below, was built in 1888 and named in his honor. The building has served as the college bookstore and post office and is now the Samuel Tyndale Wilson Center for Campus Ministry. (Courtesy of Maryville College.)

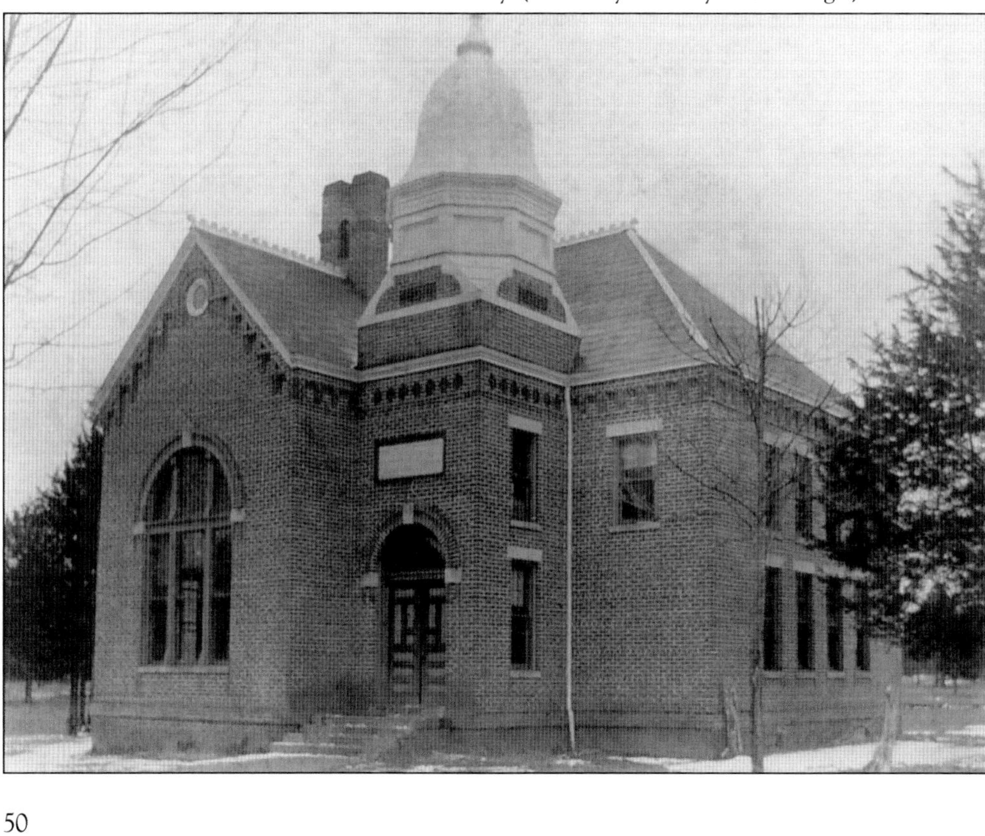

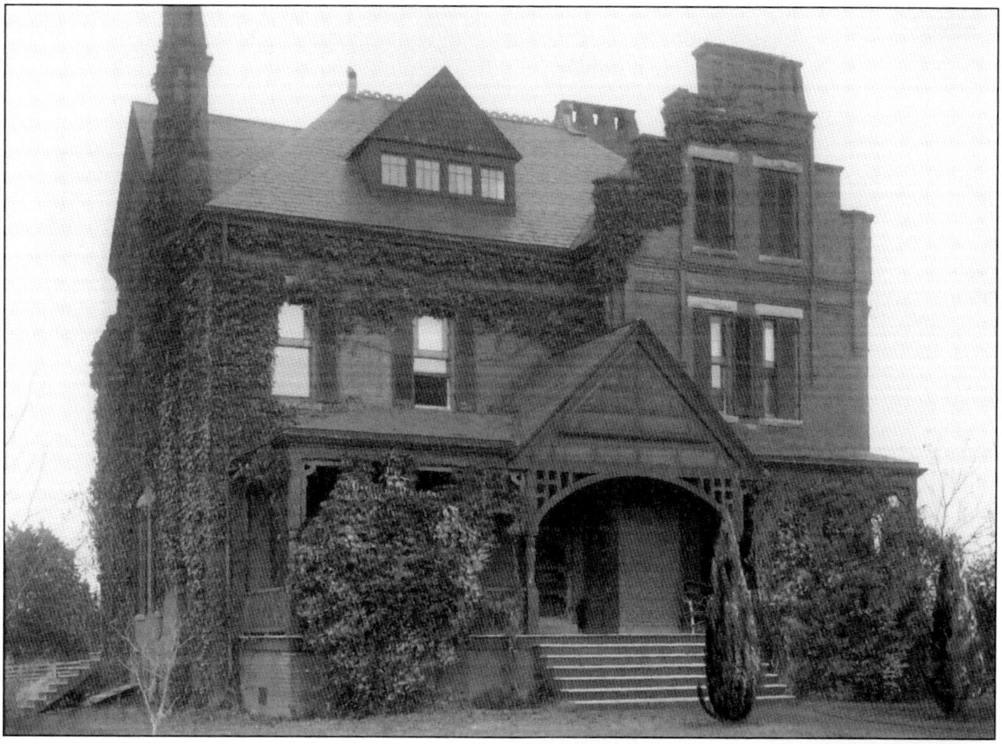

Willard Memorial, pictured above, was completed in 1890. The building was funded by Jane (Mrs. Sylvester) Willard in memory of her late husband to serve as the residence for the president of Maryville College. The gracious Queen Anne Victorian home first occupied by Dr. Samuel Ward Boardman, right, and his family was considered one of the very few truly grand houses in Maryville—and Boardman apologized for the extravagance of his "noble mansion" compared to student housing. The home included 15 rooms, not counting service areas, 15 closets, eight fireplaces, and a large bathroom with hot and cold water. After 1951, a few faculty, staff members, and students lived there, but the house fell into disrepair in the 1970s and was closed. In 1981, fundraising began for the restoration and renovation of Willard House, as it then came to be called. The building, listed in the National Register of Historic Places in 1982, houses the alumni and development offices. (Both, courtesy of Maryville College.)

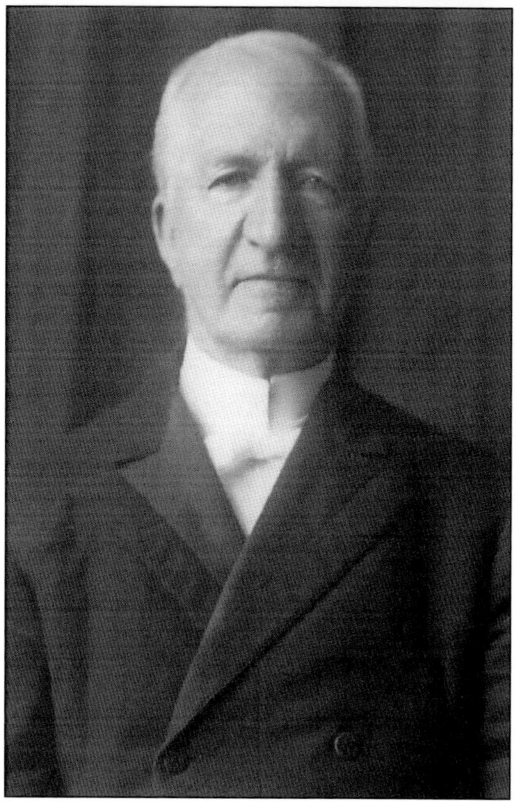

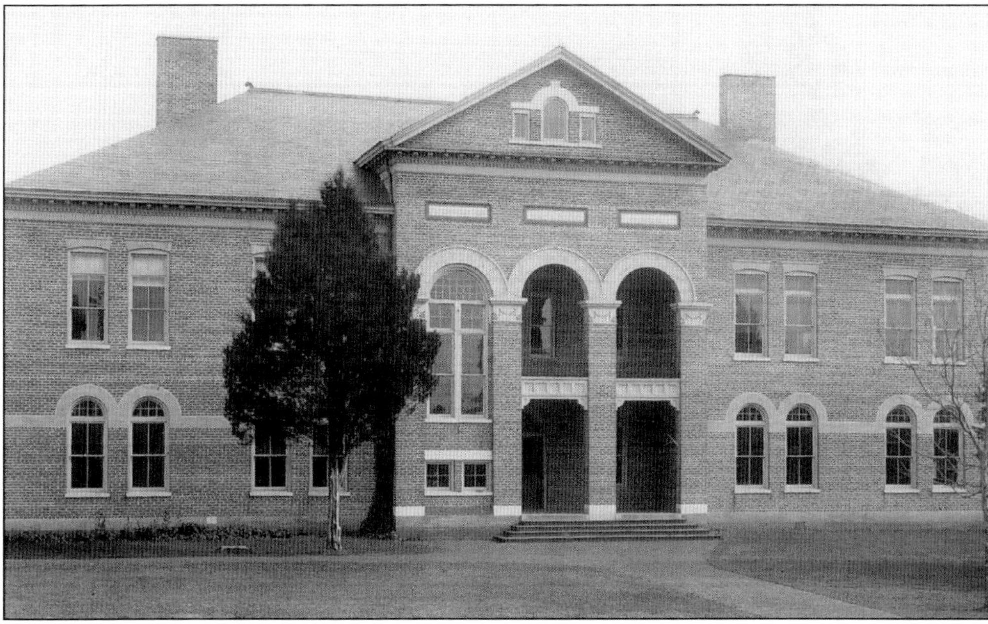

Daniel B. Fayerweather, of New York, funded the construction of Fayerweather Science Hall, above, in 1898. The building was designed by Baumann Brothers of Knoxville. A third story added to Fayerweather Hall, below, was completed in 1913, funded by an anonymous donor. The building is listed in the National Register of Historic Places in the Maryville College Historic District. (Both, courtesy of Maryville College.)

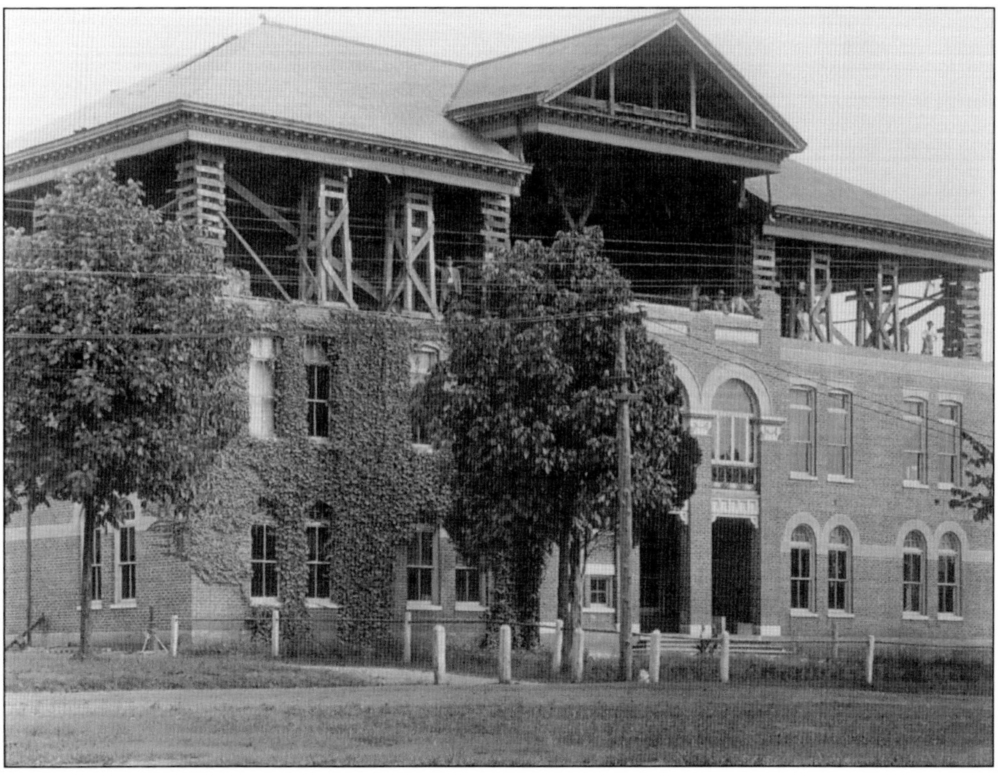

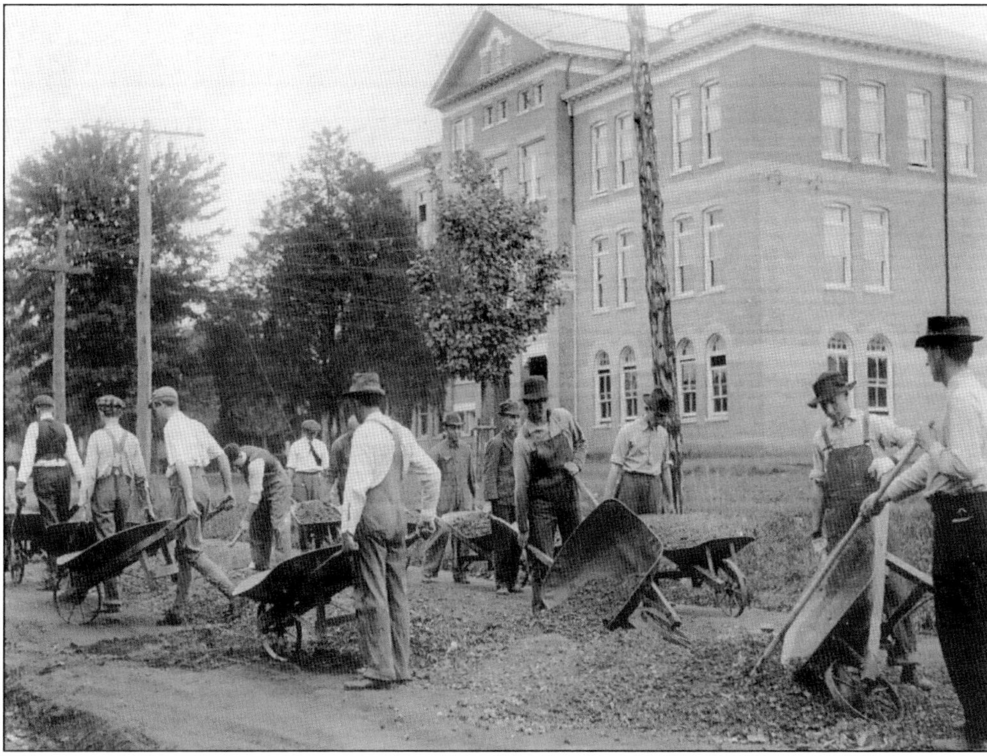

Campus road building is taking place in front of Fayerweather Hall in this photograph from around 1920. The third story of Fayerweather was completed in 1913. (Courtesy of Maryville College.)

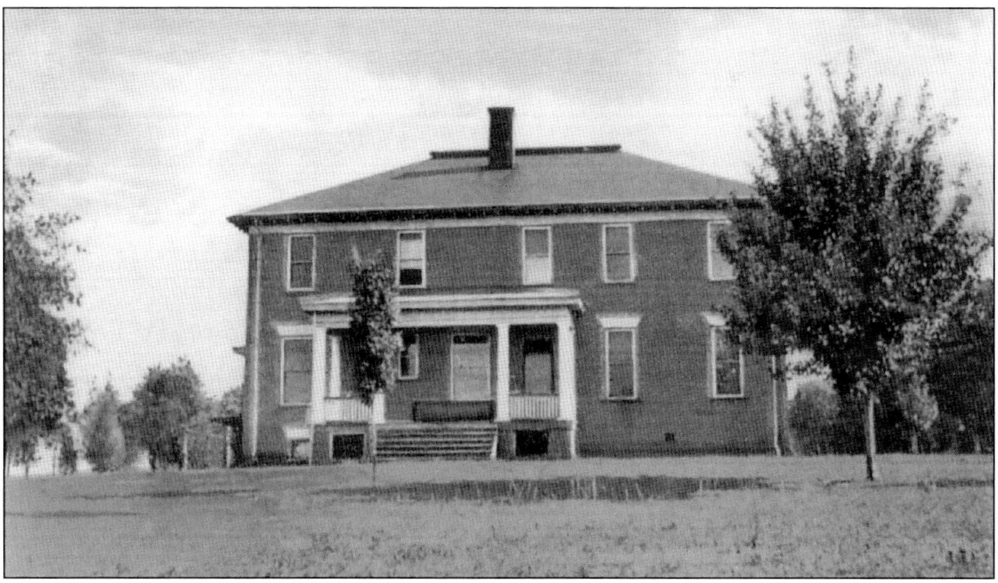

Ralph Max Lamar Memorial Hospital on the Maryville College campus was built in 1910 as the college infirmary. His mother, Mrs. Thomas J. (Martha) Lamar, provided the funding in memory of their son, who died at the age of two. The infirmary is believed to be one of the earliest hospitals of any kind in Blount County. The building is the present-day International House. (Courtesy of Ken Cornett.)

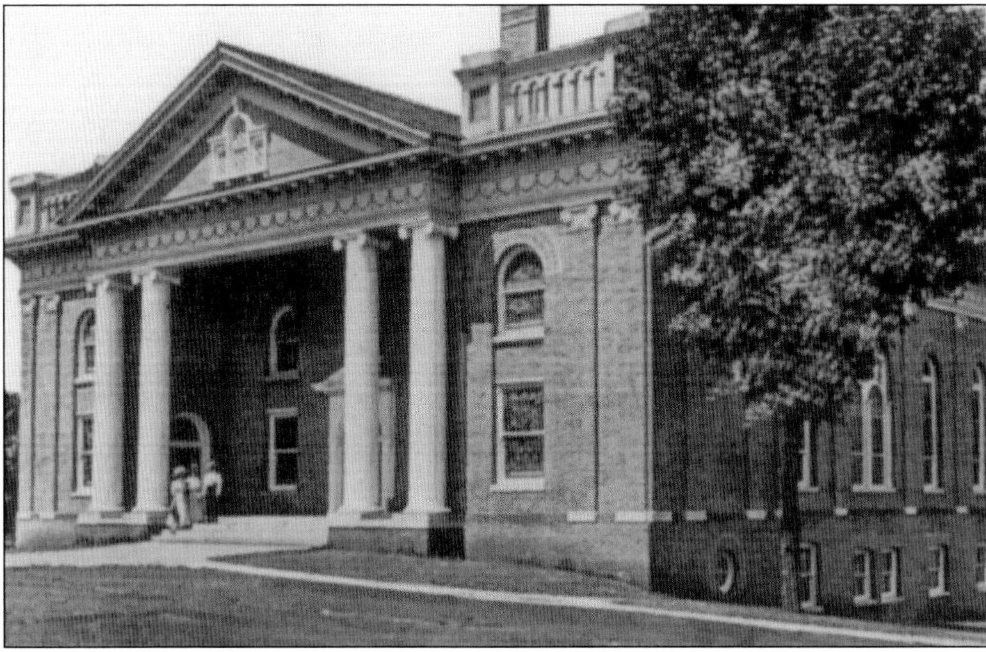

The Elizabeth R. Voorhees Chapel, above, was funded by Mr. and Mrs. Ralph Voorhees, of New Jersey. The building was completed in 1906 and was the center of campus life until it was destroyed by fire in 1947. Nita Eckles West (1877–1966), hired to head the "Expression Department" in 1899, taught drama and speech at the college for 42 years and is credited with starting the theater department. She directed theatrical productions in Voorhees Chapel or outside. In 2008, members of the West and Ramsey families, her descendants, donated $1 million toward what is now the Clayton Center for the Arts on the college campus. The Nita Eckles West Stage in the Ronald and Lynda Nutt Theatre memorializes her contributions to the arts. Pictured below is a 1939 production of *Messiah*. (Above, courtesy of B. Kenneth Cornett; below, courtesy of Maryville College.)

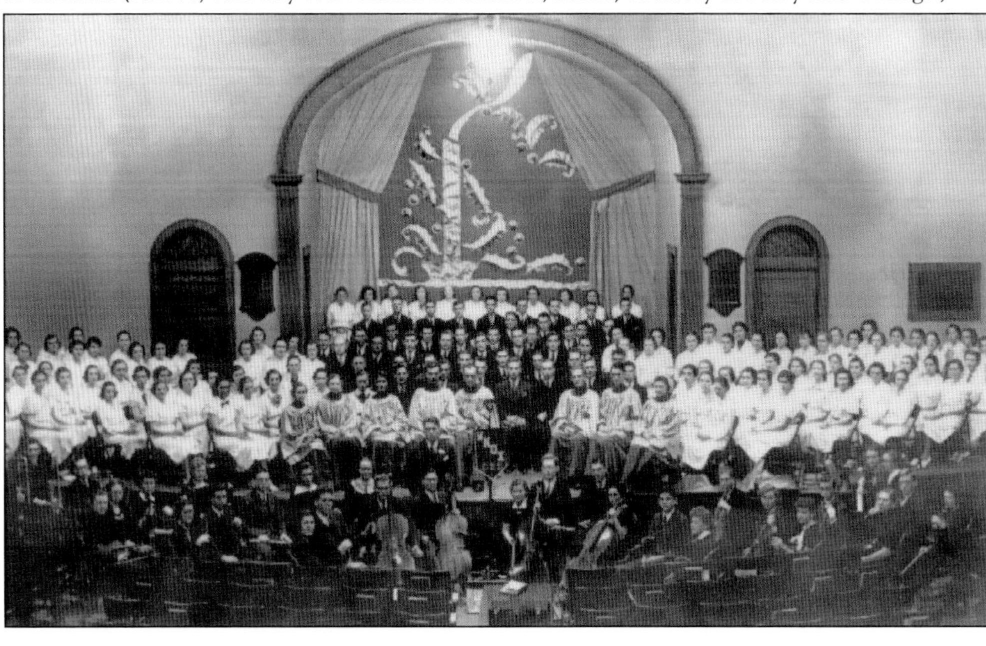

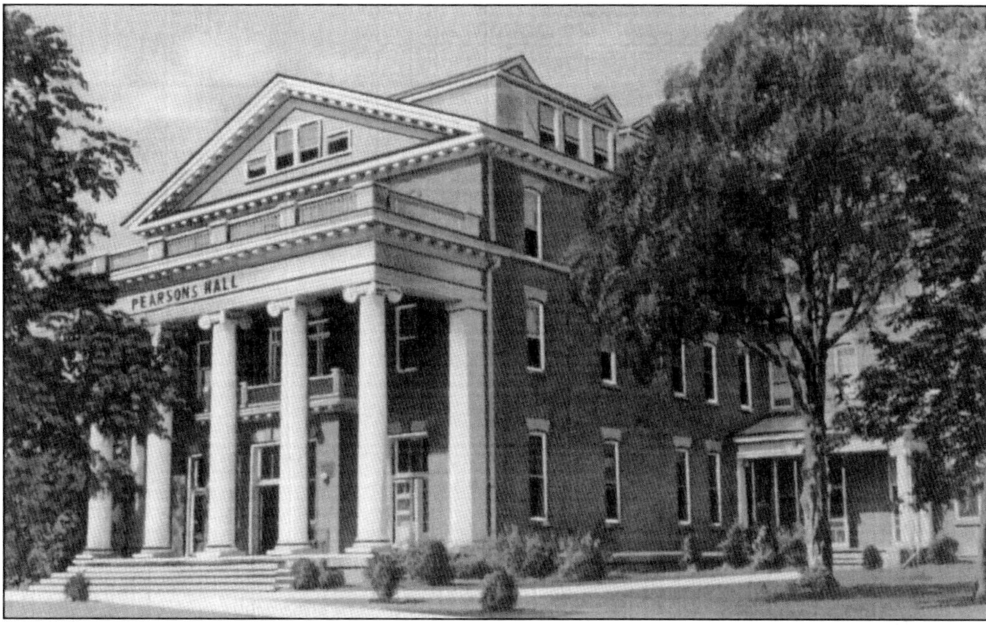

Pearsons Hall was completed in 1910 as a dormitory for women and a dining hall. Dr. Daniel K. Pearsons provided the funding. A dining hall annex was completed in 1935, and the building underwent rehabilitation in 1959. (Courtesy of B. Kenneth Cornett.)

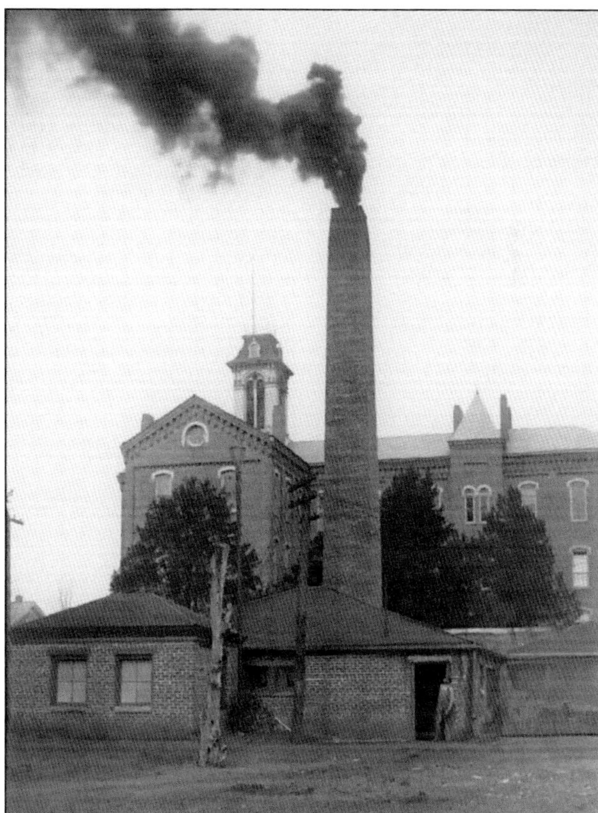

The first central heating plant on the Maryville College campus was constructed in 1893 under the administration of Dr. Samuel Ward Boardman. In 1939, a much-needed new heating plant was constructed at one edge of the campus, removing the volumes of soft-coal smoke that the old plant at the center of the campus had given off. The heating plant capacity doubled after renovations in 1951. (Courtesy of Maryville College.)

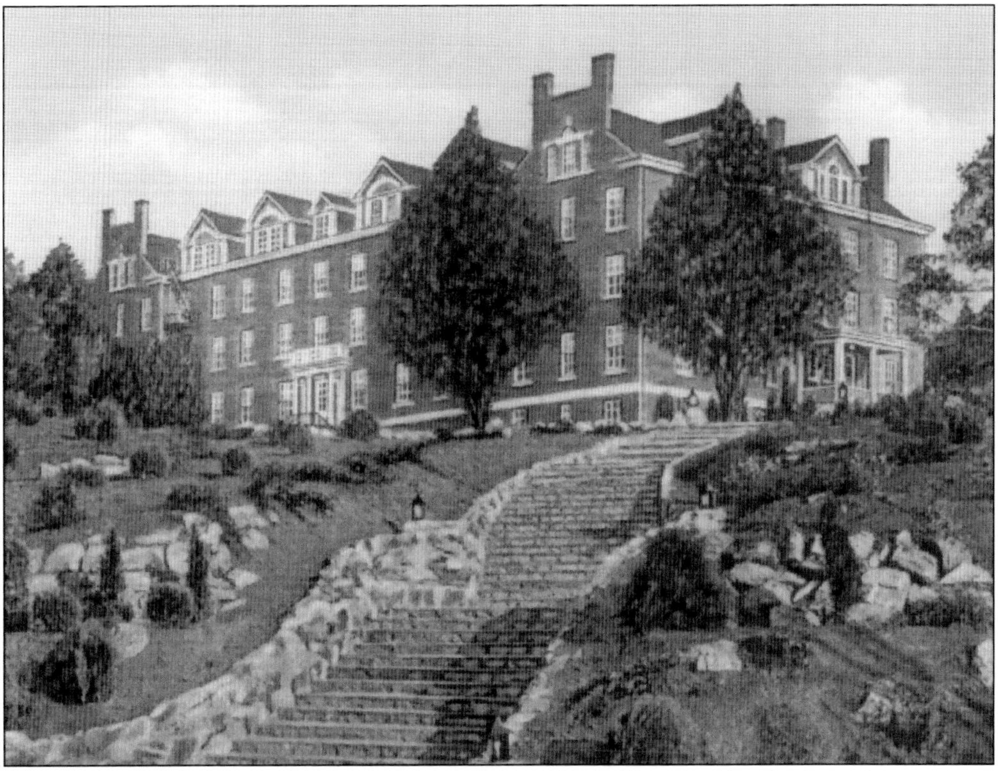

The five-story Carnegie Hall, completed in 1910, was funded by capitalist Andrew Carnegie and others as a men's dormitory. The building burned and was rebuilt, opening its doors again in 1916. (Courtesy of B. Kenneth Cornett.)

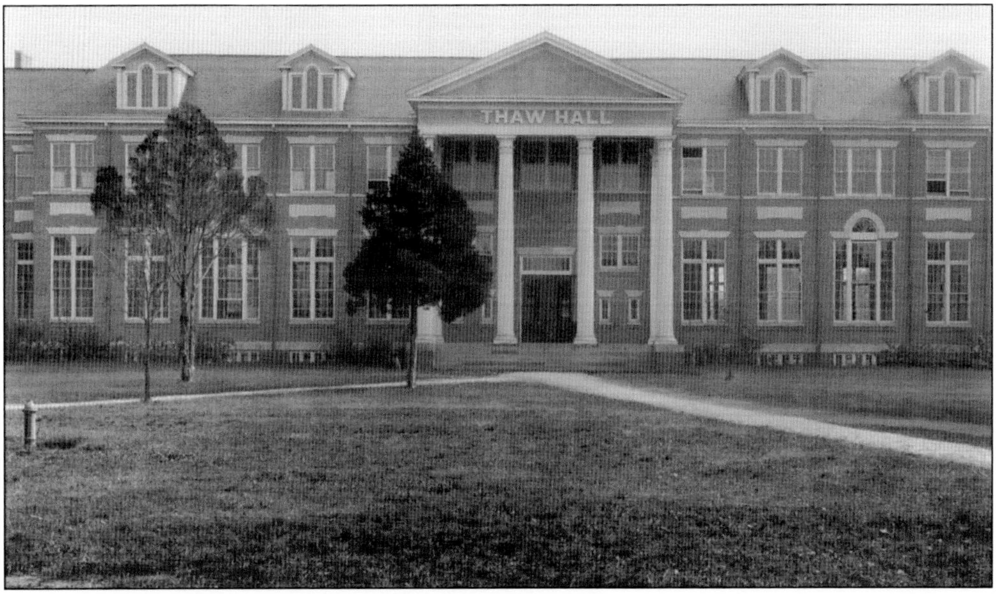

Thaw Hall, completed in 1922, was built with donations from Mrs. William (Mary C.) Thaw of Pittsburgh, Pennsylvania. The building was used for instruction and as a library. (Courtesy of Maryville College.)

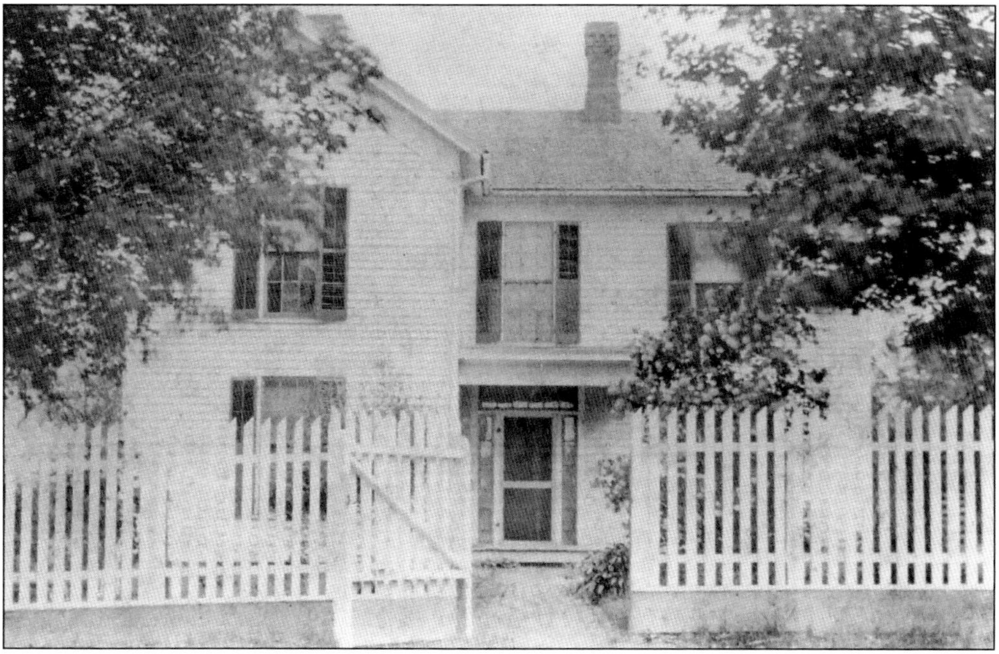

The Gideon Crawford House, built about 1875, was originally the home of Gideon Stebbins White Crawford, a mathematics professor and administrator at Maryville College who served as chairman of the Maryville College board of directors from 1876 to 1891. The college's Mountain Challenge program is housed here. The house was listed in the National Register of Historic Places in 1989. (Courtesy of Maryville College.)

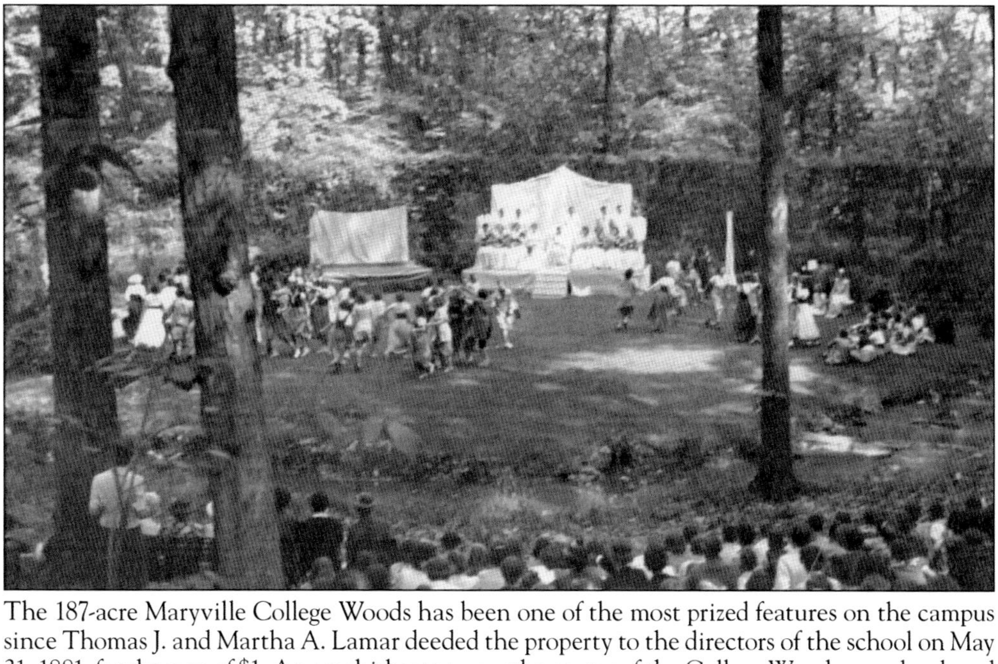

The 187-acre Maryville College Woods has been one of the most prized features on the campus since Thomas J. and Martha A. Lamar deeded the property to the directors of the school on May 31, 1881, for the sum of $1. An amphitheater, near the center of the College Woods, was developed in 1935 and succeeding years. In this c. 1905 photograph, a May Day celebration is taking place. (Courtesy of Louise Crawford Berry.)

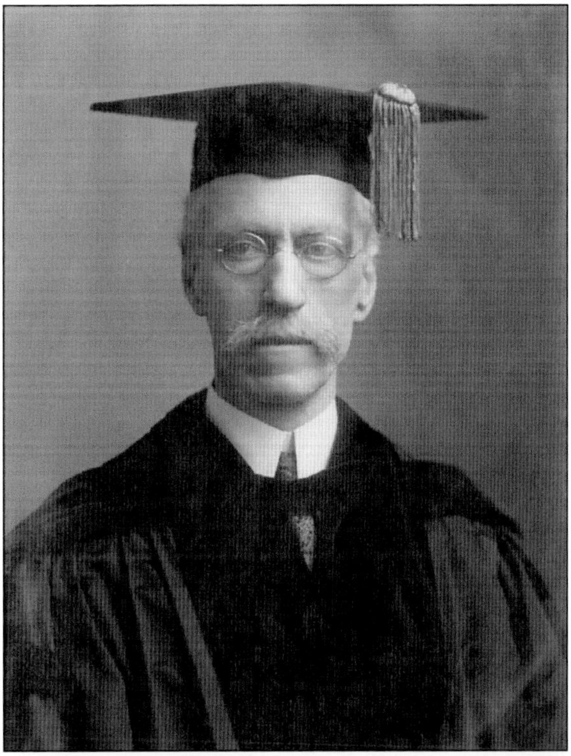

Samuel Tyndale Wilson was graduated from Maryville College in 1878. He was a professor of English and Spanish from 1884 to 1901 and was elected the fifth president of the college, serving in that capacity from 1901 to 1930. Under his presidency, the financial assets of the college multiplied approximately tenfold and the institution became established and recognized by 20th-century standards. (Courtesy of Maryville College.)

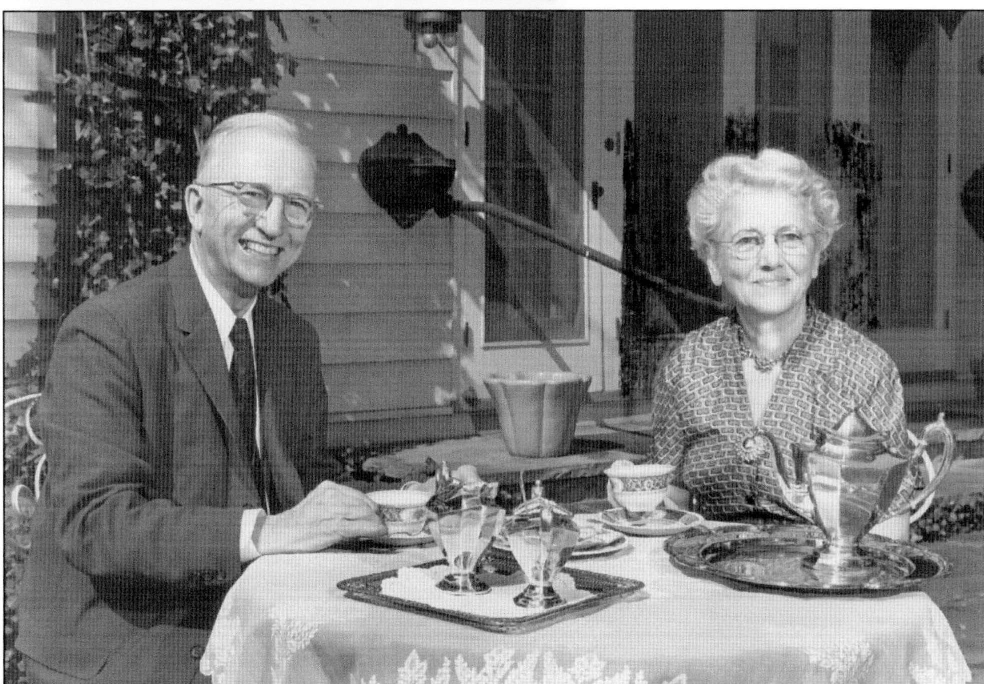

Dr. Ralph Waldo Lloyd, left, and his wife, Margaret A. Bell Lloyd, enjoy tea at Willard Memorial, the home provided to presidents of Maryville College. Lloyd, a Maryville College graduate, was the sixth president of the college, serving from 1930 to 1961. (Courtesy of Maryville College.)

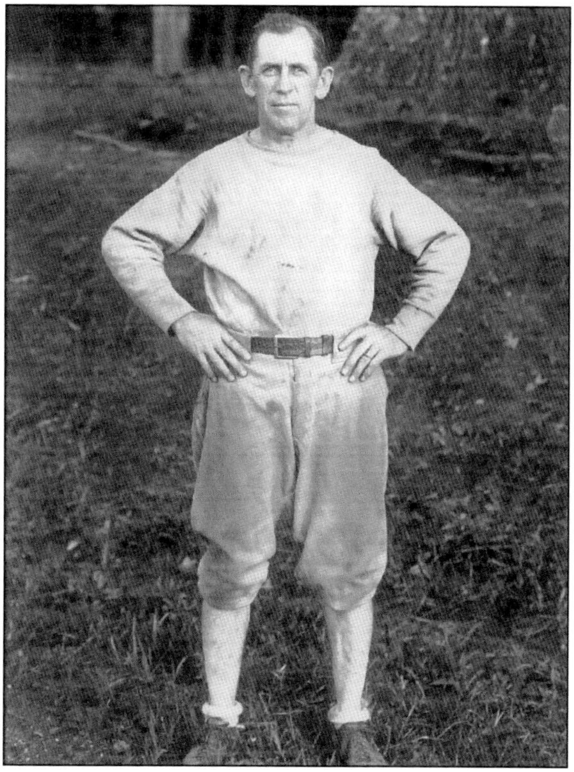

Lombe S. Honaker coached football, basketball, and baseball at Maryville College from 1921 to 1959, compiling a total record of 924-604-31 in all sports, including 408 baseball wins. In 1946, when he took his team to the Tangerine Bowl, he received votes for national football coach of the year along with Tennessee's Bob Neyland and Army's Earl Blaik. His Scot teams played the Tennessee Volunteers until the early 1930s, losing by only 6-0 and 7-0 in 1926 and 1927, and tying 14-14 in 1923. In 1956, he became only the sixth football coach to receive a Citation of Honor by the Football Writers' Association of America. The college football field is named for Honaker, who was among the initial inductees into the Blount County Sports Hall of Fame. (Courtesy of Maryville College.)

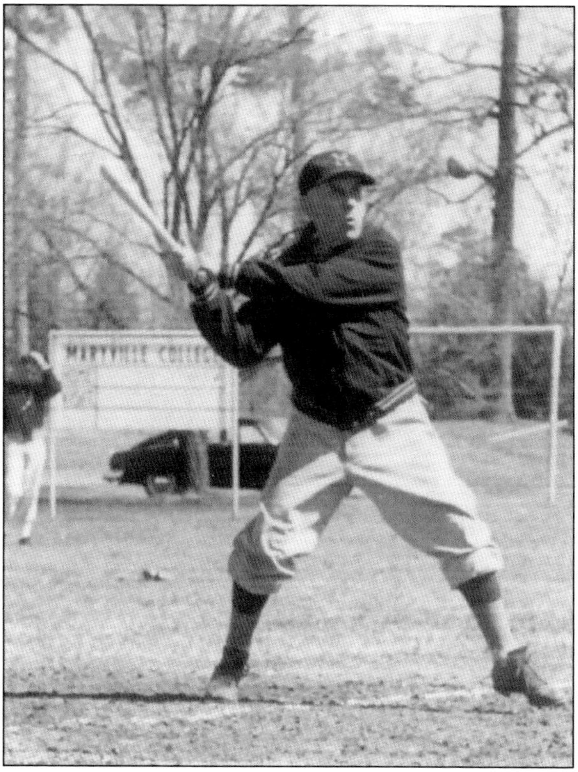

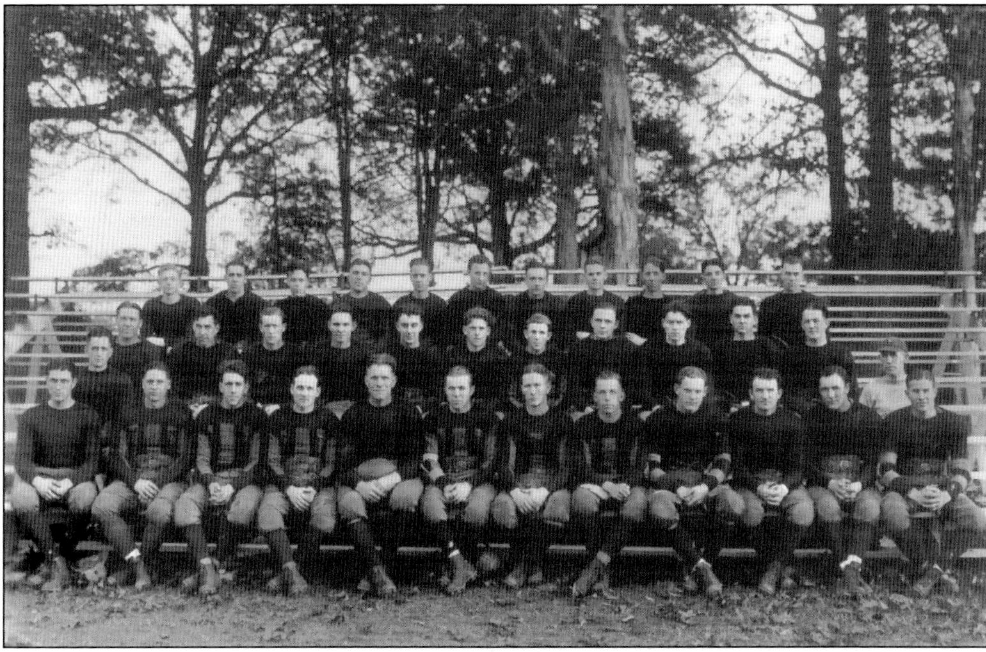

The 1923 Maryville College football team tied the University of Tennessee 14-14. The team included Bob Thrower (front row, fifth from left). Thrower was an outstanding athlete in both football and track and field. In 1999, he was named one of the 50 greatest athletes in Blount County history. (Courtesy of Maryville College.)

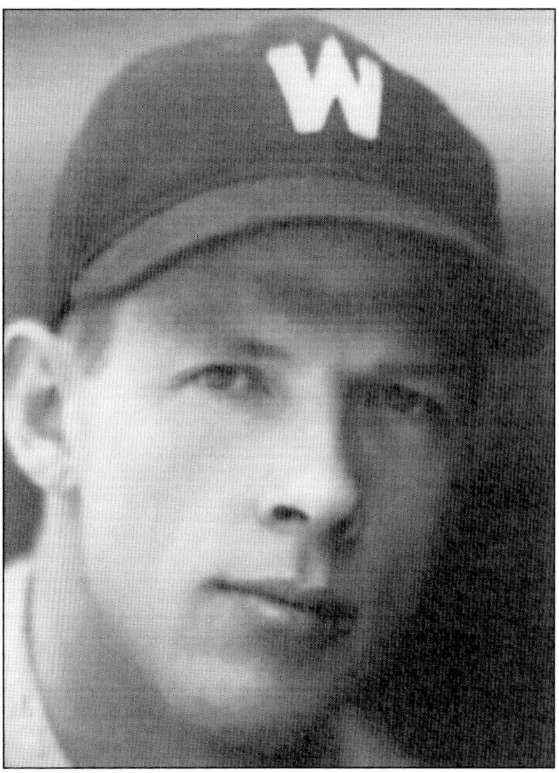

John Stone was captain of the 1927 Maryville College baseball team. He went on to a career in the major leagues as an outfielder, playing for the Detroit Tigers from 1928 to 1933, and the Washington Senators from 1934 to 1938. He had a .310 lifetime batting average. In 1999, Stone was ranked as one of the top-ten greatest Blount County athletes. He was among the initial Blount County Hall of Fame inductees. (Courtesy of Maryville College.)

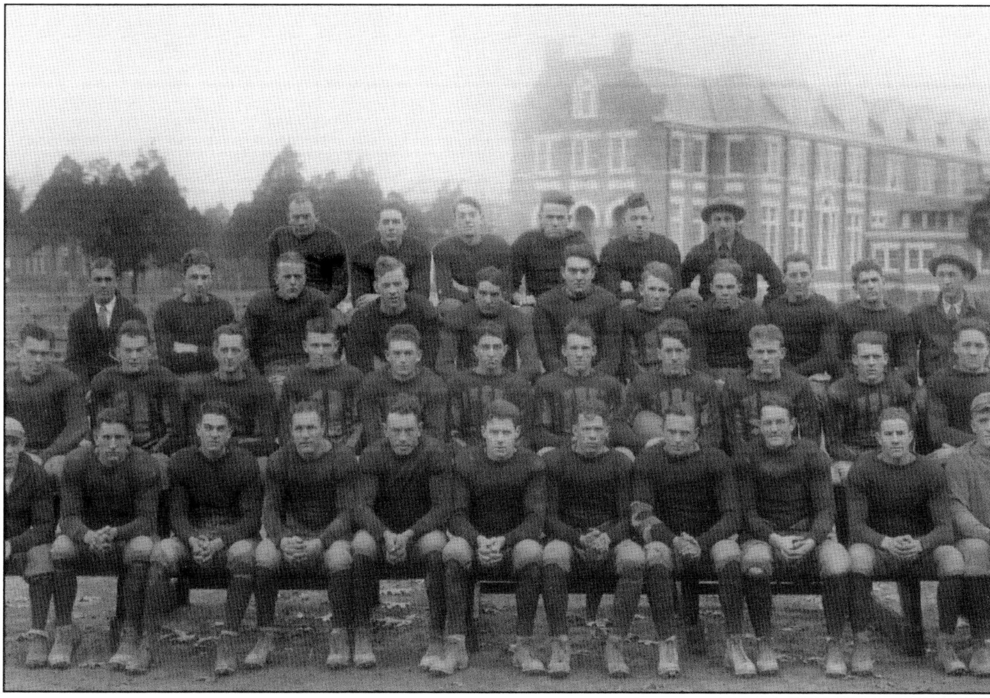

This c. 1926 Maryville College football team included Harold "Tilley" Bird (second row, seventh from left). Bird was an outstanding athlete, participating in football, basketball, and baseball. He later played professional baseball for the Knoxville Smokies. Bird was also ranked among the top-ten Blount County athletes. (Courtesy of Maryville College.)

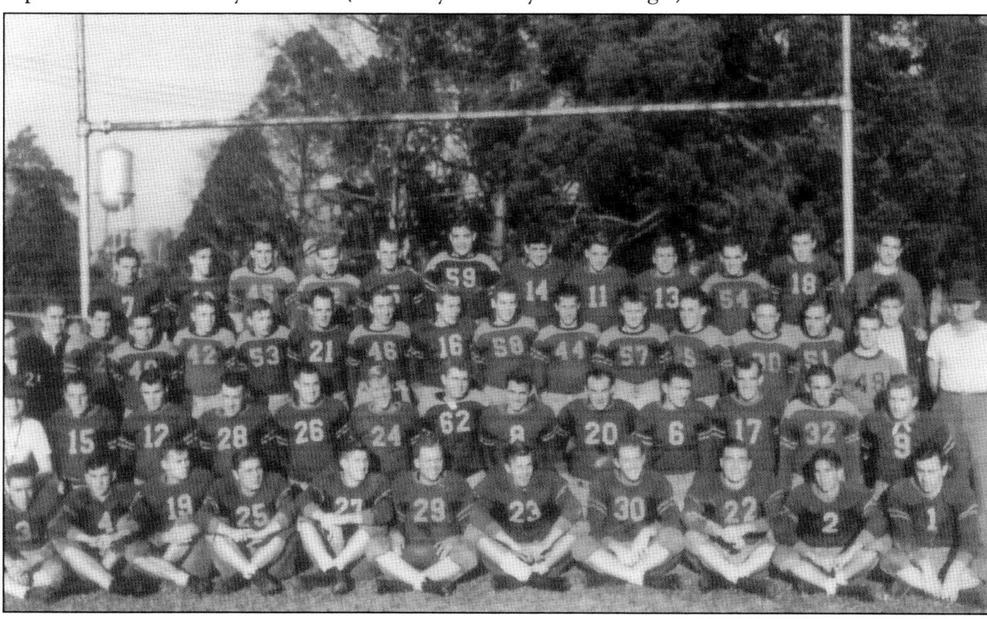

The 1946 Fighting Scots were undefeated in regular-season play. They finished 9-1 after losing to Catawba in the Tangerine Bowl. Perhaps Maryville College's finest team, the 1946 team, as well as the 1947 team, which finished 7-1-1, were among the post–World War II teams that marked coach Lombe Honaker's premier years as a football coach. (Courtesy of Maryville College.)

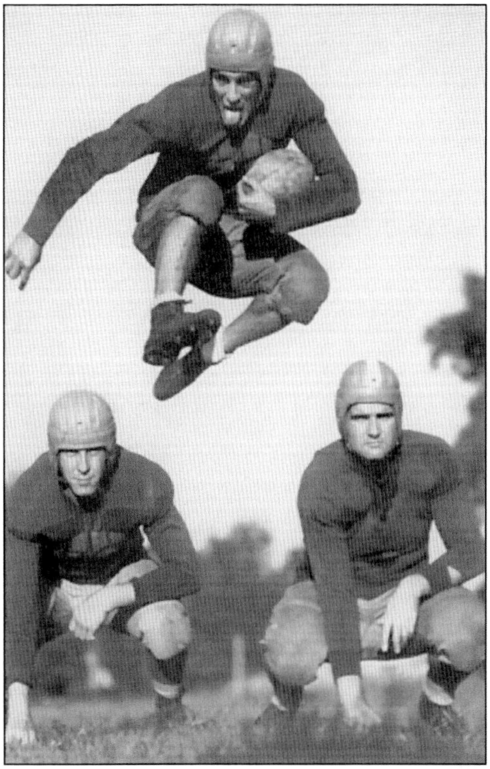

Boydson Baird, for whom the college gymnasium is named, was a nine-letter athletic star at Maryville College from 1937 to 1941. After serving as an assistant coach at Davidson and head basketball coach at William and Mary, he returned to Maryville College as head football coach and athletic director in 1959. He also coached baseball and basketball for the school. At left, he is seen leaping over linemen Cecil Tipton, left, and Gene McCurry, right, in 1940. His 1959 team finished 1-7 but defeated arch-rival Carson-Newman 14-13. The next day, a few hundred students gathered on Baird's lawn to sing and proclaim that they had rung the tower bell so long the night before that the rope broke. Baird also was among the initial inductees into the Blount County Sports Hall of Fame. (Courtesy of Maryville College.)

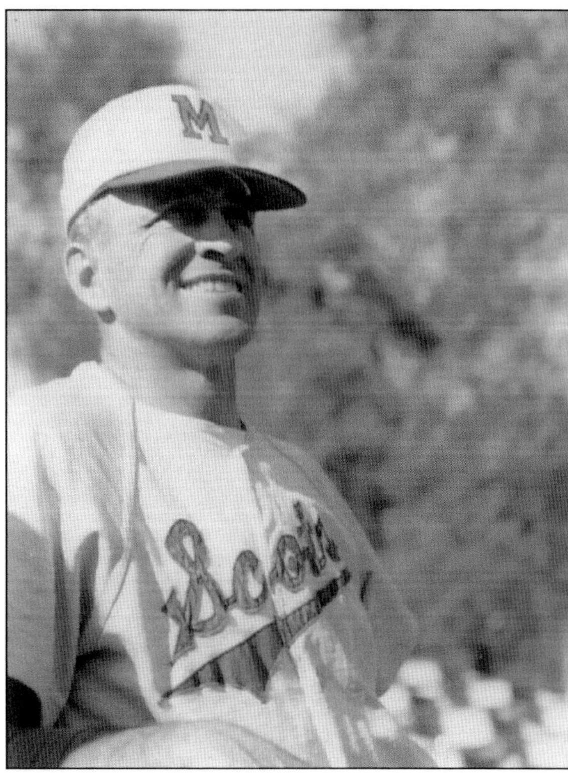

Four

Maryville's Schools

Maryville's schools have always been a source of local pride, and rightly so. The Maryville public school system is considered to be among the very finest in the state, and its athletic teams, especially in football, have established a reputation for excellence in competition, and winning state championships.

Until 1910, the local schools were private, including Freedman's Institute, the Friends Normal and Preparatory School, Maryville College's Maryville Preparatory School, and the East Tennessee Female Masonic Institute. Another private school was established in 1901, and in 1904 the school acquired the Freedman's Institute building on the present Maryville High School campus. Also in 1904, Blount County High School, later known as Maryville Polytechnic Institute, was established and educated students until 1926.

In 1910, the first Maryville public schools were constructed and opened, including West Side Elementary School on the present municipal building site, and East Side Elementary on the present Fort Craig School site. In 1913, Maryville High School was established in the East Side building where it stayed until moving to the Maryville Polytechnic building in 1927. A new high school building was constructed in 1939. West Side was closed in 1953 when its students occupied the new Sam Houston Elementary School. East Side was renamed as Fort Craig in 1928, and the new Fort Craig School was opened in 1954, its students using the West Side building after it was vacated until the new school was ready.

In the days of segregation, and from 1930 to 1966, African American students were educated at William J. Hale High School, named for the 1912 founder of Tennessee Agricultural and Industrial College (now Tennessee State University).

Fine schools are a hallmark of a great community, and nowhere is that any more true than in Maryville.

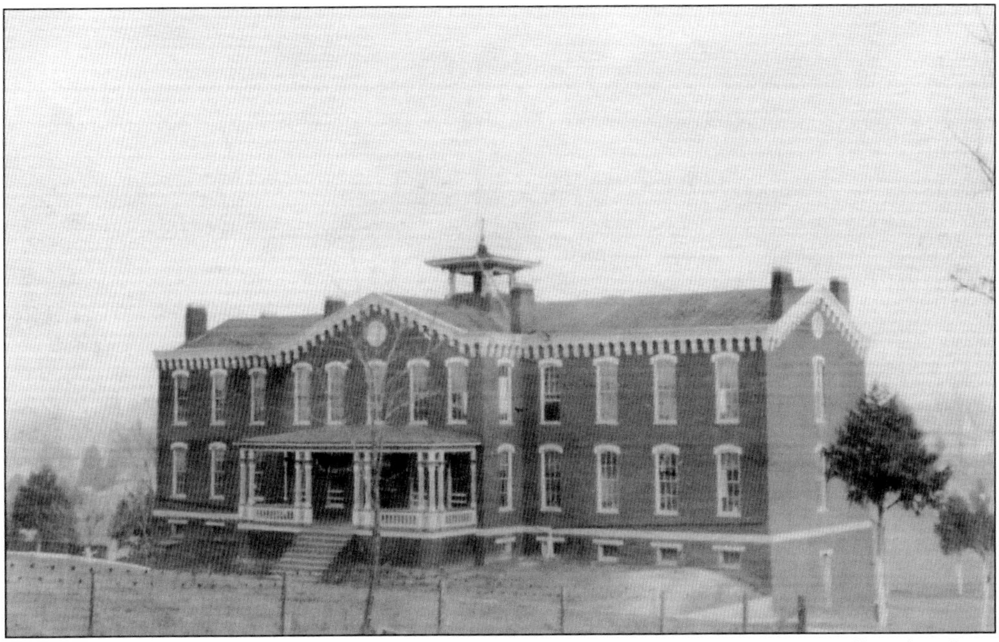

The Freedman's Institute building, pictured around 1910, would become home to Maryville Polytechnic Institute, which continued as a school until 1926. (Courtesy of Maryville City Schools.)

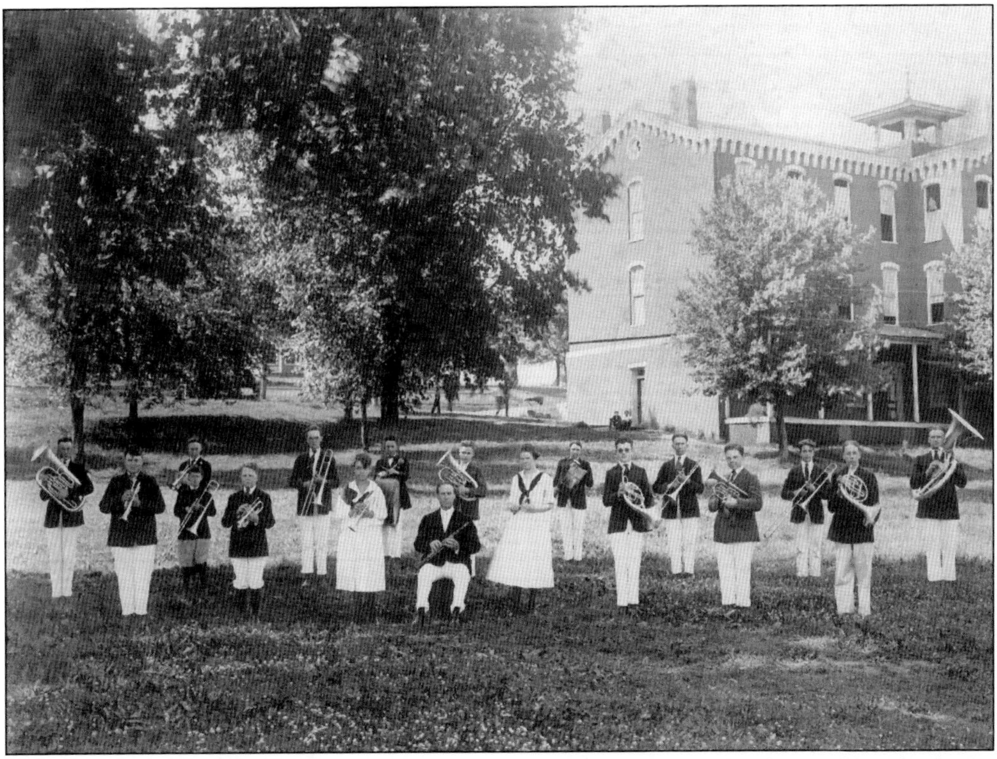

Pictured is the Maryville Polytechnic School band in 1917. A private school owned by Charles W. "Bill Joe" Henry, it was initially opened as Blount County High School. Before 1910, the name was changed to Maryville Polytechnic. (Courtesy of the Blount County Public Library.)

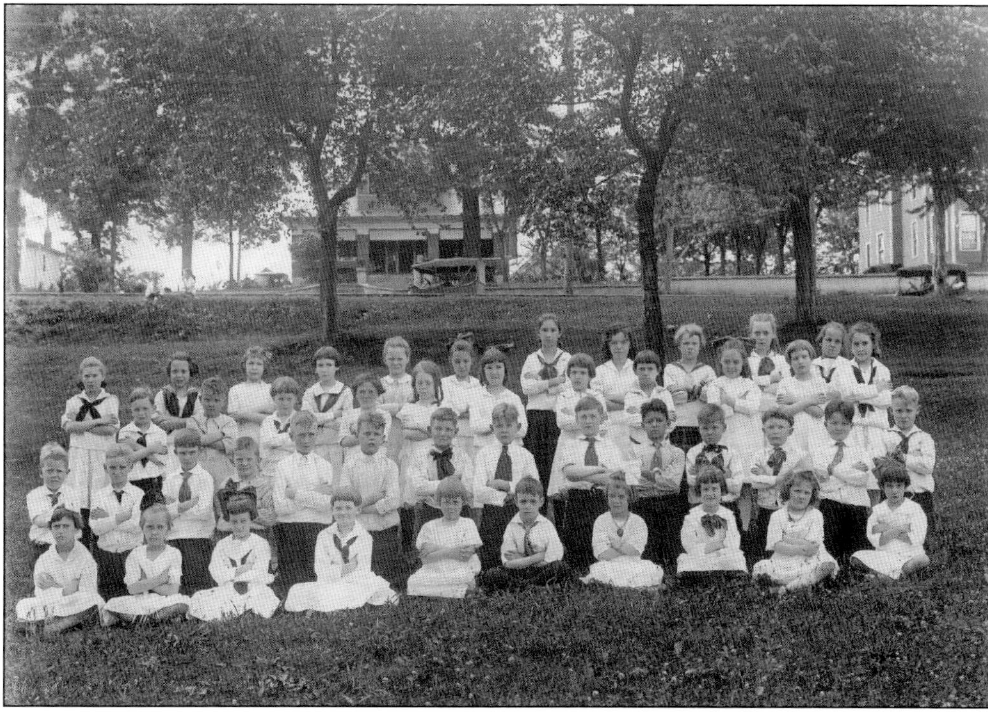

In these two photographs, homes along Main Street, now West Broadway Avenue, can be seen in the background. Shown above is the Maryville Polytechnic primary class in 1918–1919. Below are the girls enrolled in the school at the time, also around 1919, from elementary school through high school. (Above, courtesy of Blount County Public Library; below, courtesy of City of Maryville.)

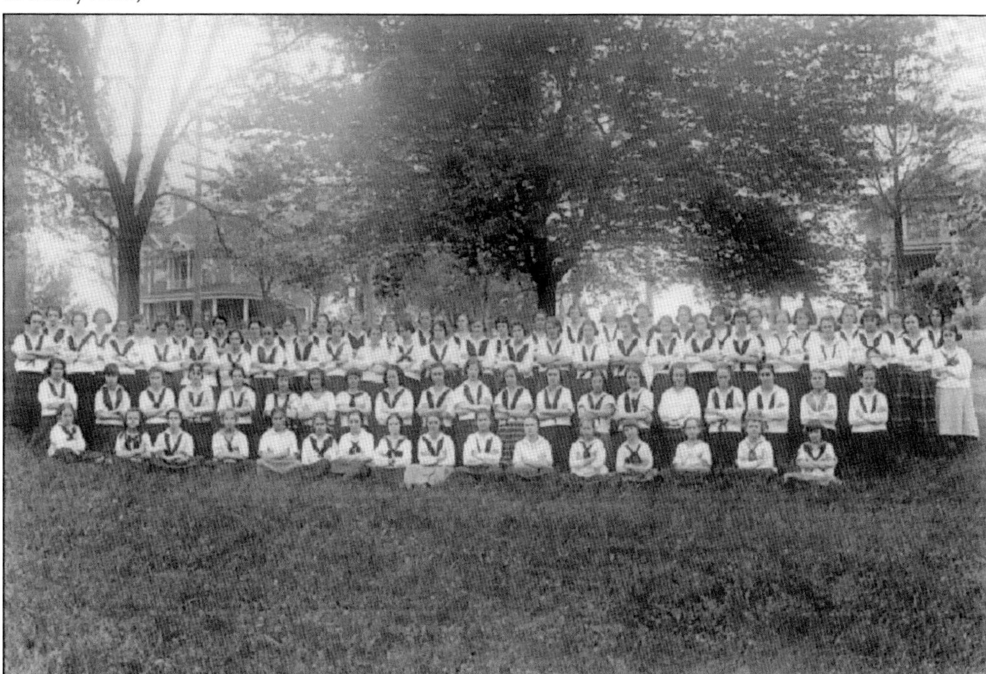

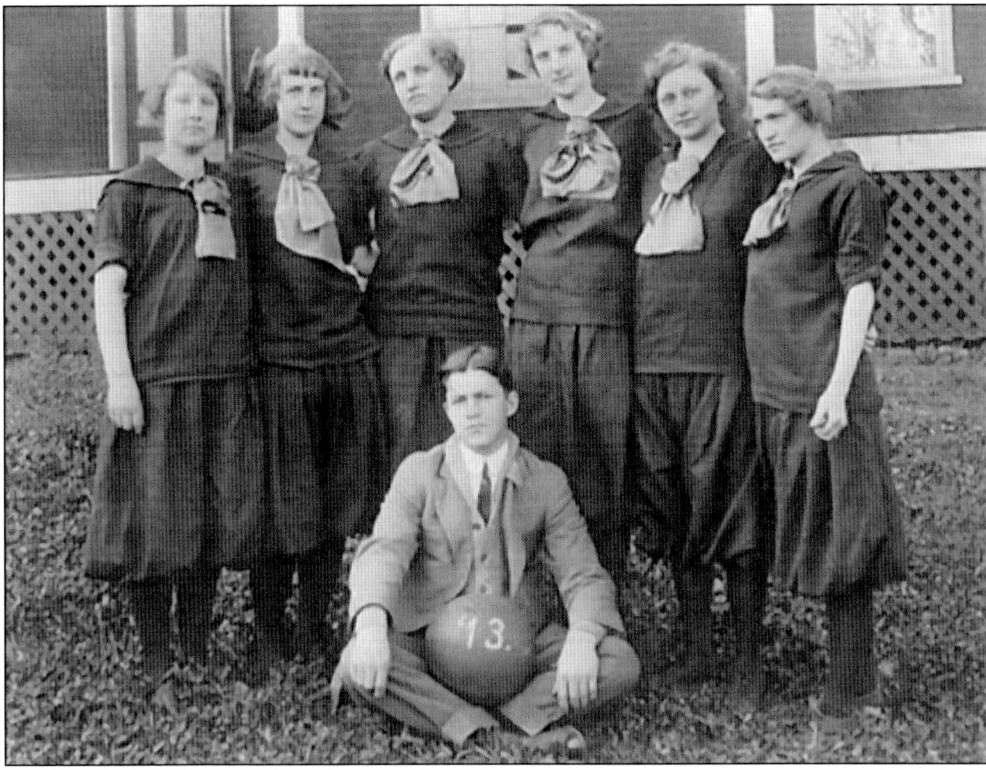

Maryville Polytechnic fielded athletic teams, including football and basketball teams. Pictured here is the 1913 girls basketball team. Shown from left to right are Dollie Cook, Stella Henry, E. Davis, K. Cornwell, Flora Lowe, and P. Browning. The male in front is unidentified. (Courtesy of City of Maryville.)

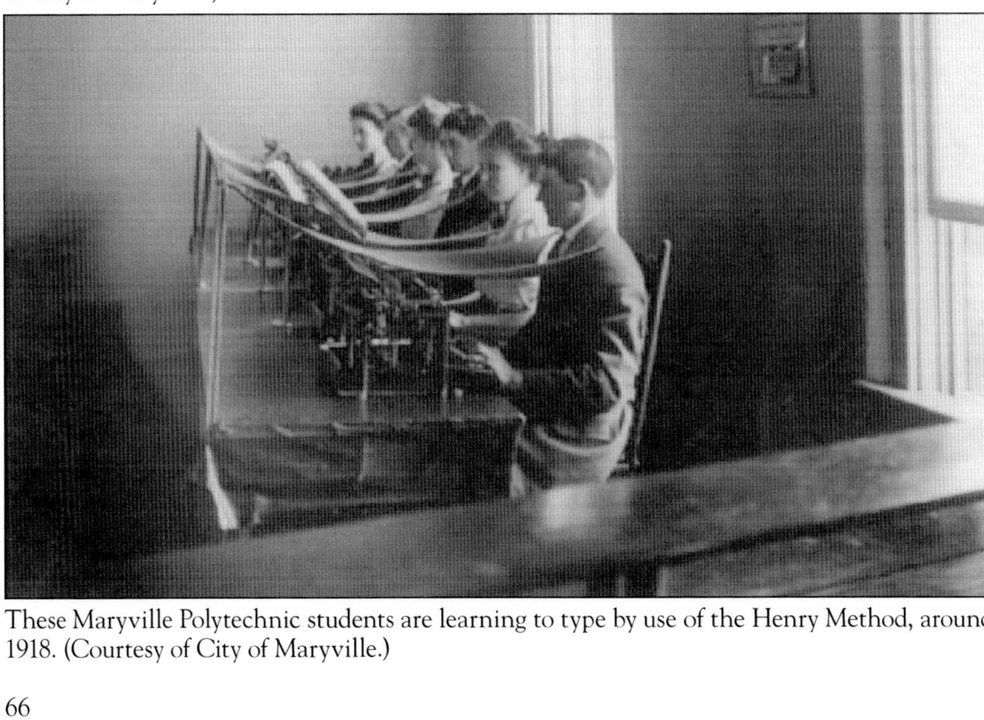

These Maryville Polytechnic students are learning to type by use of the Henry Method, around 1918. (Courtesy of City of Maryville.)

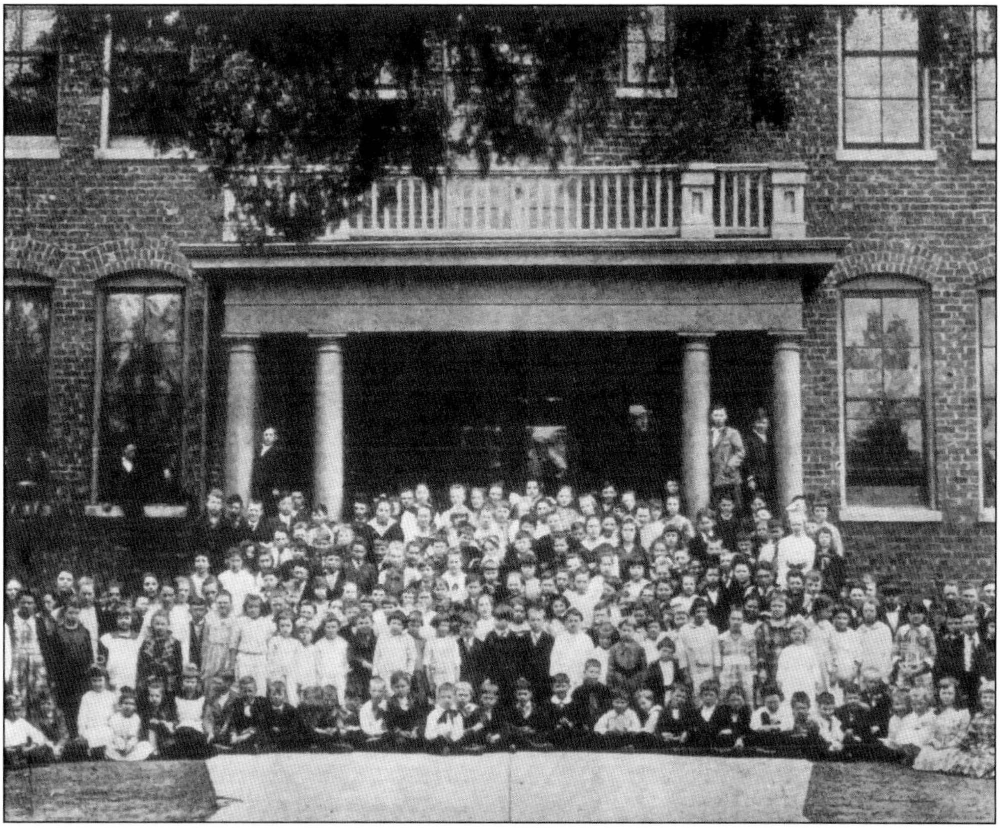

Pictured here are Maryville's first two public schools, opened in 1910. At right is East Side School. Maryville High School was opened there in 1913. It stood on the present Fort Craig School grounds. The first high school class graduated in 1919. Above is West Side School, which stood on the present municipal building site until about 1954. Shown are the West Side grammar grades in 1919. (Both, courtesy of Maryville City Schools.)

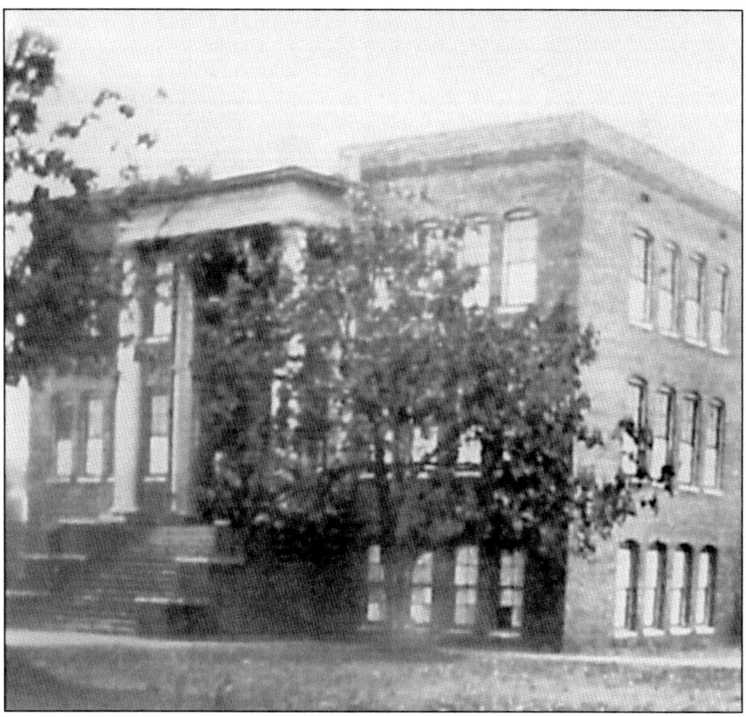

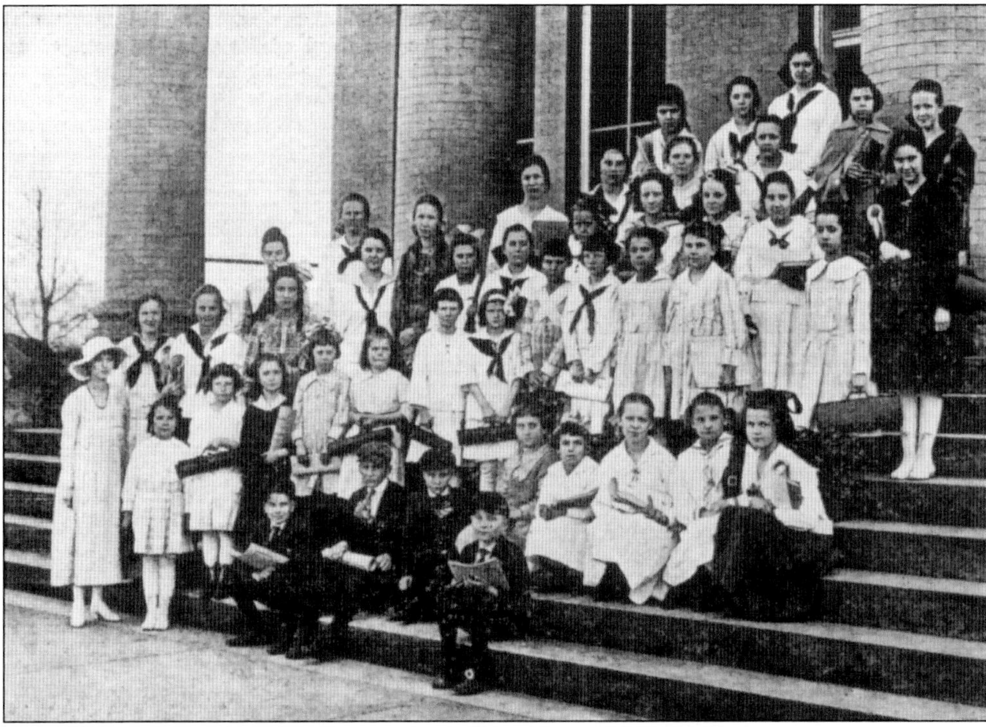

Maryville City Schools music department students are pictured on the front steps of the Blount County Courthouse in 1919. (Courtesy of Maryville City Schools.)

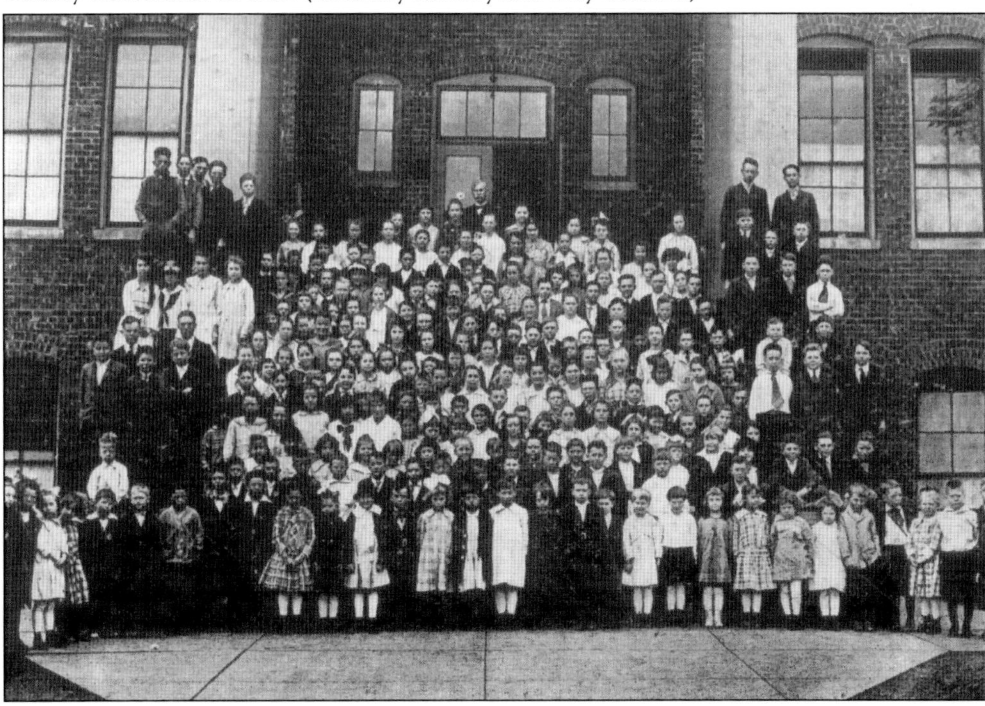

The grammar grades of East Side School are pictured in front of the school in 1919. (Courtesy of Maryville City Schools.)

The Maryville High Schools girls' basketball team is pictured in 1919. Shown from left to right are (first row) Grace Brown; (second row) Pauline Goyne Nash and Mable Williams Richmond; (third row) Isabel Brown Yearout, Erma Hall Crawford, and Elizabeth Stanley Parrish. (Courtesy of Maryville City Schools.)

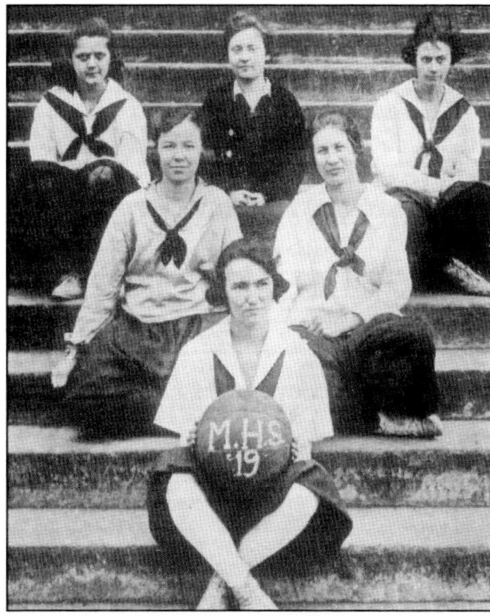

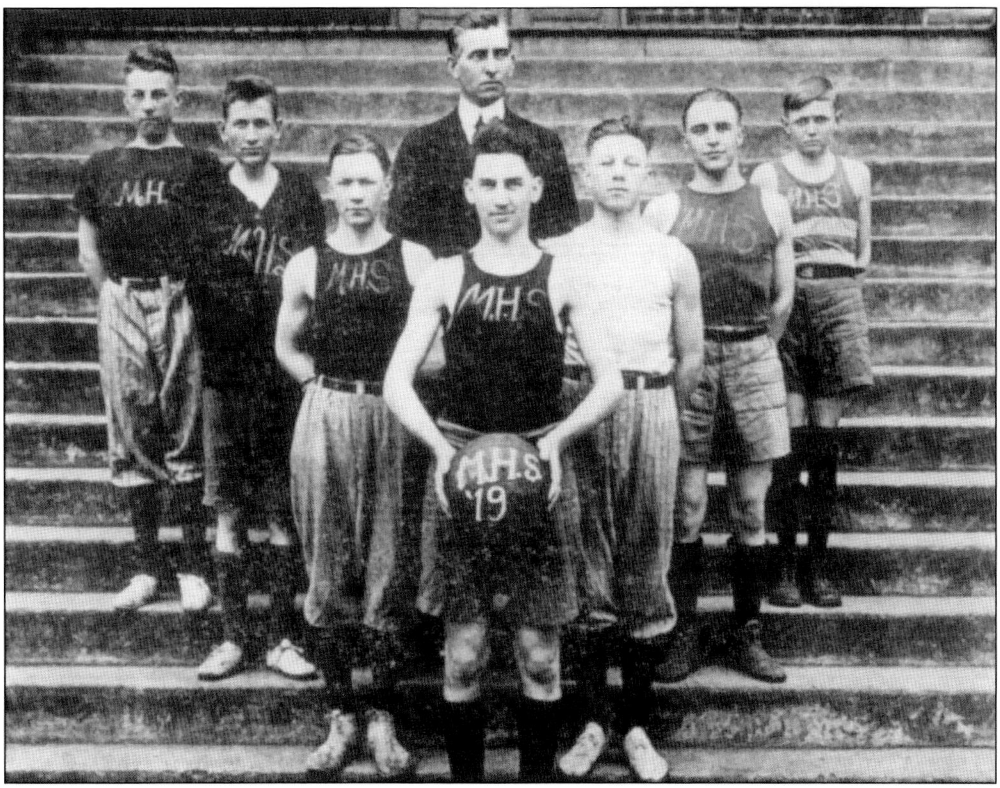

The 1919 Maryville High School basketball team included, from left to right, Ross Birchfiel, Oren Lowe, Kenneth Johnson, Howard Sullinger, Arthur "Speedy" Ruble, Hugh Clabough, and Joe Scott. Superintendent of Schools Clyde D. Curtis, behind, coached both the boys and girls teams. Ruble, a member of the Blount County Sports Hall of Fame and selected one of Blount County's 50 all-time greatest athletes, played with the Detroit Tigers in 1927 and the Philadelphia Phillies in 1934. (Courtesy of Maryville City Schools.)

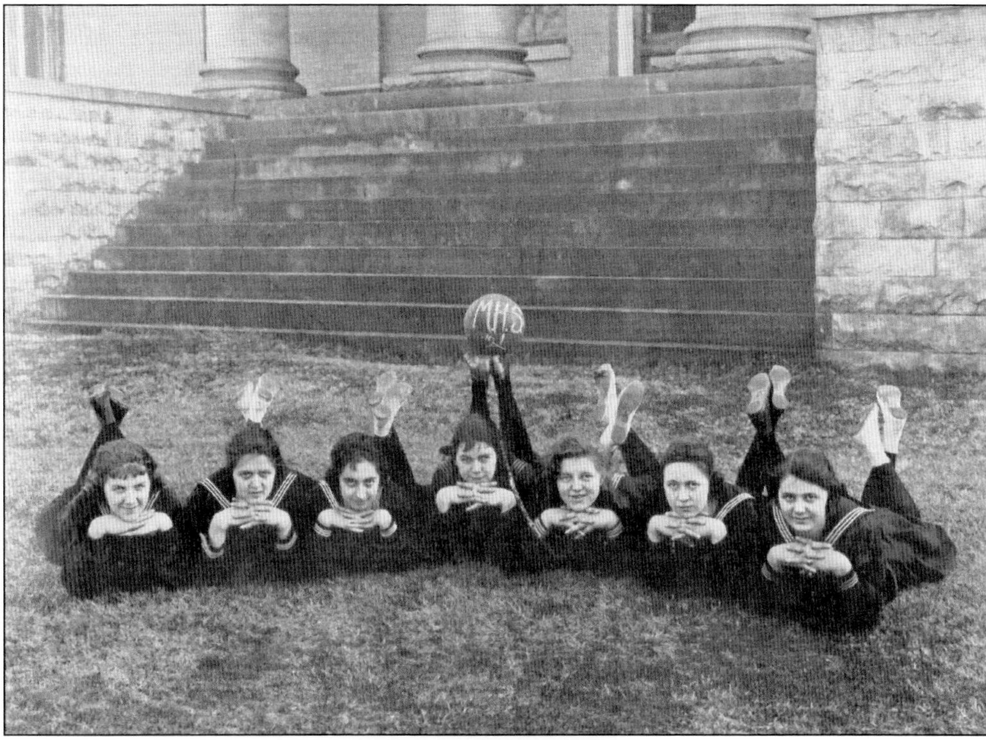

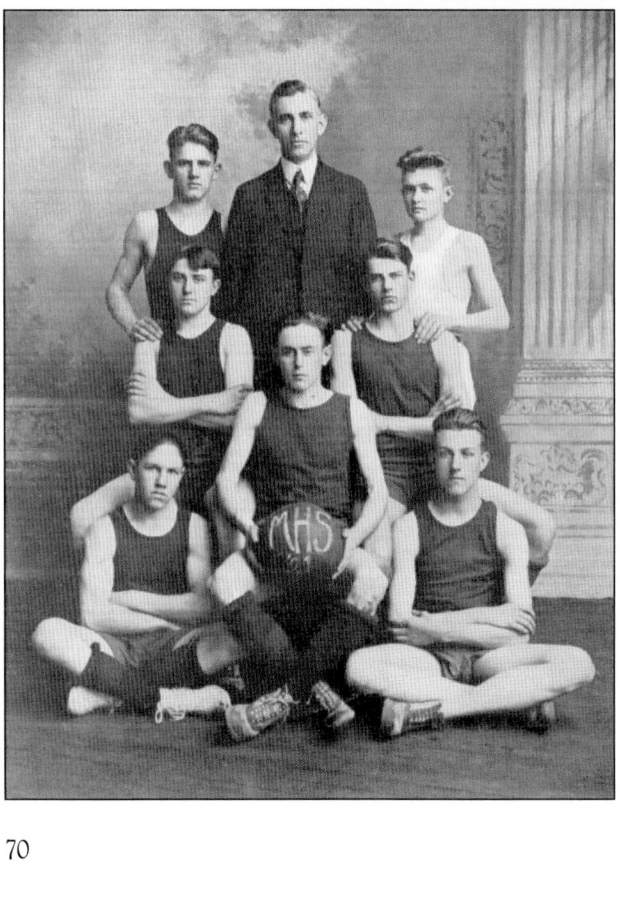

Pictured are the 1921 Maryville High School basketball teams. Shown above, second and third from left, are Isabel Brown and Annie Moore and, fifth and sixth from left, Jeanette Sturgeon and Lois Painter. The other team members were Edith Bell Dikes, Louise Trotter, and Mary Williamson, in unknown order. Shown in the photograph to the left are Robert Pickens (holding the ball) and, front right, Ross Birchfiel. Standing to the right, beside coach Clyde Curtis, is Joe Scott. The order of the other boys is unknown, but team members were Julian Crookshank, Earl Ammons, Len Stanberry, and Horace Clemons Jr. (Courtesy of Maryville City Schools.)

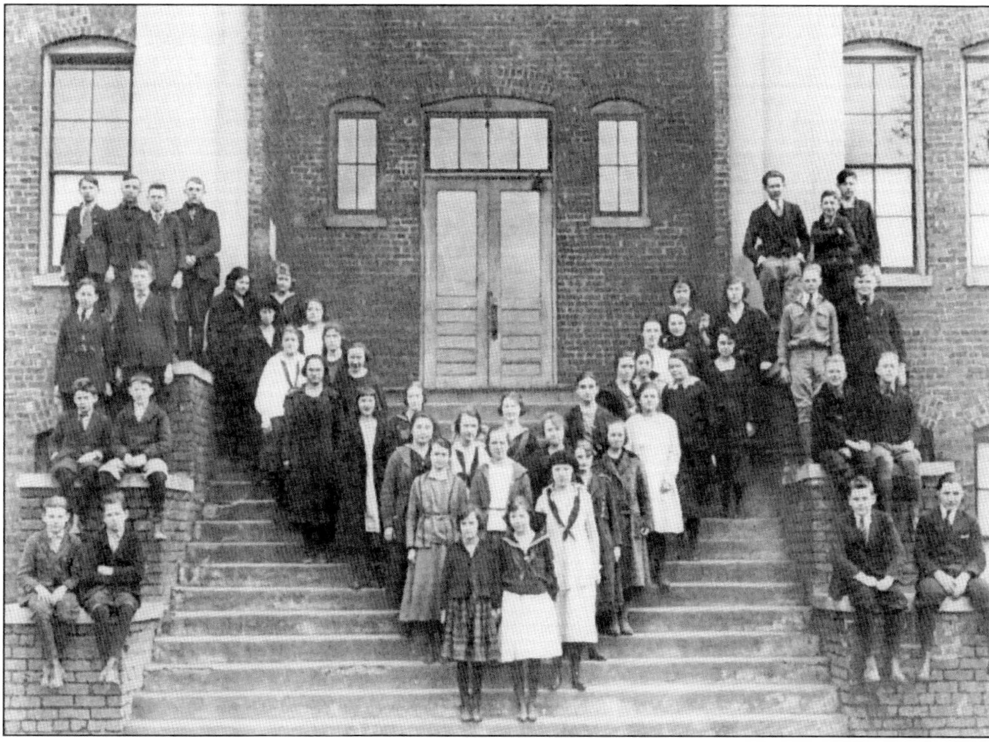

Maryville High School students form an "M" on the steps of East Side School in 1921. (Courtesy of Maryville City Schools.)

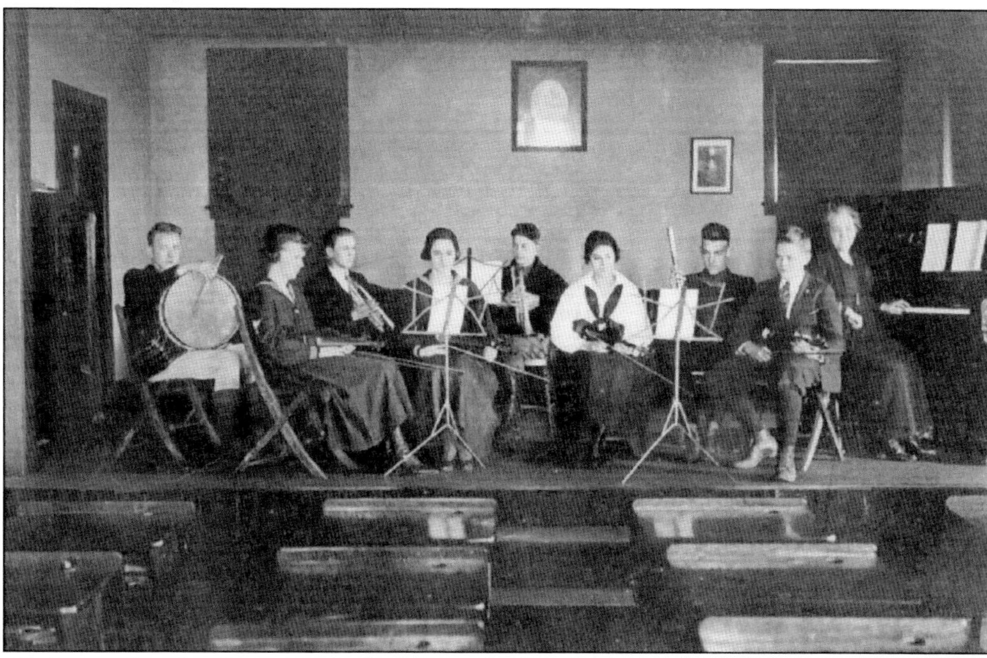

The Maryville school system has offered instruction in the fine arts, including orchestra. Shown in 1921 are high school music students, featuring stringed instruments. (Courtesy of Maryville City Schools.)

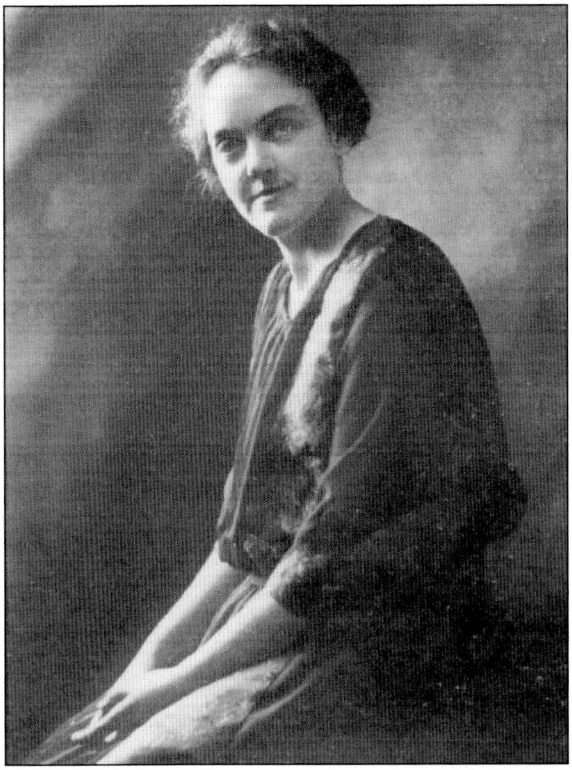

Belle Pickens was the principal of Maryville High School when this photograph was taken in 1921. She was the mother of Maryville attorneys A.B. and Houston Goddard. (Courtesy of Maryville City Schools.)

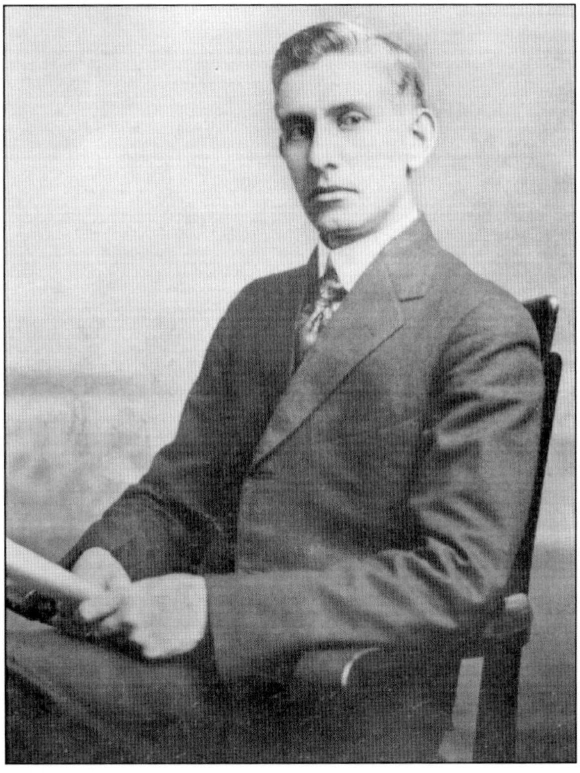

Claude D. Curtis was the superintendent of Maryville city schools. He had taught at Maryville Polytechnic Institute from 1907 to 1914 when he became superintendent and served two terms from 1914 to 1923, then from 1952 to 1958. He was Blount County superintendent from 1932 to 1938, and previously was president of Martha Washington College in Abingdon, Virginia, from 1923 to 1931. (Courtesy of Maryville City Schools.)

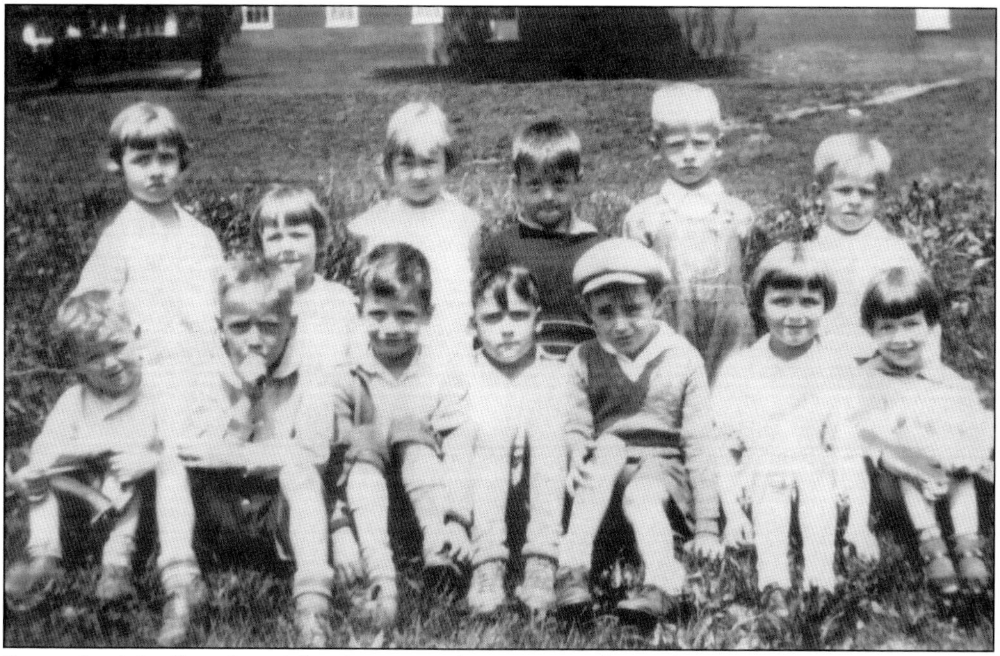

Pictured is Mrs. Boardman's kindergarten class in 1931. Shown from left to right are (first row) Jack Tarvin, Raymond "Bicky" Smith, Carl Murray, Bill Hoyt, Bill Manley, Helen Wilhoit, and Rella Anderson; (second row) Ernestine Harrison, unidentified, Lillian Badgett, A.B. Goddard, Bill Orr, and Jack Young. Orr was killed in World War II. (Courtesy of A.B. Goddard.)

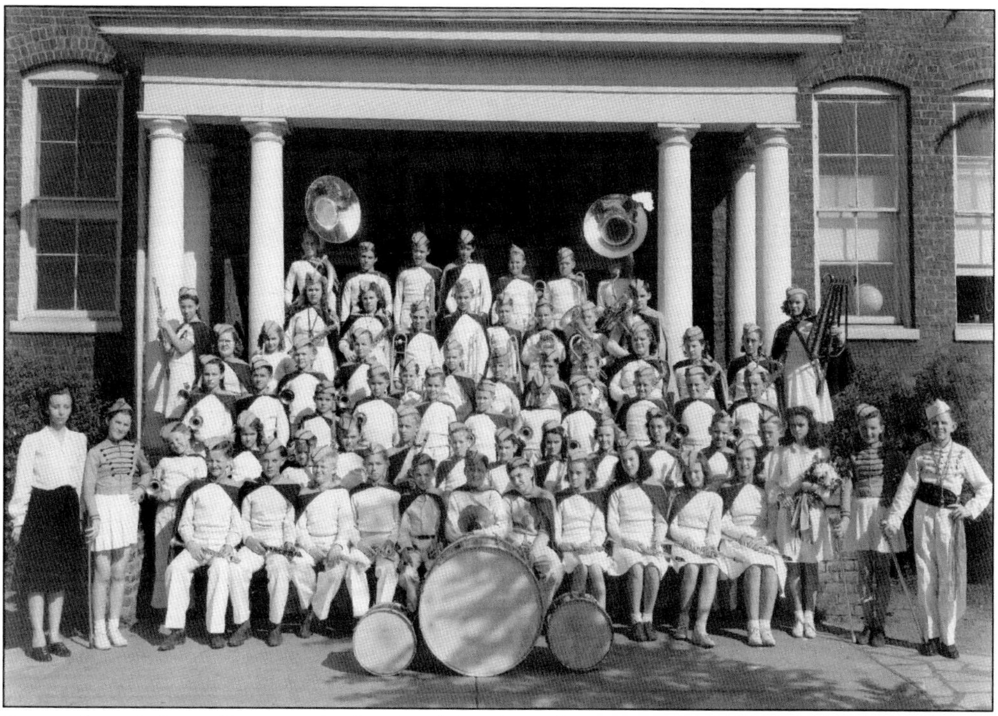

Pictured is a Maryville junior high school band on the steps of West Side School, around the 1940s. (Courtesy of Maryville City Schools.)

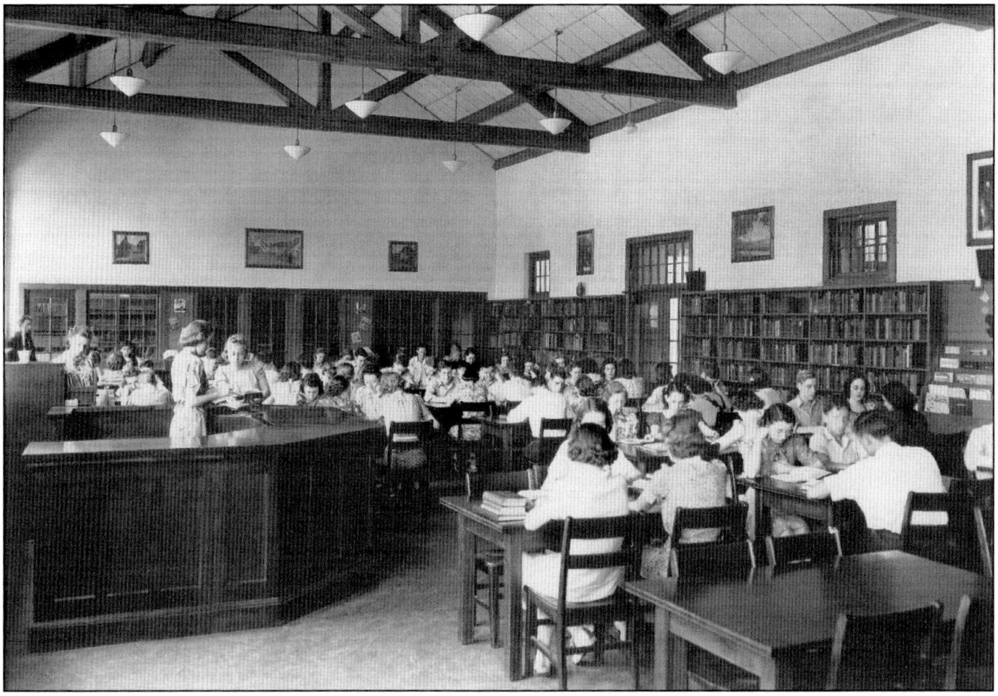

Above, Maryville High School students are pictured in the library around the 1940s. Below, Helen Ott was the first librarian in the present building. A dedicated and well-respected faculty member, Ott established a library club to promote appreciation of good books. (Courtesy of Maryville City Schools.)

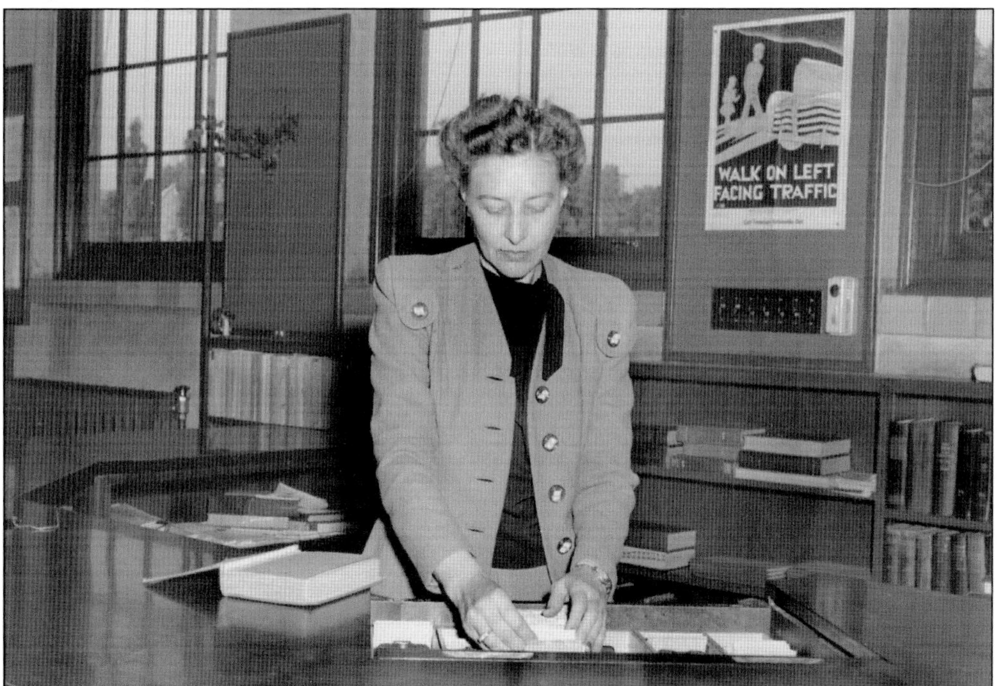

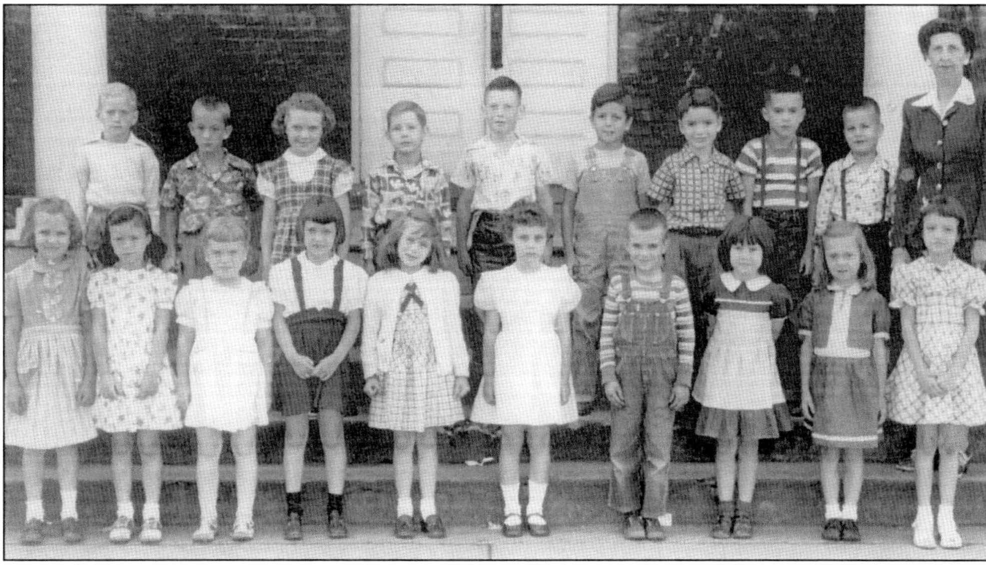

Mrs. Lane's first grade class at West Side School, around 1950, included, from, left to right, (first row) Judy Johnson, unidentified, ? Huddleston, Carolyn Cruze, Andrea Trotter, Jenny Cutler, Kenneth Irwin, Judy Green, Rosalyn Everett, and Beth Hitch; (second row) Jimmy Huffman, unidentified, Linda Clark, Kenneth Carver, James Haworth, Marvin Walker, Parks Hitch, Lynn Howard, unidentified, and teacher Lois Lane. (Courtesy of Maryville High School Class of 1962 Album.)

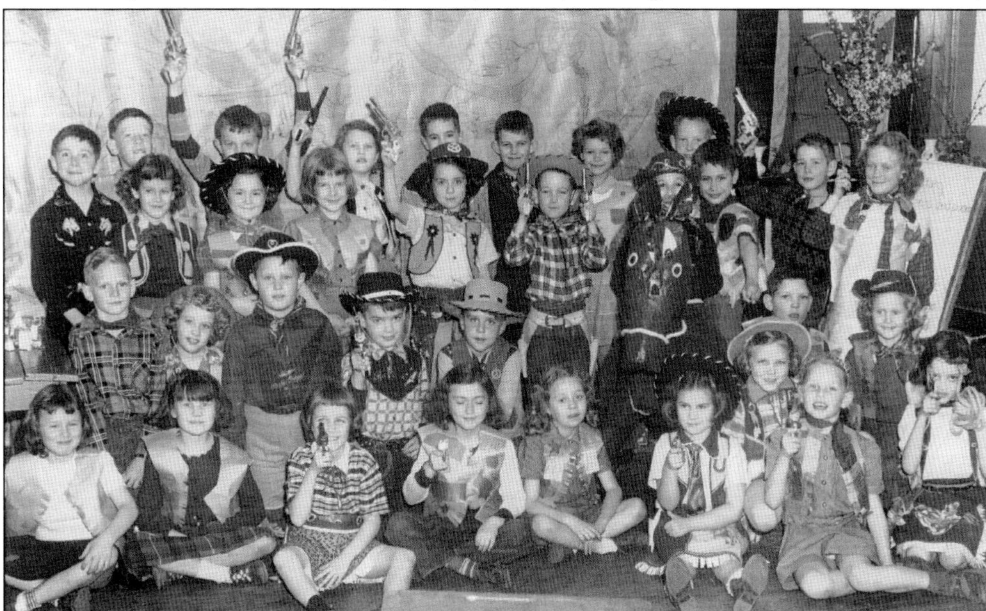

West Side's second grade students, around 1951, included, from left to right, (first row) Sandra Barraso, Judy Green, Carolyn Cruze, Susan Camper, Rosalyn Everett, Romilda Cox, Lynn LeQuire, and Beth Hitch; (second row) Jimmy Huffman, Sandra Long, John Beals, Parks Hitch, Tom Badgett, Judy Johnson, Calvin Free, and Peggy Frishe; (third row) Billy Gass, Jane Lentz, Sandy Humphrey, Becky Blankenship, Sandy Burnett, unidentified, Sammy Wilkinson, Bobby Crabtree, Kenneth Carver, and Linda Clark; (fourth row) James Haworth, Joe Atchison, Jane Kizer, Lynn Howard, Harold Belt, Linda Chapman, and Roger Blair. (Courtesy of Maryville High School Class of 1962 Album.)

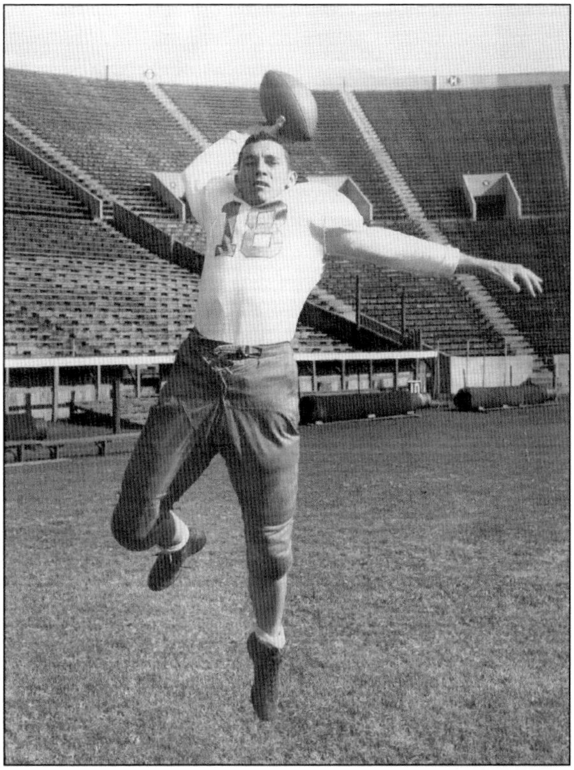

Ollie Keller, an outstanding Maryville High School football player, played at the University of Tennessee and Memphis State and then became a successful college and high school coach. In 1999, he was named one of Blount County's 50 all-time greatest athletes, and he is a member of the Blount County Sports Hall of Fame. (Courtesy of the *Daily Times*.)

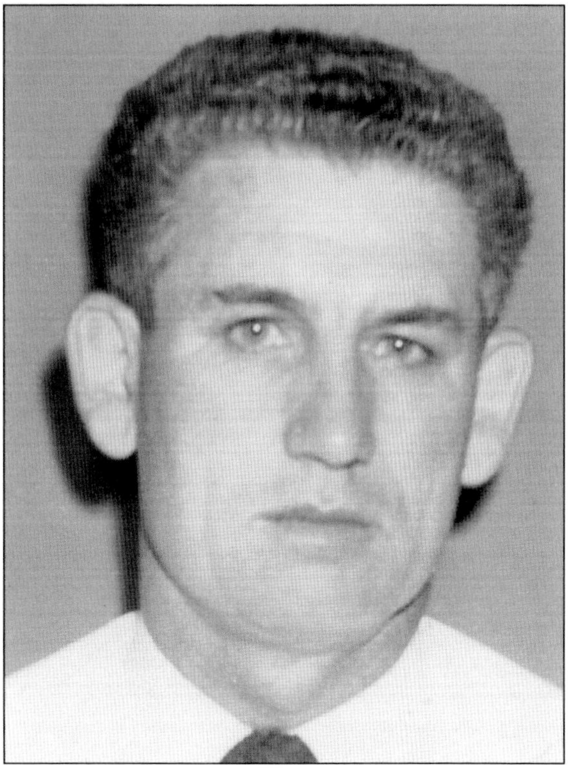

Jim Renfro coached at Maryville High School from 1943 to 1955, establishing a record of 79-40-8, including an undefeated 9-0-1 record in 1946. His 1948 team lost only one game. Renfro is a member of the Blount County Sports Hall of Fame. (Courtesy of the *Daily Times*.)

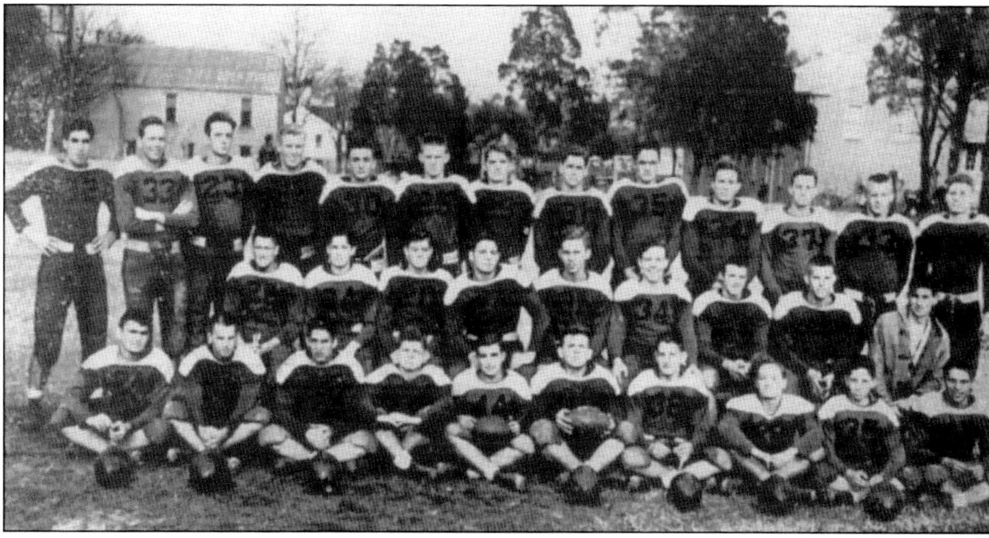

Maryville's 1944 team included, from left to right (front row), Bobby Kizer, Robert Lindsay, Jimmy Wilson, Frank Shepard, Jack Young, Fred Morton Jr., Homer Stinnett, Jimmy Hill, Fred Waggoner, and Charles Aytes; (second row) Roy Beaver, J.S. Henderson, Jimmy Russell, Otis Beaver, Mac Law, Roy Kramer, Bill Stinnett, Don King, and coach Jim Renfro; (third row) Grant Sharp, Winfred Davis, Don Farmer, David Clark, Tommy Long, Raymond Keny, Lowry Holt, Knox Ramsey, Curtis Smith, Robert Roylston, Richard Roylston, Allen Law, and Hoyt Mull. Clark, Hill, Law and Ramsey were named among the county's 50 all-time greatest athletes. Clark was the first Blount Countian named All-Southern in football, Hill and Law played at the University of Tennessee, and Hill and Ramsey played in the National Football League. Kramer became SEC commissioner. (Courtesy of Maryville City Schools.)

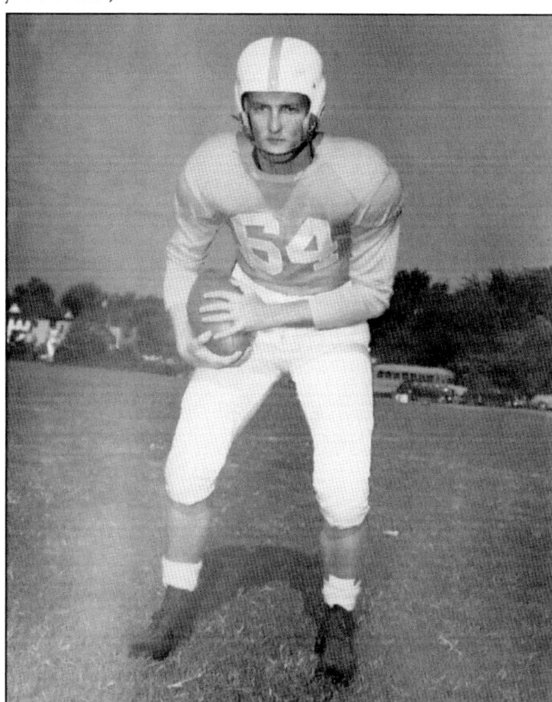

Jim Hill played for the Detroit Lions and Pittsburgh Steelers in the National Football League. He was a key defensive player in his senior season when Tennessee defeated Texas in the Cotton Bowl, and he played on Detroit's 1952 world championship team. (Courtesy of the *Daily Times*.)

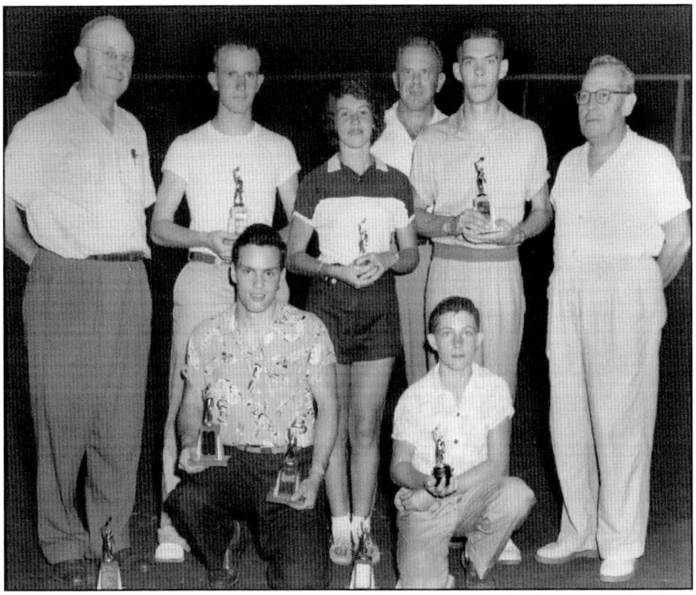

These tennis winners, shown around 1950, included Maryville High School students. Pictured from left to right are (first row) Bill Crowder Jr. and George Paine; (second row) Bitsy Howard, Pat Flynn, Peggy Watts Thompson, Bill Anderson, and two unidentified. (Courtesy of Blount County Genealogical and Historical Society, Ned Sherer Collection.)

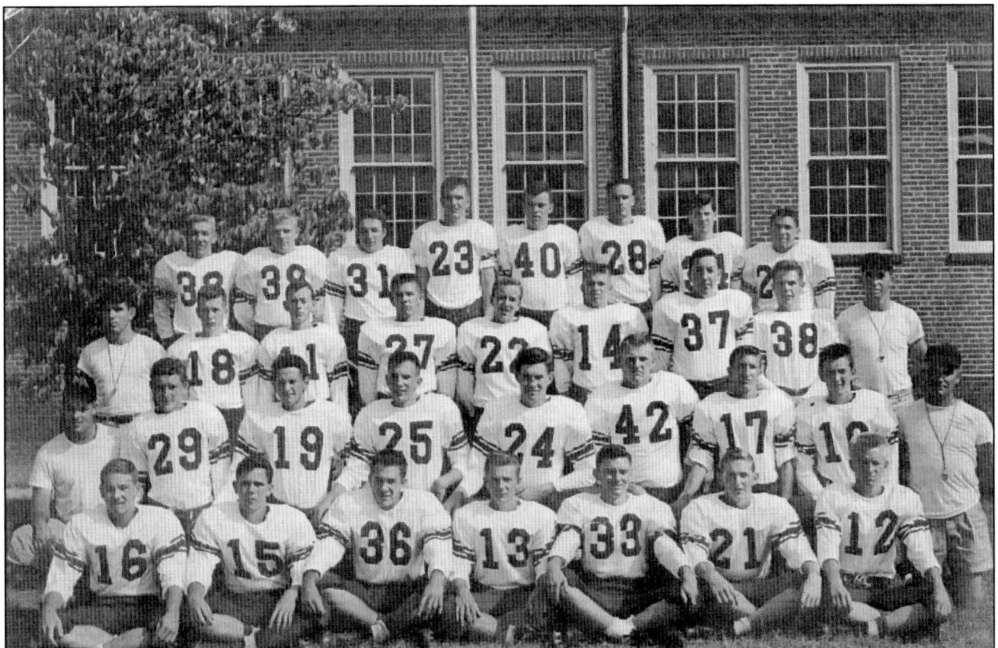

The 1956 Maryville team included, from left to right, (first row) Jimmy Renfro, David Erwin, Bob Henry, Jerry West, Joe Caldwell, Andy Tinker, and Larry Miller; (second row) coach Jim Campbell, Charles Thomas, Bill Bradley, Bill Thatch, John Cropp, Scott Trundle, Ralph Morrison, Larry Cupp, and coach Bill Largen; (third row) coach Buddy Gilbert, Wendell Carpenter, Kenneth Edwards, Dick Williams, Don Hurst, Lynn Webb, Eddie Lambert, Steve Corbett, and head coach Ollie Keller; (fourth row) Robert Henry, Mike Christian, Bill Lyons, Tony Koella, Richard Leatherwood, Alvin Cruze, David Stapleton, and Eddie Greene. (Courtesy of Ken Cornett.)

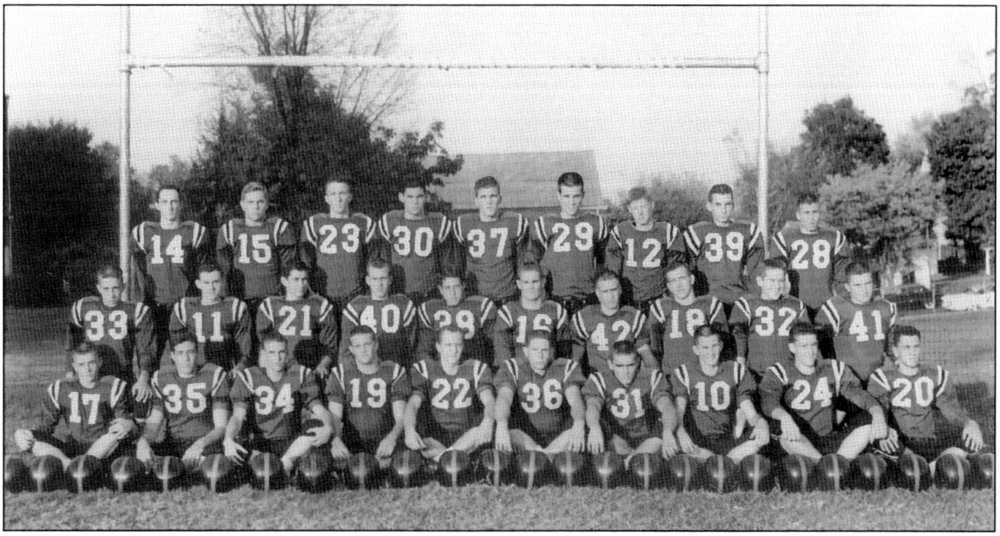

The 1958 team members were, from left to right, (first row) Bob McMurray, Bob Stepp, Bob Stinnett, Lowell Ridings, Don Hurst, Ray Henderson, Vernon Bremberg, Larry Cupp, Charles Thomas, and John Bradley; (second row) Pat Reed, Kenneth Edwards, Jerry Cunningham, Ralph Maples, Harold Hannah, Dale Long, Bud Watters, Wendell Carpenter, Dick Cowan, and Frank Atchison; (third row) Glenn Gregory, Sandy Cunningham, Roy Gregory, Graham McArthur, Dennie Sparks, Jerry Hodge, Roy Stinnett, Tom Stafford, and John Burns. (Courtesy of Ray Henderson.)

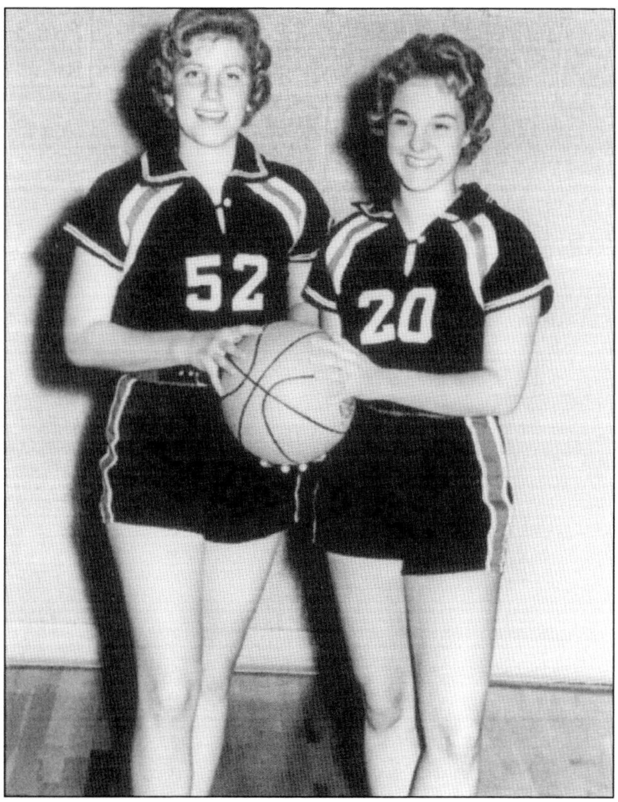

Ann Baker Furrow, left, and Jenny Sweitzer are pictured in 1963. Furrow, an initial inductee into the Blount County Sports Hall of Fame, was selected in 1999 as the best all-around female athlete in the county's history. A basketball star and five-time Tennessee women's golf champion, she won 12 Knox Area Women's Golf Association titles, the 1961 Western Junior championship, and was runner-up in the 1962 USGA National Amateur when she was ranked the nation's 10th best female golfer. (Courtesy of Maryville City Schools.)

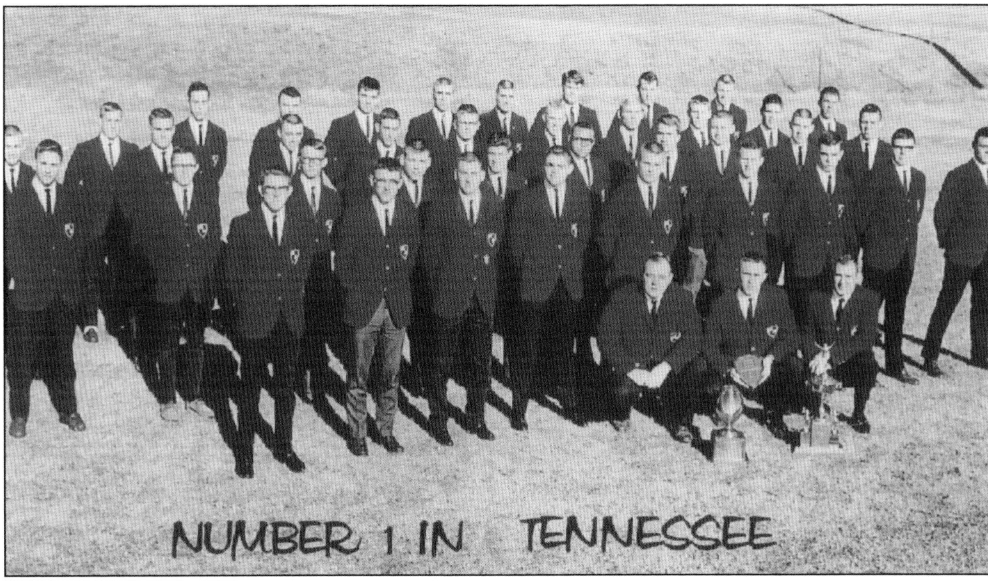

The undefeated 1964 Rebel football team was ranked number one in the state in the final Associated Press poll. It gave up only 13 points, and *Sports Illustrated* ranked the team the best among AP state champions in that regard. The coaches were coaches of the year Don Rawls and Ted Wilson. John Moscript was All-East Tennessee and second team All-State. (Courtesy of Maryville City Schools.)

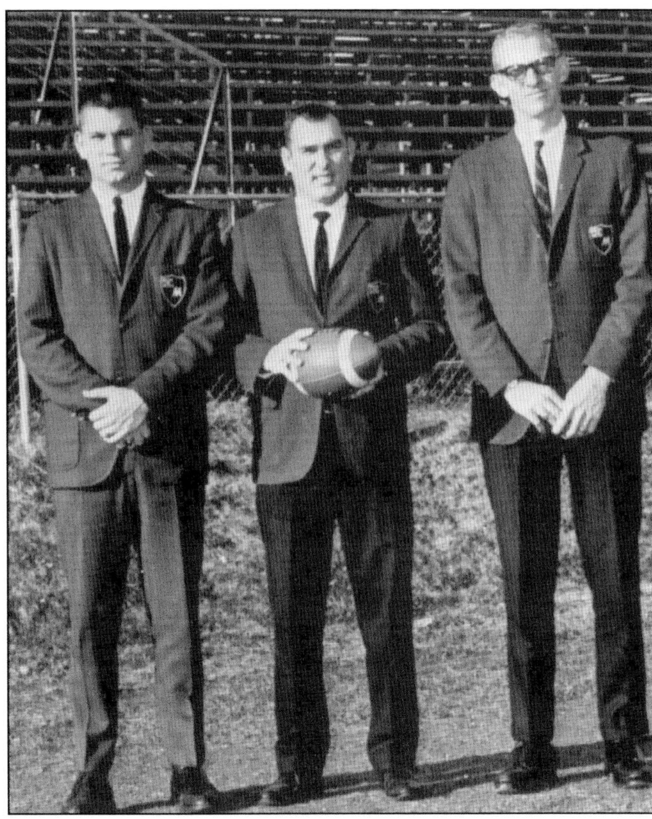

The 1967 football coaches were, from left to right, Benny Monroe, head coach Ted Wilson, and Bill Phillips. Wilson, an initial inductee into the Blount County Sports Hall of Fame, compiled a phenomenal 150-25-2 record and led his teams to state championships in 1970, 1976, and 1978. His 1978 team was undefeated. (Courtesy of Maryville City Schools.)

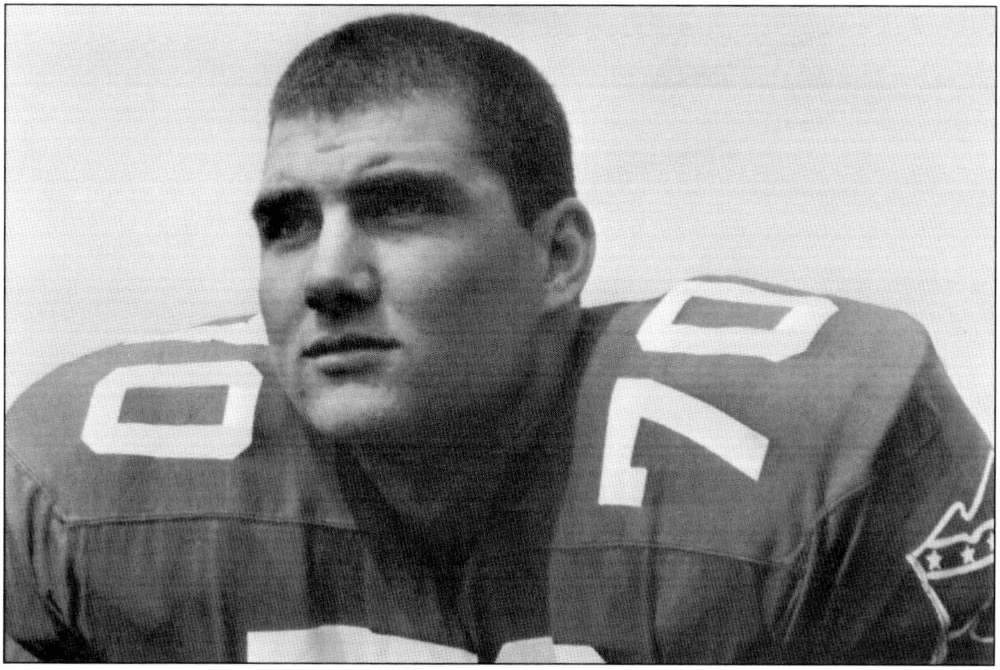

Larry Johnston played offensive and defensive tackle at MHS from 1964 to 1966. He received a scholarship to the University of Tennessee, where a knee injury ended his career. Ted Wilson called him the smartest player he ever had, and in 1983 he was named to the All Blount County Quarter Century Team. (Courtesy of Maryville City Schools.)

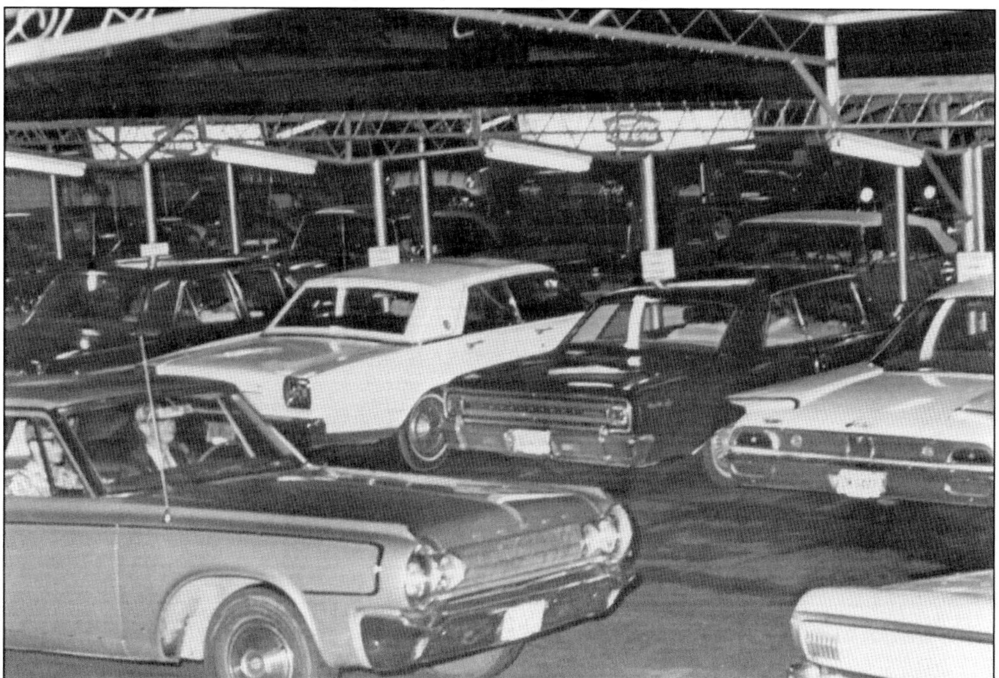

Maryville High students, and students from around the county, enjoyed "circling the Dwarf" drive-in. This picture was taken around 1967. (Courtesy of Maryville City Schools.)

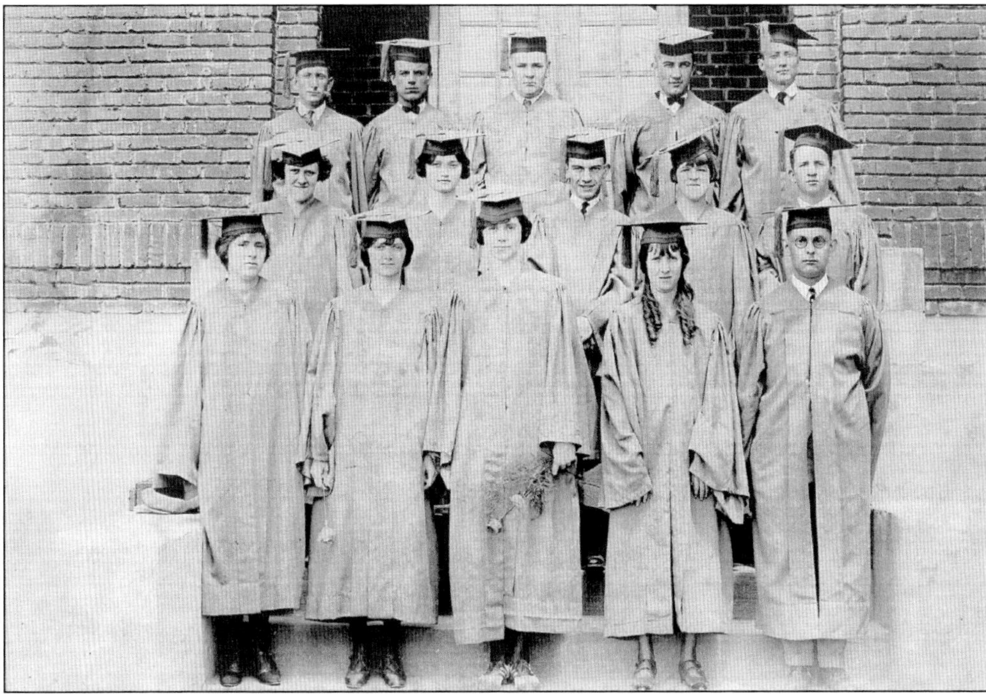

Everett High School, although part of the Blount County School System, would today be within the city of Maryville. The school welcomed students from 1922 until 1977, when Heritage High School opened. The first graduating class was in 1924 and included, from left to right, (first row) Ina Atchley, Bess Mynatt, Mazelle Hall, Myrtle Russell, and Nat Farmer; (second row) Bessie Bowman, Pearl Mynatt, Earnest Hautz, Lucille Everett, and Steve Jett; (third row) Virgil Davis, Barney Ballard, Perry Wrinkle, Paul Everett, and Hobart Davis. (Courtesy of Linda Keller West, Everett High School Alumni Association.)

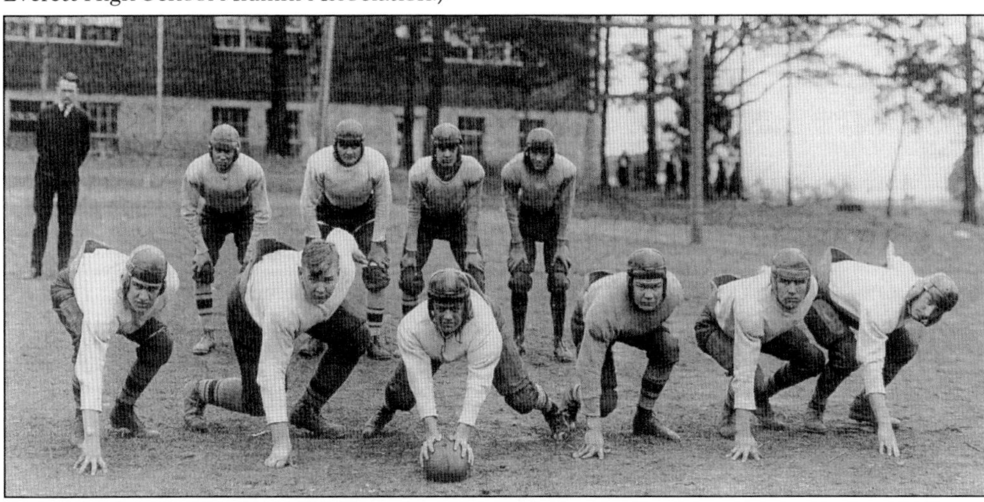

The 1923 Everett High School Bulldogs football team included, from left to right, (first row) Glenn Garner, John Grant, Perry Wrinkle, Gatman Shamblin, Robert Black, Ben Rogers, and Virgil Davis; (second row) Clifford Large, John Harrison, Barney Ballard, and H.B. "Bud" McCall. Coach Ralph McConnell is standing behind the team. (Courtesy of Linda Keller West, Everett High School Alumni Association.)

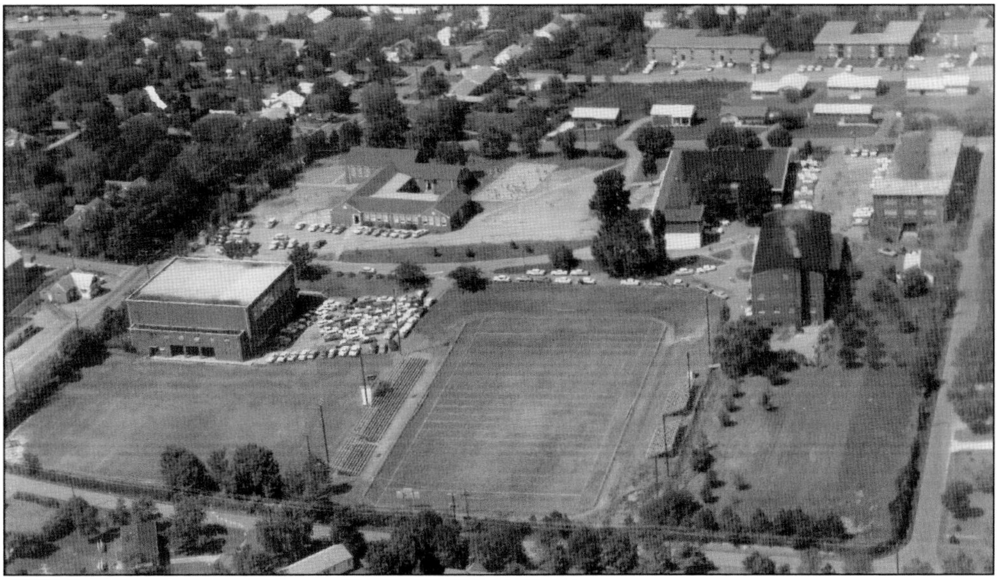

The Everett High School campus, shown above, was located on Everett Hill, known affectionately to students simply as "The Hill." Below is the undefeated 1941 Bulldog football team. Shown are, from left to right, (first row) Wayne Davis, Dean Stone, Marion Goodman, captain Dale Jones, Elmer White, Bill Jones, and A.R. Archer; (second row) principal J. Hobart Davis, Ralph Mitchell, Buddy Bird, E. J. Hutsell Jr., Fred Smith, Charles Harmon, Hayden Proctor, Leon Wilson, and coach Walter Coker; (third row) Bill Cross, George Rutherford, Edwin Webb, King Berrong Jr., Calvin Rule, Charles Lawson, Hershell Merriman, and Charles Burger; (fourth row, white shirts) Larson Everett, Don Ammons, Jack Young, Ralph Effler, and Leon Berrong; (fifth row) Joe Downey, Otie Smith, Mayford Marine, Alvin Walker, Jim Millard, and Ben Talbott. Burger was the first Blount Countian named to an All-State team. (Courtesy of Linda Keller West, Everett High School Alumni Association.)

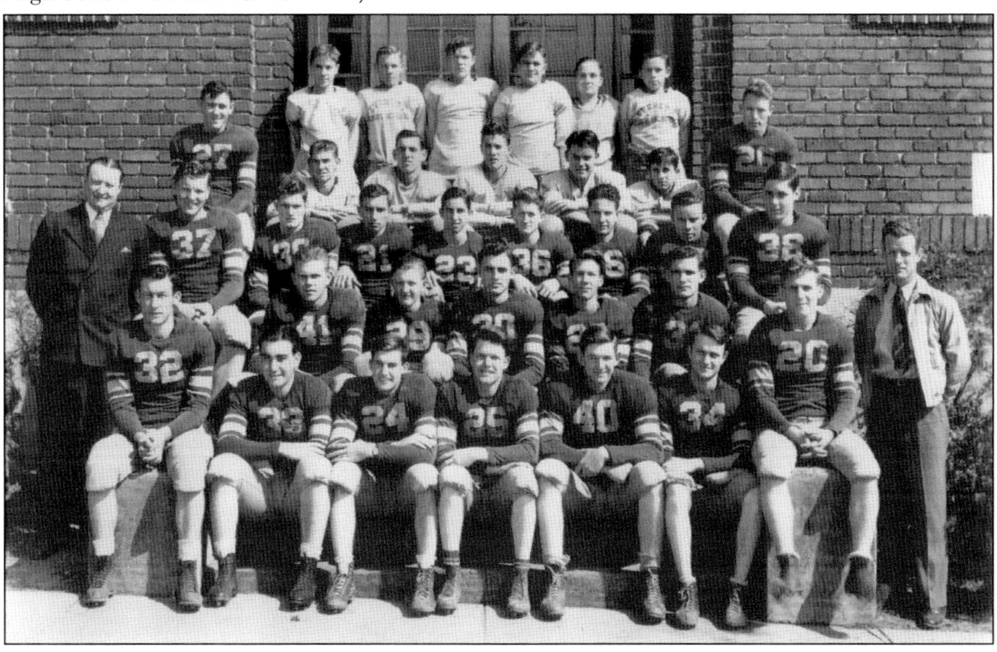

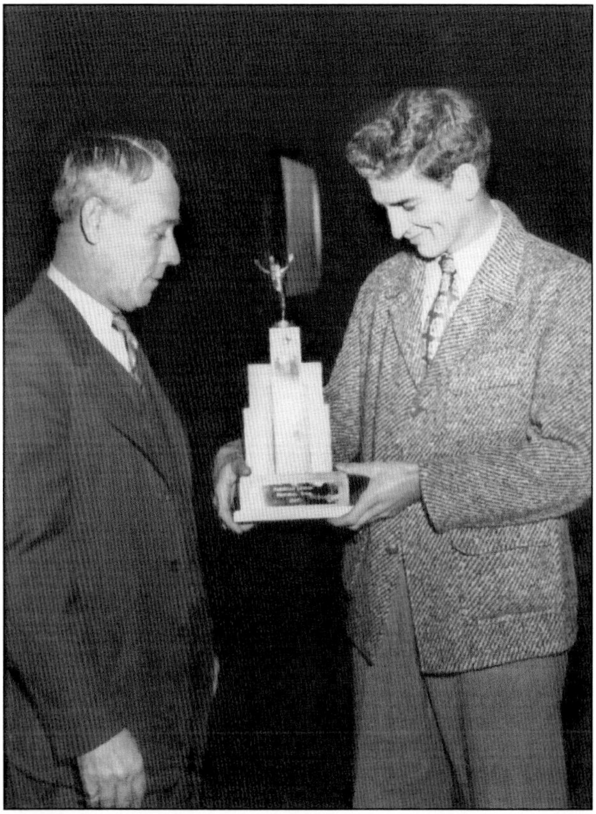

Everett coach Spence Renfro, left, was an initial inductee into the Blount County Sports Hall of Fame. He coached football from 1946 to 1948 and basketball from 1946 to 1955. His basketball record was 207-36, and his 1951 team went to the state tournament, losing to eventual state champion Selmer. Below is Renfro's 1954 team. Pictured from left to right are (first row) Renfro, Dan Webb, Don Spencer, Ronnie McBrayer, Kenny Coulter, Ken Thacker, and Bud Keeble; (second row) James Brown, Ronald Huffstetler, Maurice Bell, Ed Atchley, Earl Smith, Eddie Lowe, and manager Bill West. Webb and Coulter, also initial Hall of Fame inductees, played for Tennessee, Webb in football and Coulter winning 12 letters in basketball, baseball, and track. In 1999, Webb was selected the best all-around male athlete in Blount County history. (Courtesy of Max Renfro.)

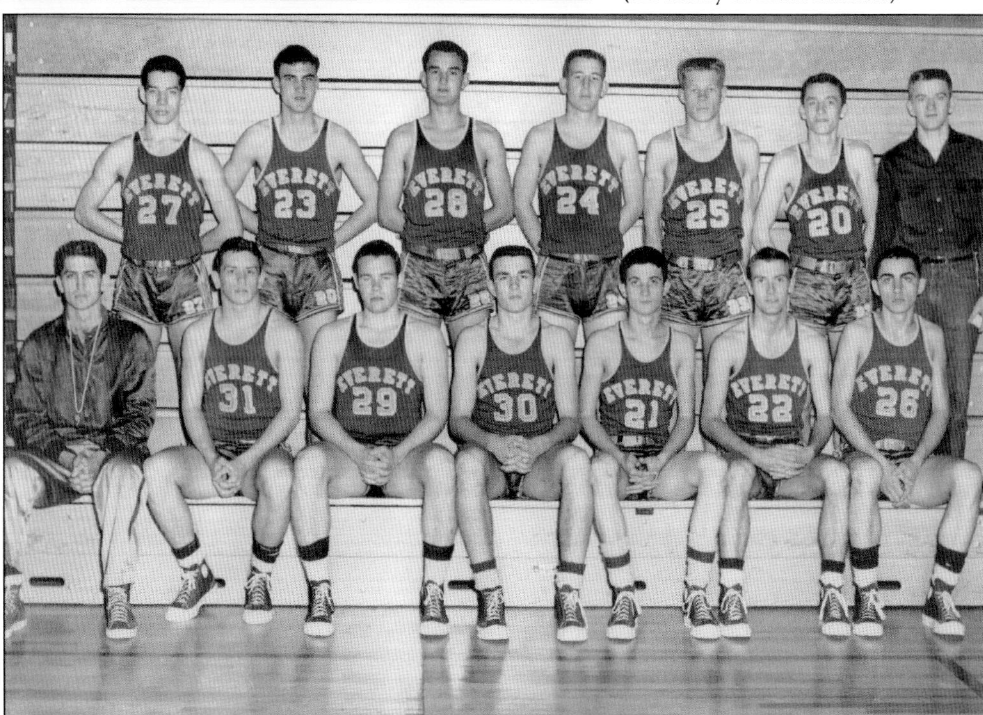

Five

Professionals and Government

Both Blount County and Maryville were founded in 1795, with Maryville being the county seat. Accordingly, the proper administration of local government—both county and municipal—has been among the most important responsibilities of Maryville's citizens from the inception of the city.

For more than 200 years, the lawyers and judges who have comprised the Blount County bar have established a reputation for integrity and excellence in the practice of law. By the early 20th century, many prominent names in the history of the Blount County bar, including families whose members have practiced here for a hundred years or more, had offices in Maryville, including Will A. McTeer Sr. and Jr., M.H. Gamble Sr., John C. Crawford Sr., Sam H. Dunn, Homer A. Goddard, and R.R. Kramer. After World War II, other prominent lawyers included John C. Crawford Jr., Roy Crawford, Joe and Mose Gamble, A.B. and Houston Goddard, Rom Meares Sr., William B. Felknor, Dave Rosier, Hugh E. Delozier Sr., D.K. Thomas, Frank Bird, Bob Navratil, Ben W. Kizer, and Maryville's first female attorney, Marinell Ross Waggoner.

Likewise our physicians have established a tradition of excellence in the practice of medicine. By the early 20th century, many prominent medical families were established here, represented by C.C. Vinsant, C.F. Crowder, W.B. Lovingood, G.D. LeQuire, and A.M. Gamble, who would also serve as mayor. By the 1950s, local doctors included Henry and Lea Callaway, J.W. Christofferson, Mary Cragan, William C. Crowder, Lynn Curtis, Bob Haralson Jr., Joe Henderson, Cecil Howard, Homer Isbell, Sam Lambeth, Roy Laughmiller, J.C. Lentz, Robert Leyen, F.S. Lovingood, J. Frank Manning, N.A. McKinnon, Bob Mynatt, Jim Proffitt, B.P. Ramsey, O.L. Simpson, T.H. Vandergriff, Lowell Vinsant, and John Yarborough.

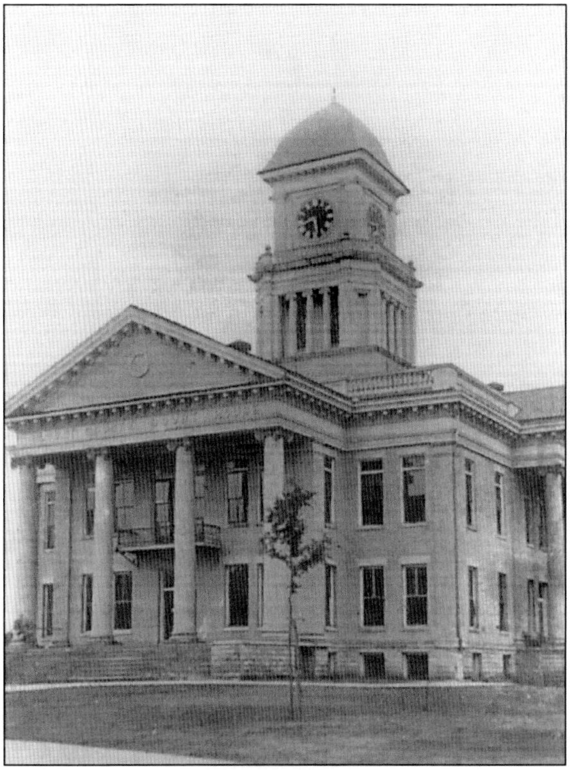

Pictured to the left is the Blount County Courthouse around 1908. After the previous courthouse on Main Street burned in 1906, a committee recommended moving the courthouse from Main Street due to traffic noise. Shown below is the courthouse, from its southern side, around 1956, before additional expansion on that side. A quaint feature of the courthouse, still unnoticed by many, is that over the main entrance a period follows the words "Blount County Court House." (Left, courtesy of City of Maryville; below, courtesy of Karen Kenst.)

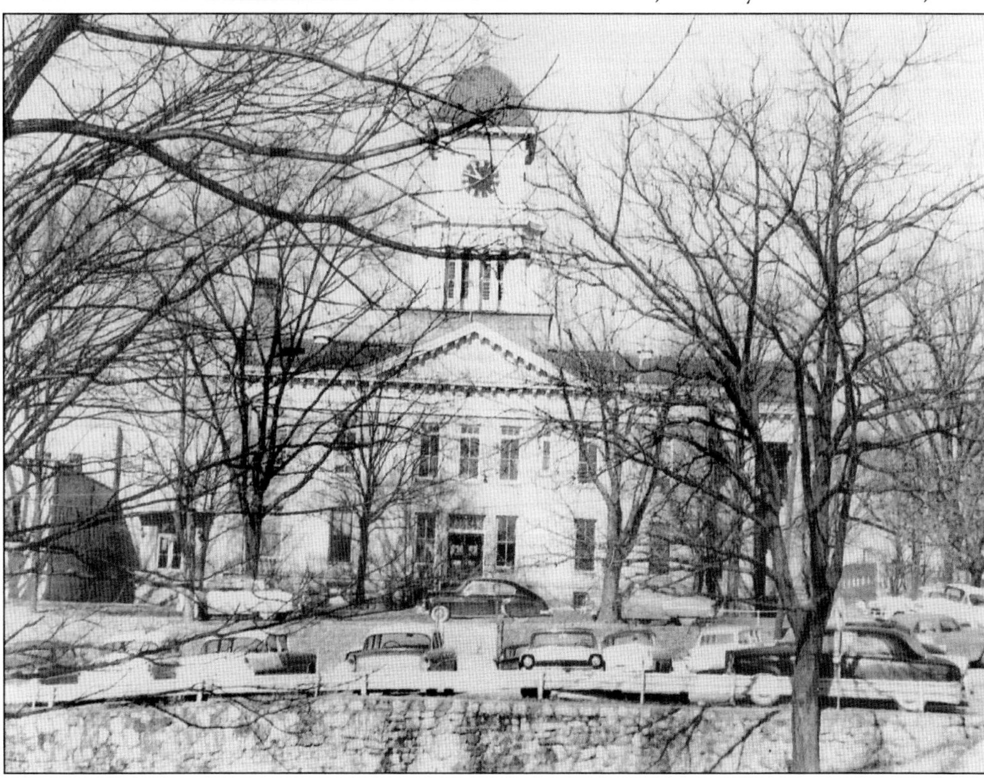

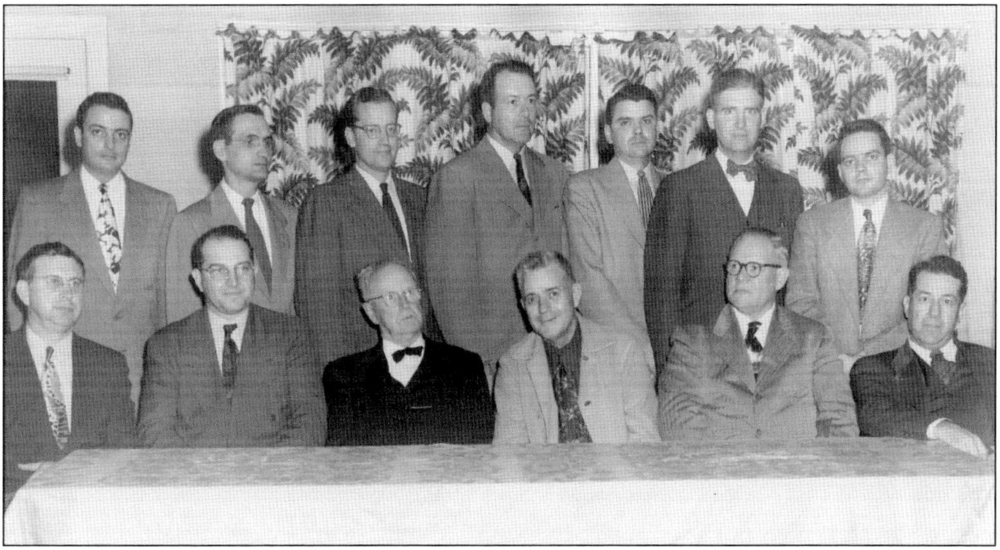

Above are members of the Blount County Bar Association in the late 1950s. From left to right are (first row) Hugh E. Delozier Sr., John Crawford Jr., Sam H. Dunn, Homer A. Goddard, Dave Rosier, and Joe C. Gamble; (second row) A.B. Goddard, William B. Felknor, Ralph Reed, Mose H. Gamble Jr., D. K. Thomas, Frank Bird, and Houston M. Goddard. Pictured below are members of the bar around 1964. From left to right are (first row) Rom Meares Sr., Hugh E. Delozier Sr., Beecher Witt, Sam H. Dunn, Russell Kramer, Dave Rosier, Joe C. Gamble, and Glenn Flack; (second row) Frank Drinnen, Ben Kizer, Bob Navratil, Jimmy Witt, William B. Felknor, Houston M. Goddard, Frank Bird, Will A. McTeer, ? Watkins, Roy Crawford, and D.K. Thomas; (third row) Ed Lynch, Bill Shields, John Crawford Jr., Carl O. Koella Jr., Arnold Kramer, A.B. Goddard, and Mose H. Gamble Jr. (Courtesy of A.B. Goddard.)

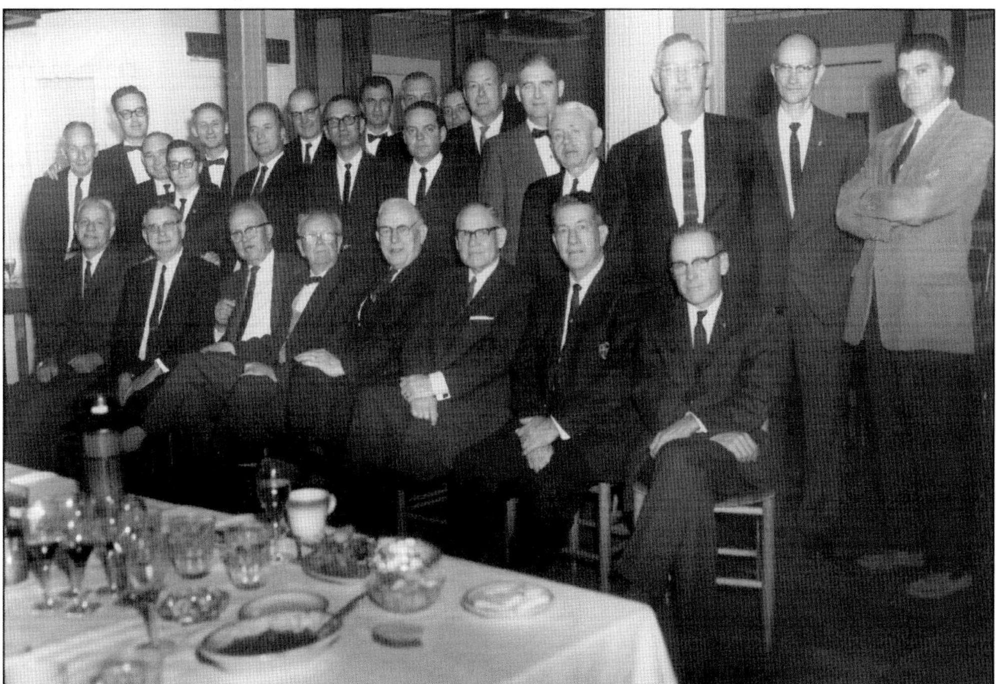

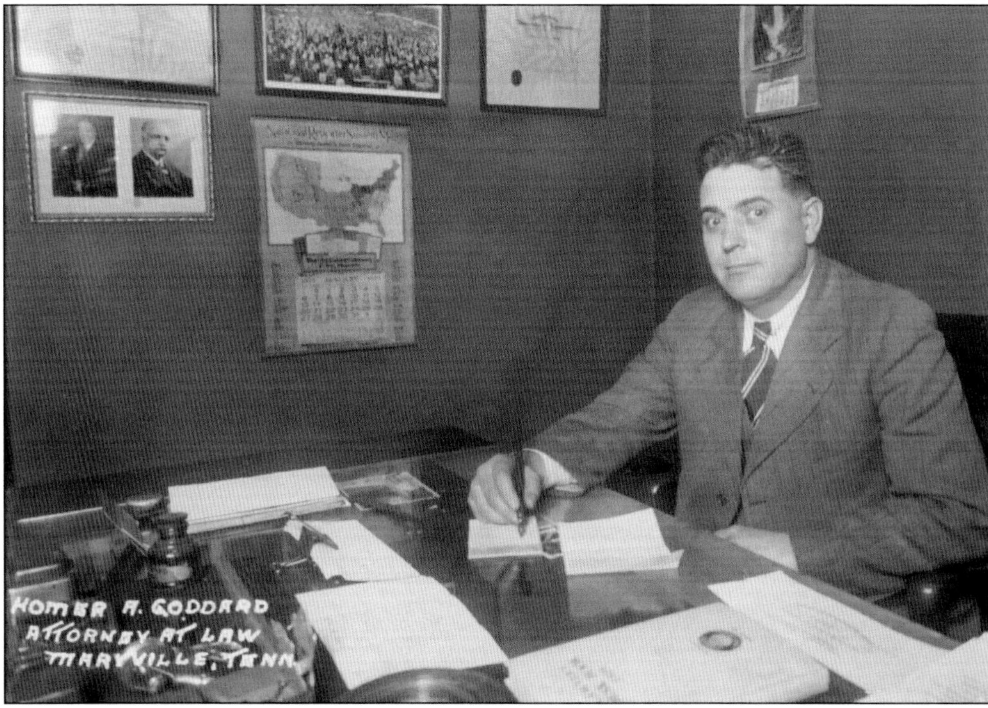

Homer A. "Bully" Goddard is pictured inside his Gamble, Crawford, and Goddard office in 1929. Goddard and Gamble was established around 1932. Goddard's sons A.B. and Houston M. Goddard would join him in the firm. Goddard was instrumental in the establishment of the city of Alcoa as its city attorney. (Courtesy of A.B. Goddard.)

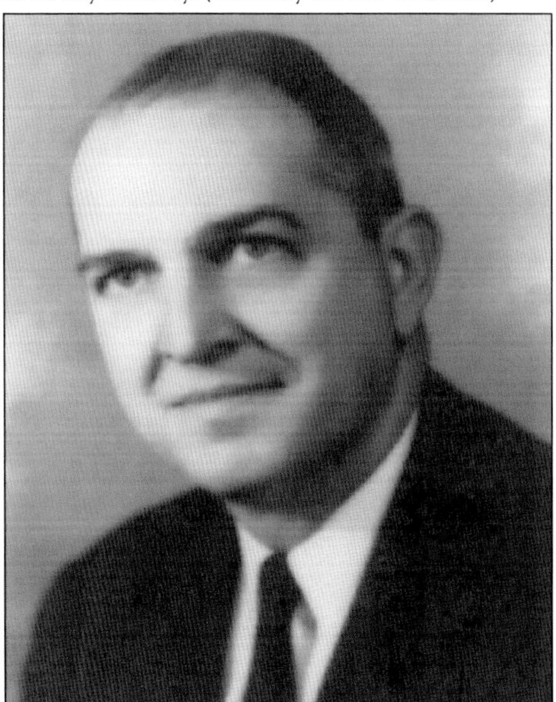

John C. Crawford Jr. joined his father in forming Crawford and Crawford in 1932. His brother Roy Crawford later joined the practice, as did his sons John C. Crawford III and Duncan V. Crawford. Crawford served as mayor from 1947 to 1953. The picture shown is his official portrait when he served as US Attorney for the Eastern District of Tennessee under Pres. Dwight D. Eisenhower from 1953 to 1961. (Courtesy of Duncan V. Crawford.)

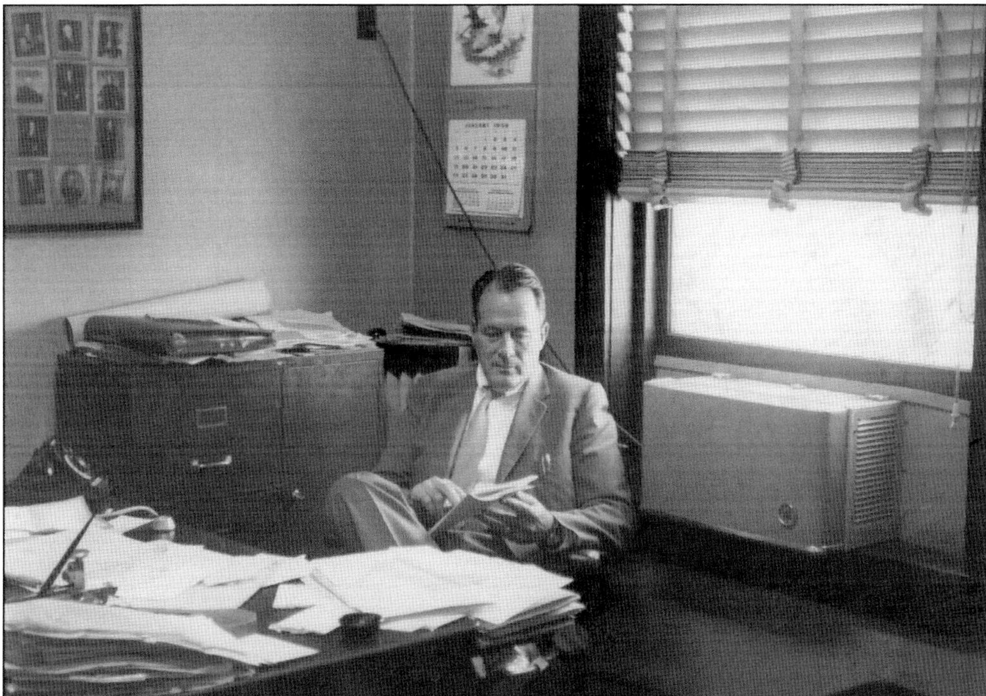

Pictured are Mose H. Gamble (above) and Joe C. Gamble (below) in their offices at Goddard and Gamble in 1958. Their father, Moses H. Gamble Sr., was previously a partner in the firm. Joe served on the Maryville College board of directors for 31 years and as chairman from 1953 to 1970. Mose succeeded Homer Goddard as Alcoa city attorney. (Courtesy of A.B. Goddard.)

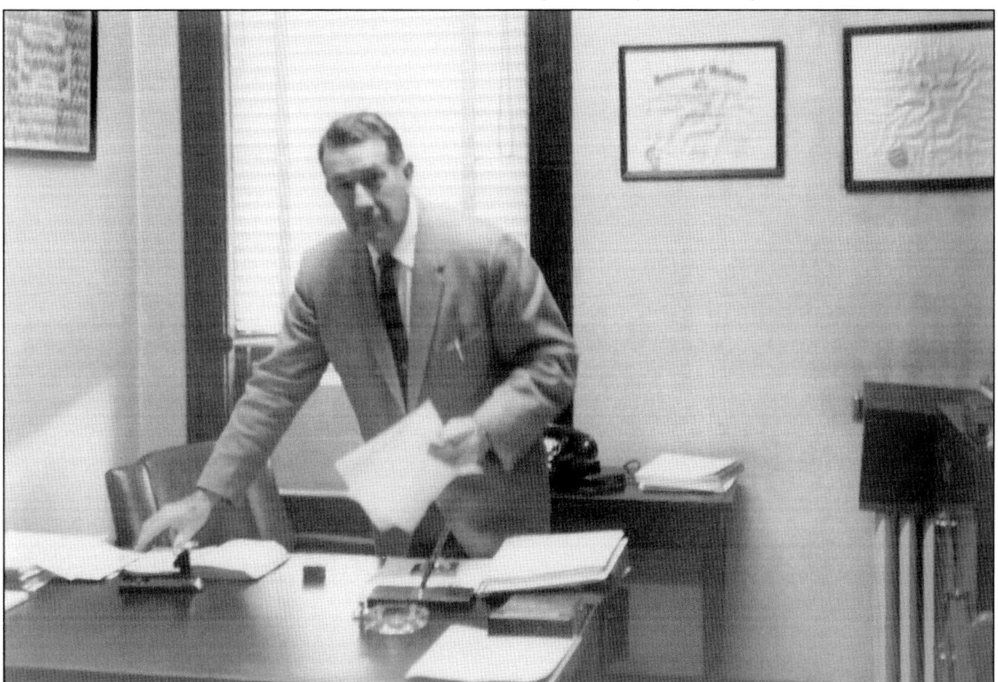

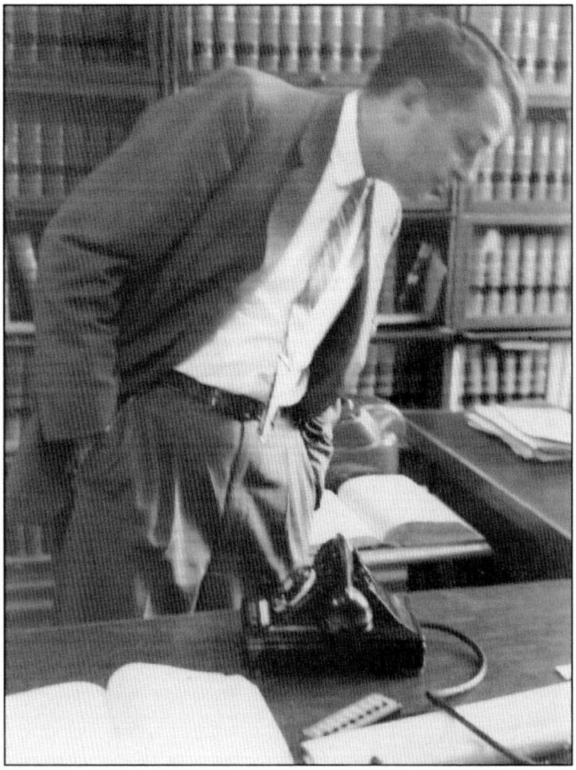

A.B. Goddard is shown at Goddard and Gamble in 1959 using a spittoon. At that time, spittoons were standard fixtures in Blount County courtrooms. (Courtesy of A.B. Goddard.)

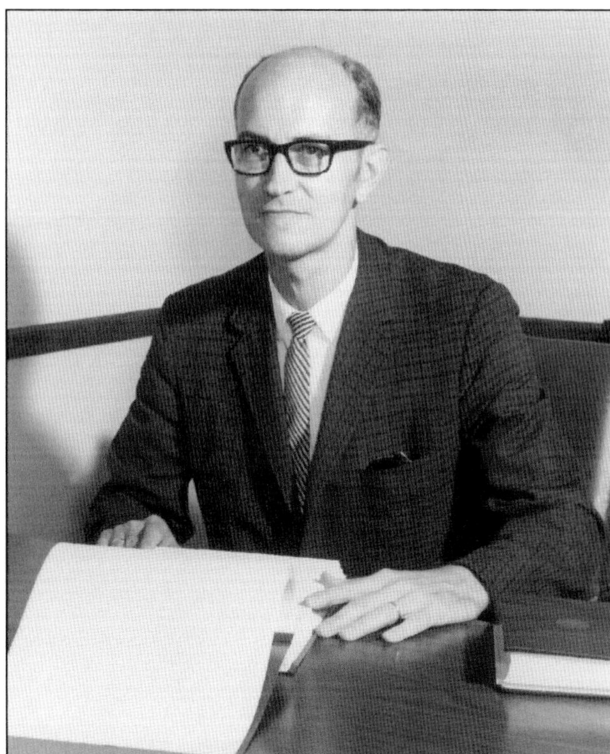

Roy D. Crawford, a partner at Crawford and Crawford, served as Maryville city attorney from 1966 to 1999. He was a state senator from 1960 to 1966. (Courtesy of City of Maryville.)

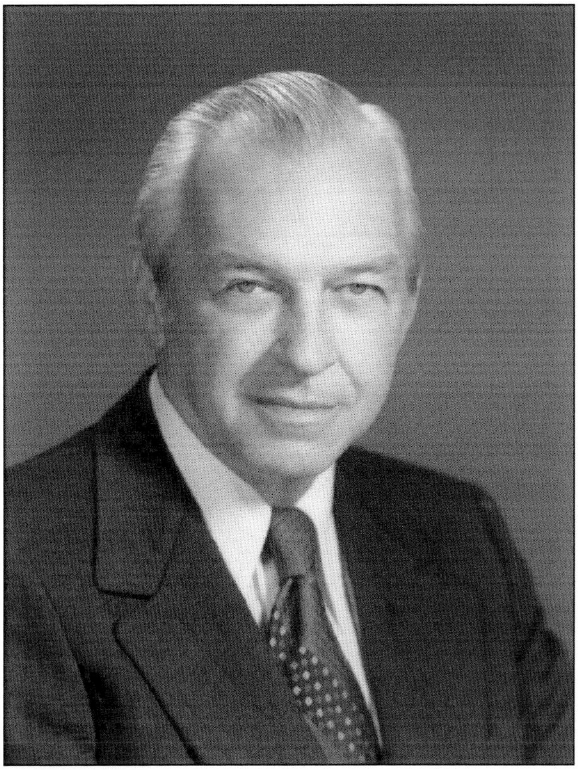

R. Arnold Kramer's father, R.R. Kramer, opened his practice in Maryville in 1913, forming a partnership with Will A. McTeer. He moved his practice to Knoxville in 1934, and his son joined him there. The present firm of Kramer Rayson is the successor firm. Arnold Kramer served as general counsel, and as a director and officer, of the Aluminum Company of America. (Courtesy of the *Daily Times*.)

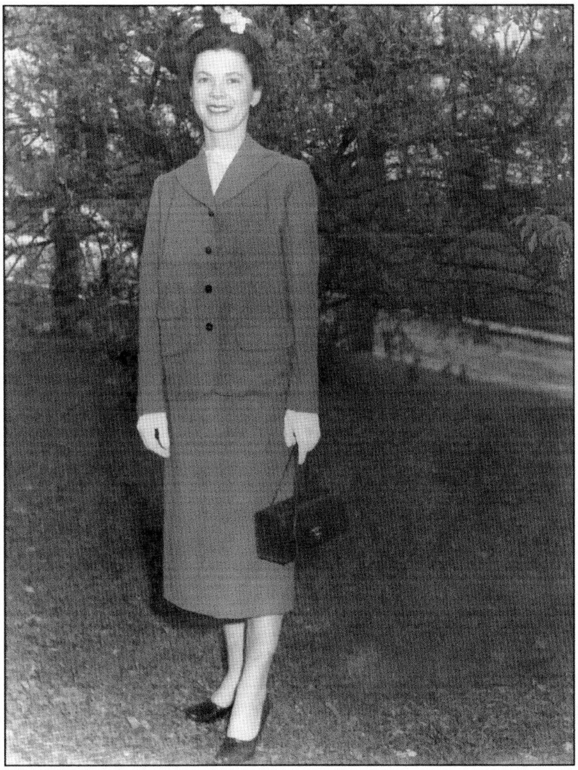

Marinell Ross Waggoner was Blount County's first female attorney. She attended Maryville High School and Maryville College, then earned her law degree from Vanderbilt University after attending the University of North Carolina. She was in private practice until she married A.B. Waggoner Jr. (Courtesy of Nell Waggoner.)

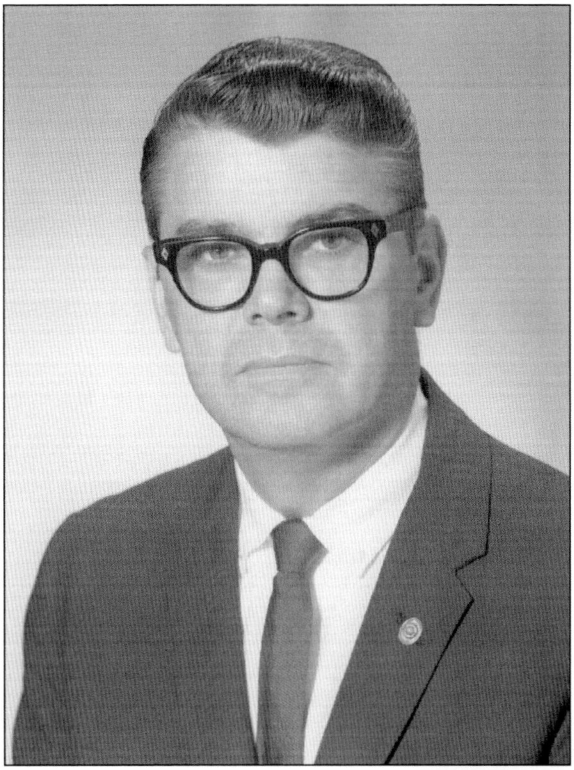

D.K. Thomas practiced law for 36 years beginning in 1949. His son D. Kelly Thomas served as Blount County circuit judge from 1990 until 2006, and presently sits on the Tennessee Court of Criminal Appeals. Another son, Oliver "Buzz" Thomas, practiced with them before becoming general counsel for the Baptist Joint Committee on Public Affairs in Washington, then director of the Great Schools Partnership for Knox County. (Courtesy of the *Daily Times*.)

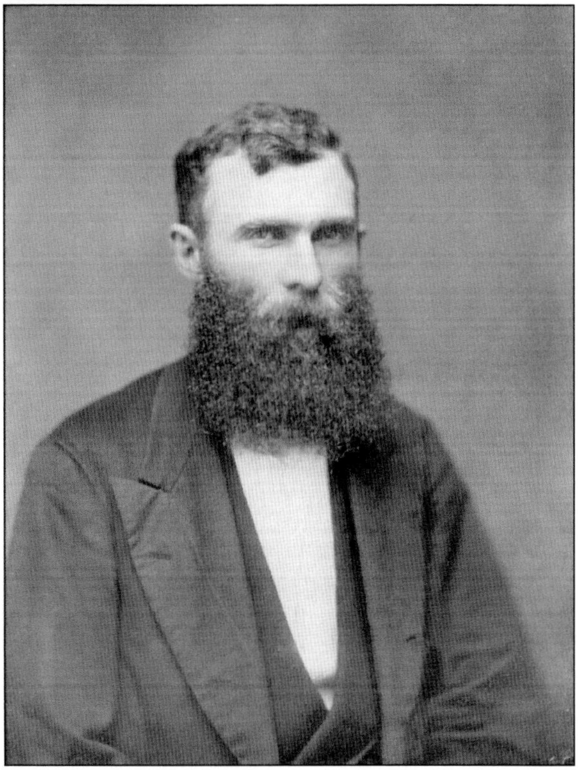

Dr. John Patton Blankenship attended Friendsville Institute, later Friendsville Academy, and became a physician by "reading" medicine with Drs. Isaac Taylor and Benjamin Morton. After serving as an assistant surgeon during the Civil War with the 3rd Tennessee Infantry, US Army, he returned to Maryville to practice medicine. In 1874, he became the founding president of the Blount County Medical Society. (Courtesy of Becky Blankenship Darrell.)

John W. Cates graduated from Maryville College in 1851 and then from Nashville Medical School. In 1857, he began his Maryville practice as a physician and surgeon and served as a Confederate army surgeon during the Civil War. He returned to Maryville after the war and constructed his home, "Sunny Hill," on the site of the present courthouse. (Courtesy of A.B. Goddard.)

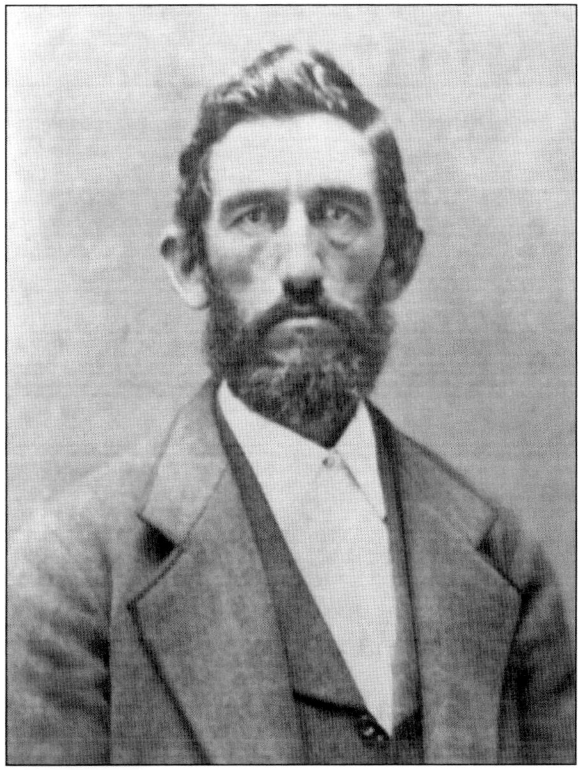

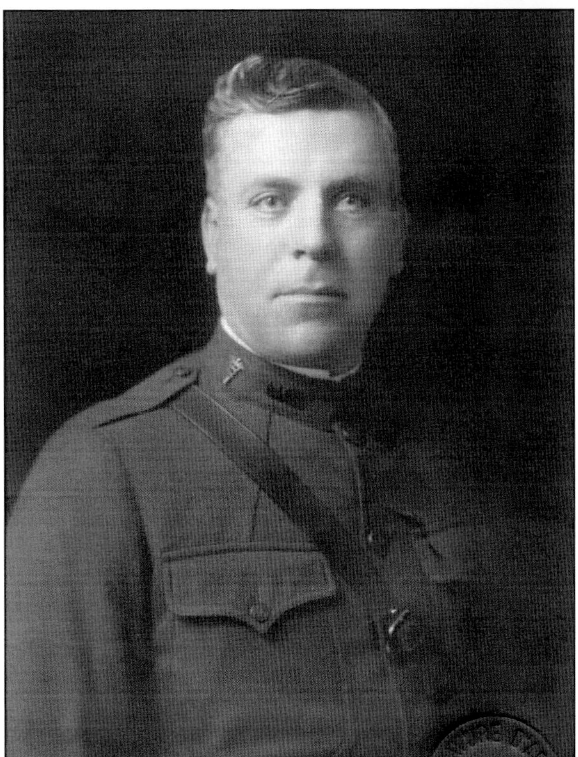

G.D. LeQuire was a prominent Maryville physician. He served in World War I and was instrumental in the establishment of Blount Memorial Hospital. (Courtesy of Karen Kenst.)

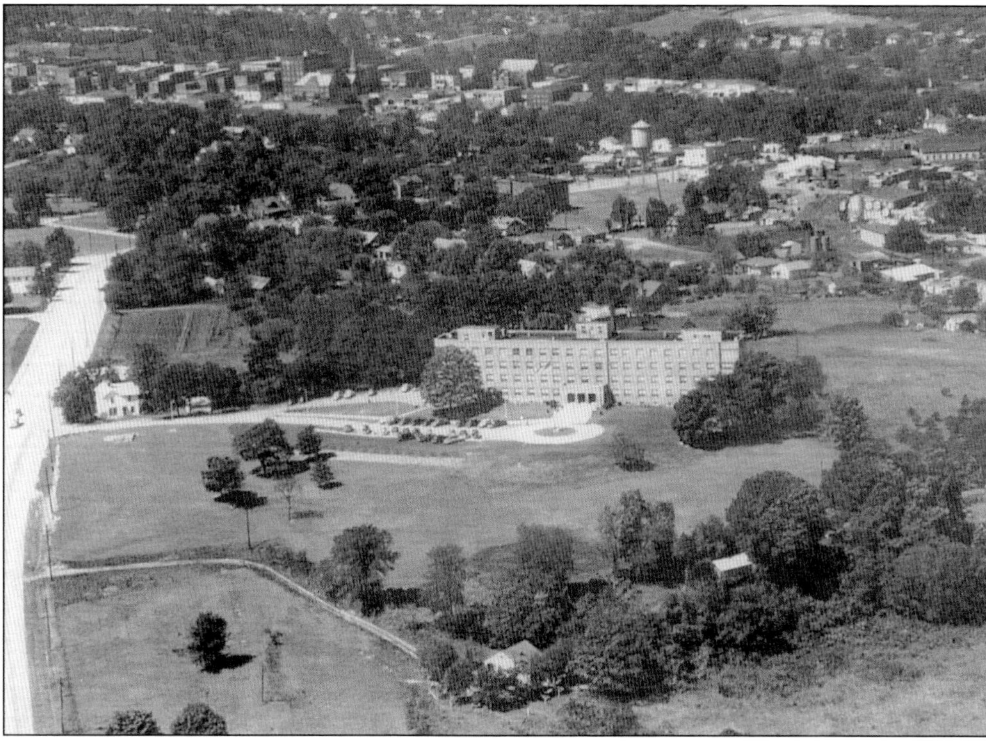

Blount Memorial Hospital is shown above and below at the time of its opening in 1947. Prior to Blount Memorial, most of the hospitals had been small and privately owned, often located in a doctor's office. Two doctors opened Fort Craig Hospital, on the present chamber of commerce site, in 1928; it was in operation until the 1940s. Doctors' Hospital, at the corner of Ellis Avenue and College Street, operated from 1943 to 1947. Blount Memorial was opened as a 50-bed, nonprofit facility. (Courtesy of Blount Memorial Hospital.)

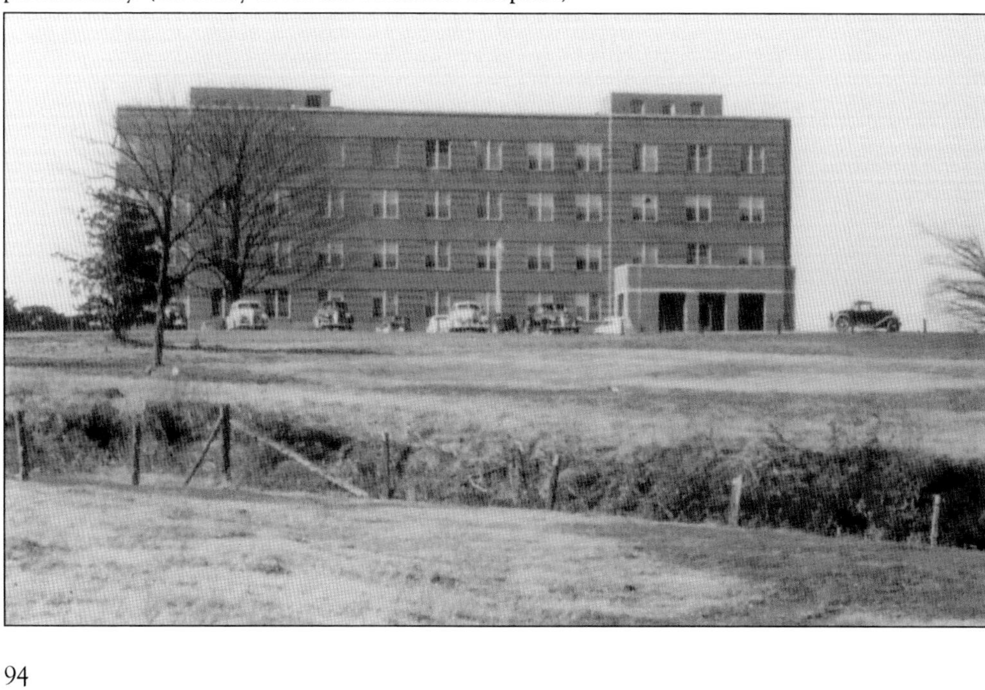

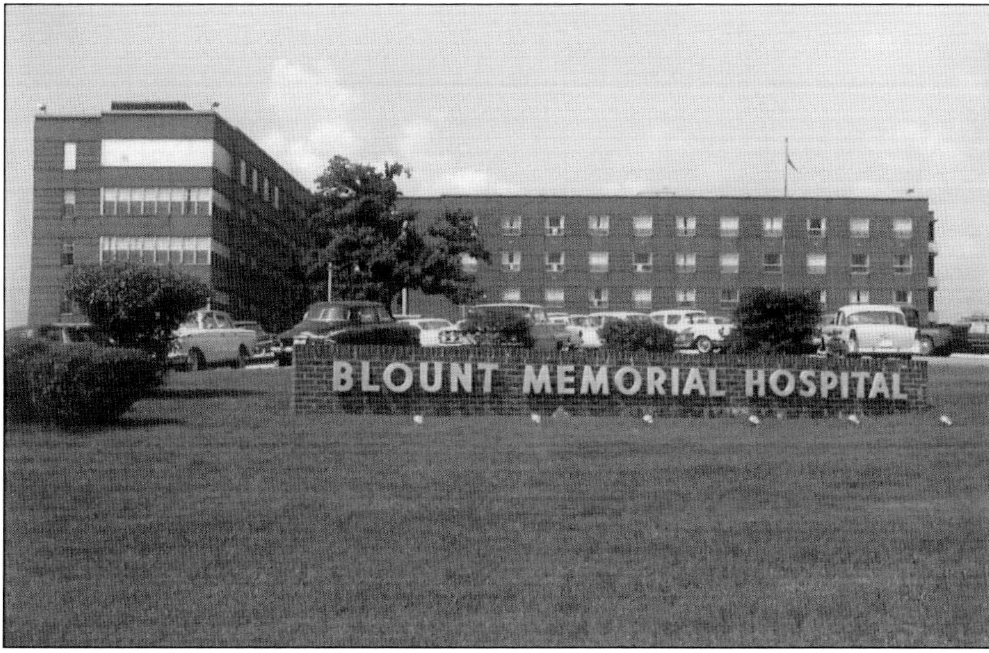

Blount Memorial Hospital is shown here in 1957 after it was expanded to a 210-bed facility. (Courtesy of Blount Memorial Hospital.)

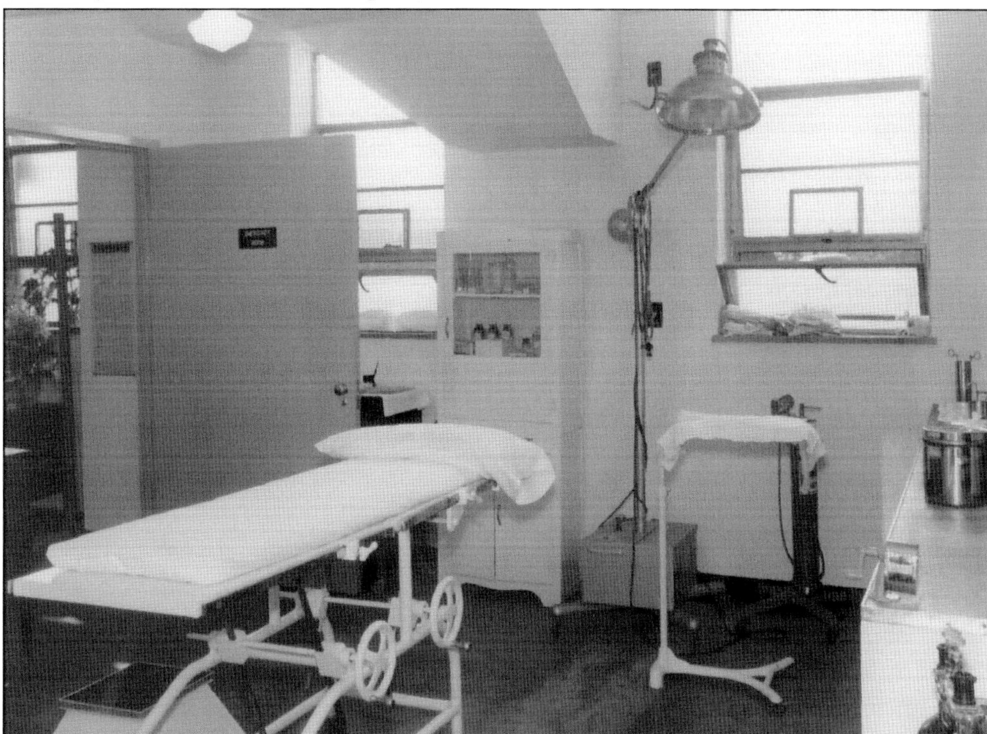
A Blount Memorial Hospital surgical operation room is shown in 1947. (Courtesy of Blount Memorial Hospital.)

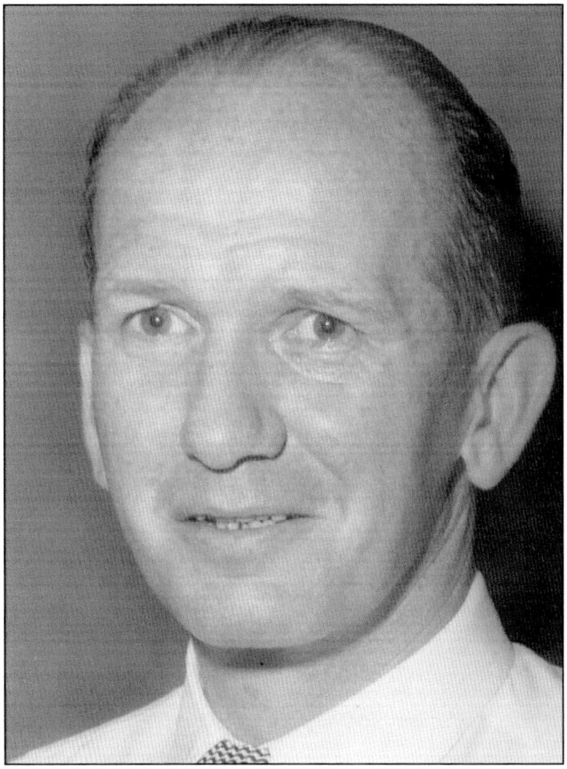

Dr. Lea Callaway, a physician, also served as mayor. During his 1953–1961 administration, he oversaw the fluoridation of city water, extension of the corporate boundaries on Morganton Road, and the construction of the new Fort Craig School. As a young man he was an outstanding athlete in football and wrestling and in 1999 was selected as one of the 50 all-time greatest athletes in Blount County history. (Courtesy of the *Daily Times*.)

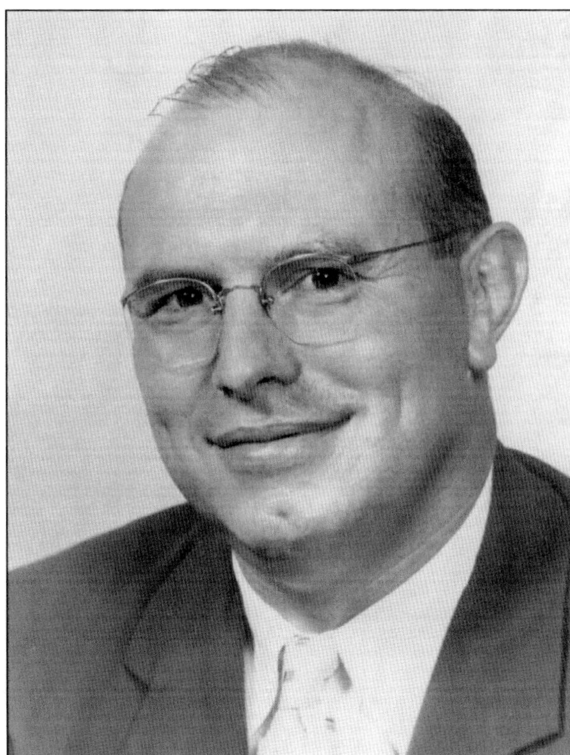

Dr. James N. Proffitt was a surgeon who served his community in many ways, including as a city councilman. (Courtesy of the *Daily Times*.)

Sam Everett served as Maryville's mayor from 1911 to 1919. During his tenure, an ordinance was passed to require children to attend school, and Maryville High School was established. He experienced strong opposition to the location of the Aluminum Company of America in unincorporated North Maryville, due to fears about how industrialization would impact community life. There was allegedly a plan to "tar and feather" him. (Courtesy of City of Maryville.)

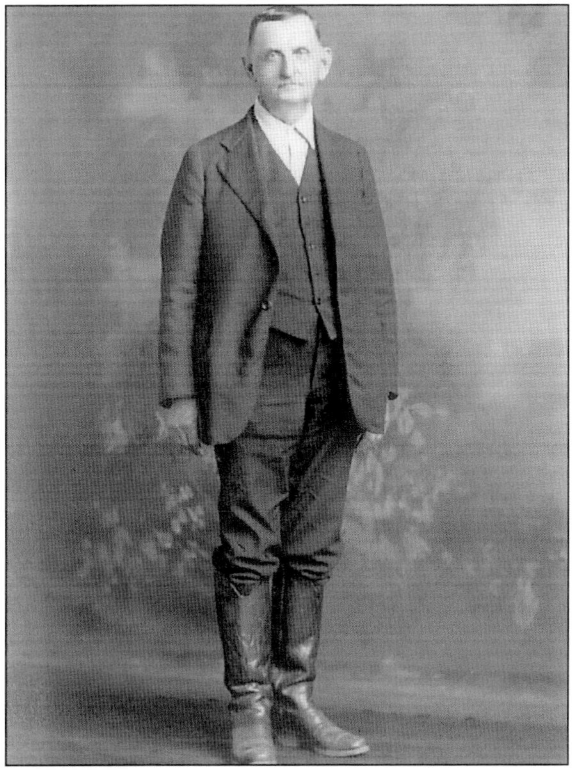

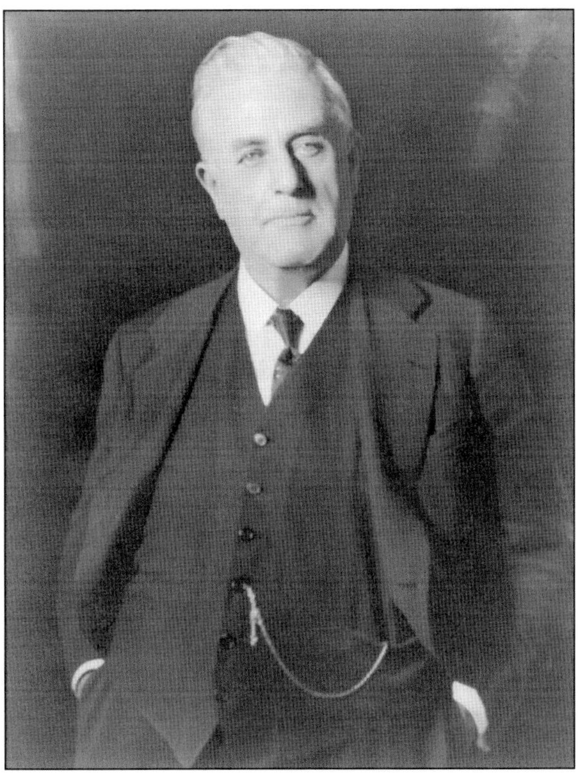

Dr. A.M. Gamble was a physician who served as mayor from 1939 to 1947. His accomplishments included initiating accreditation of the Maryville schools and abolition of the poll tax so that citizens could vote without cost. (Courtesy of A.B. Goddard.)

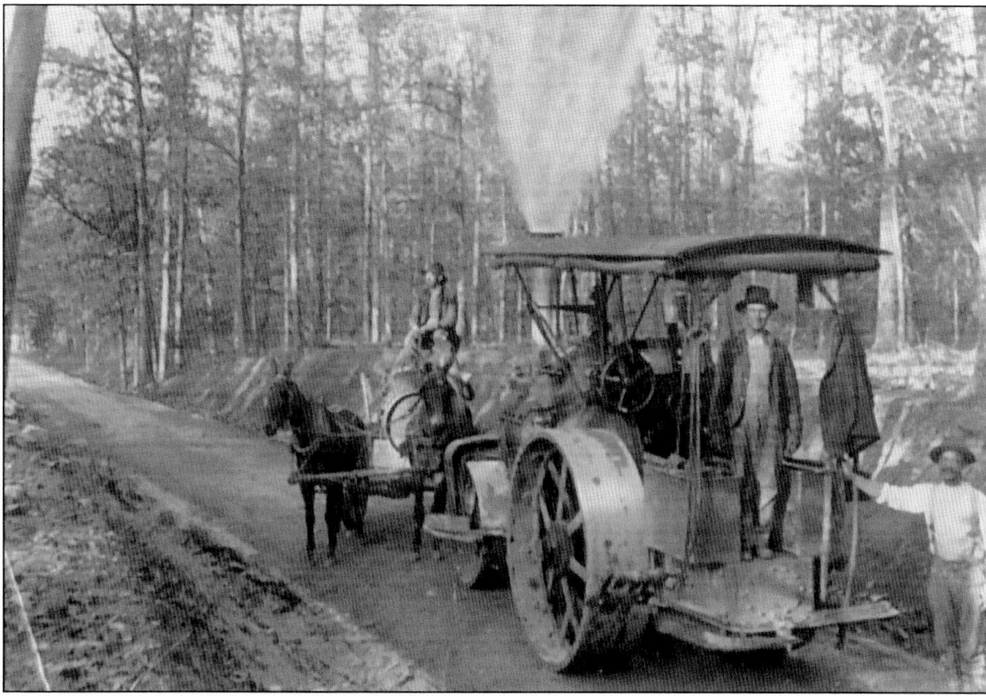

Maryville has taken pride in the provision of quality city services. Shown are early examples of such services. Above, a black-topping crew is working with a steam engine on Montvale Road near Broady Lane around 1910. Below is a department of public works truck and crew around 1920. (Courtesy of City of Maryville.)

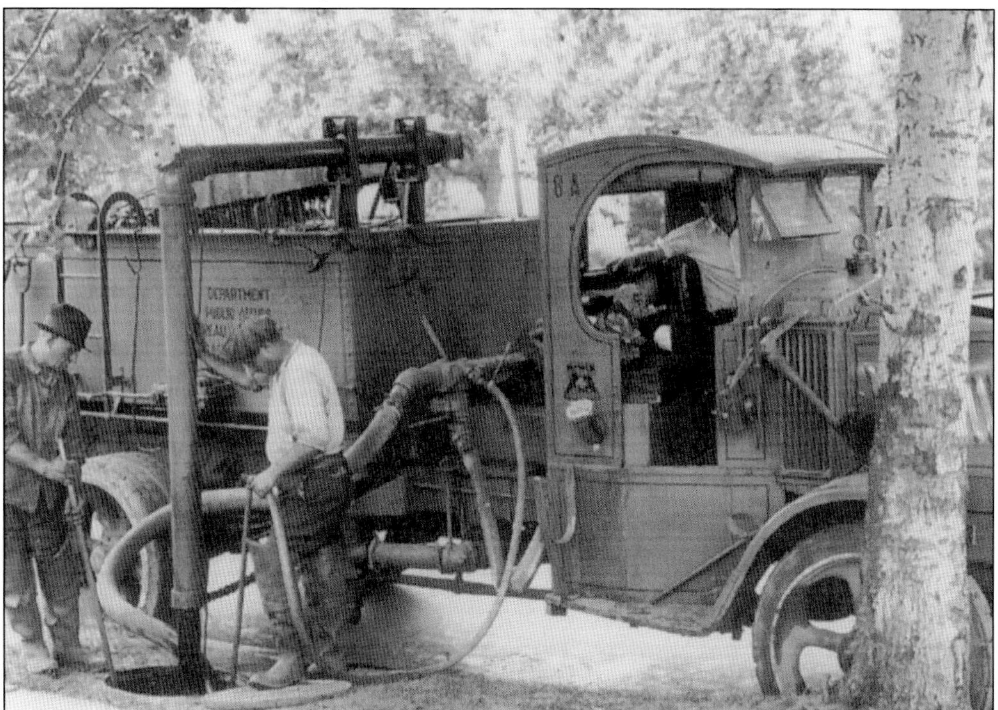

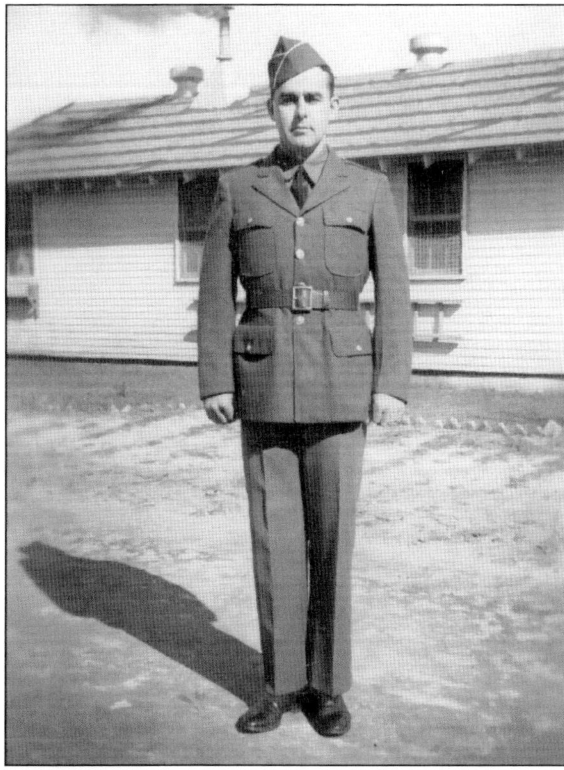

T. Ned Lee served as mayor from 1965 to 1967. He began the move toward Maryville's third form of government, the present manager-council form, and the construction of John Sevier Elementary School. He is pictured at right in his World War II uniform and below, right, receiving the Jaycees Tennessee's Young Man of the Year award in 1952. (Courtesy of Sandra Lee Stevens.)

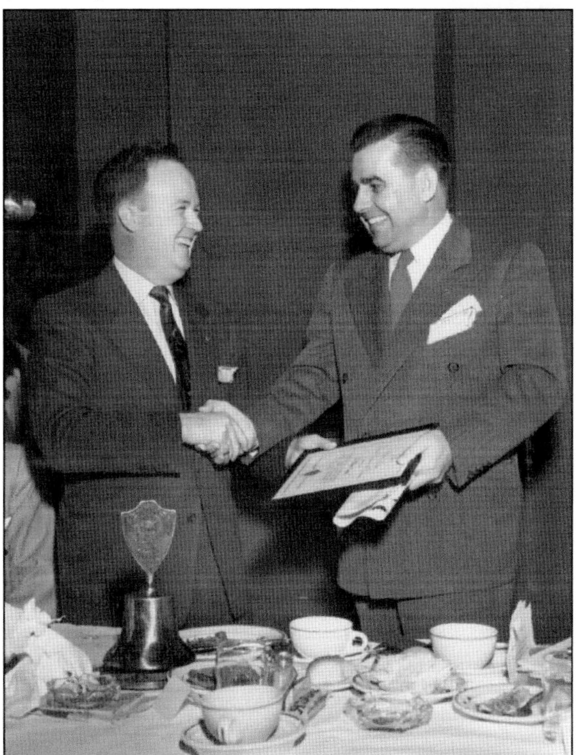

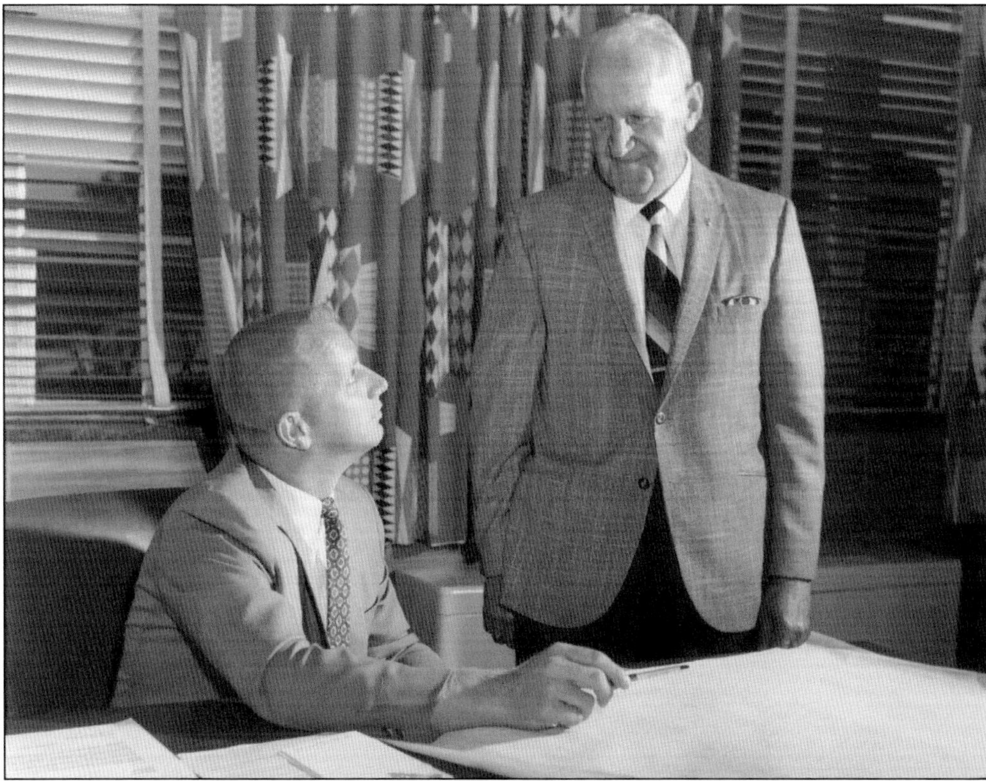

After adoption of the manager-council form of government, Rodney Lawler, left, served as Maryville's first city manager. Col. Merle Delaney, right, was chairman of the Maryville Housing Authority. (Courtesy of City of Maryville.)

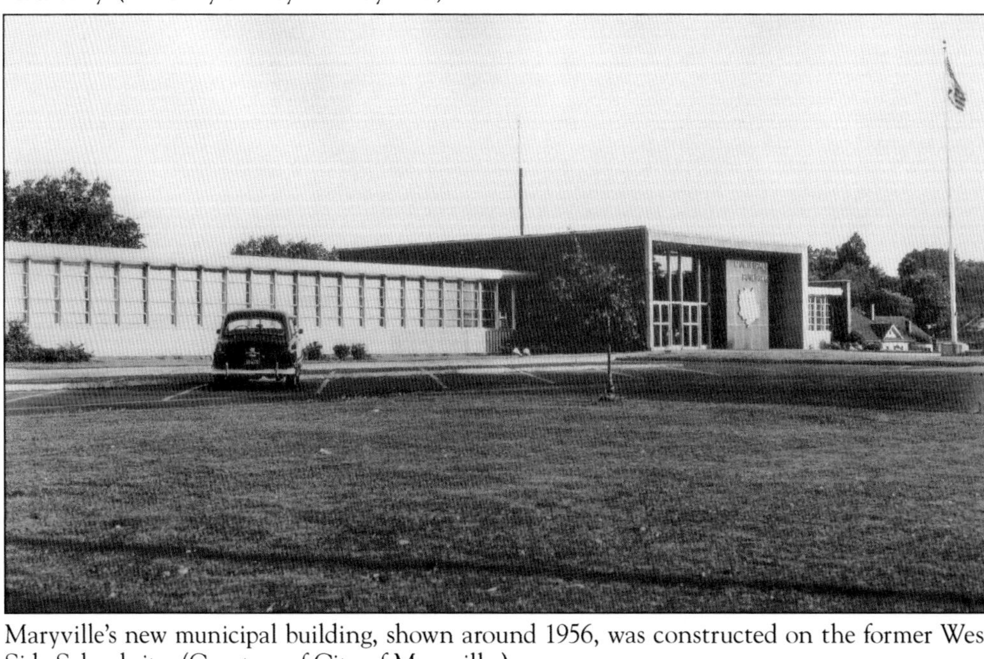

Maryville's new municipal building, shown around 1956, was constructed on the former West Side School site. (Courtesy of City of Maryville.)

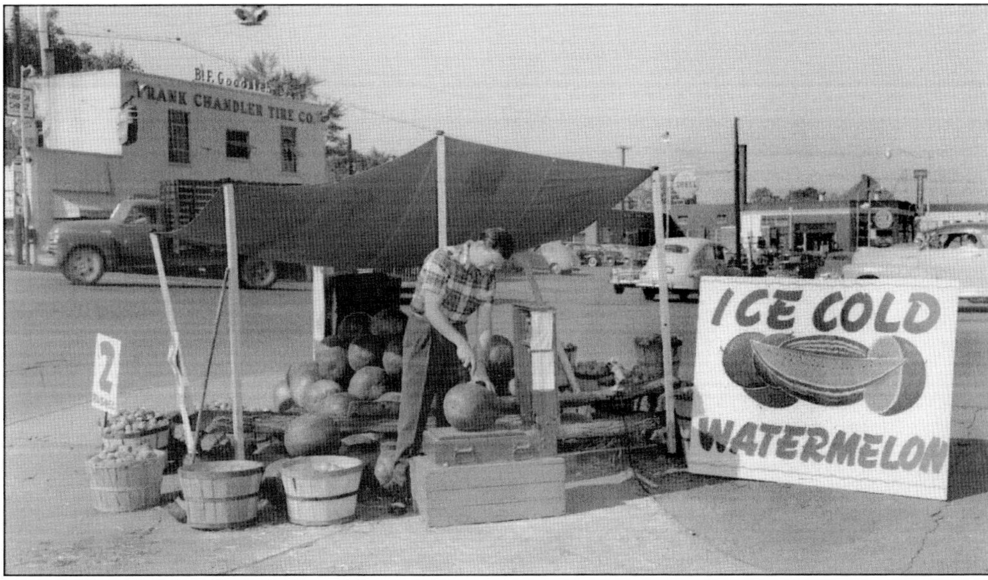

Maryville has experienced a variety of political activity. In the picture above, Gordon Huddleston is shown selling watermelons at the corner of Washington Street and East Broadway. Because he sold on Sundays in violation of the "Blue Laws," there was an effort to enforce the ordinance, which became an issue in the reelection campaign of Mayor John C. Crawford Jr. Crawford won the election, but Huddleston won the legal action, in part because Joe Gamble successfully argued in defending Huddleston that no one prosecuted Gamble when he went to his law office on Sunday. Below, Maryville native Lamar Alexander, now a US senator, campaigned for governor in Maryville in 1978. (Above, courtesy of David Duggan and the Aluminum Company of America; below, courtesy of the *Daily Times*.)

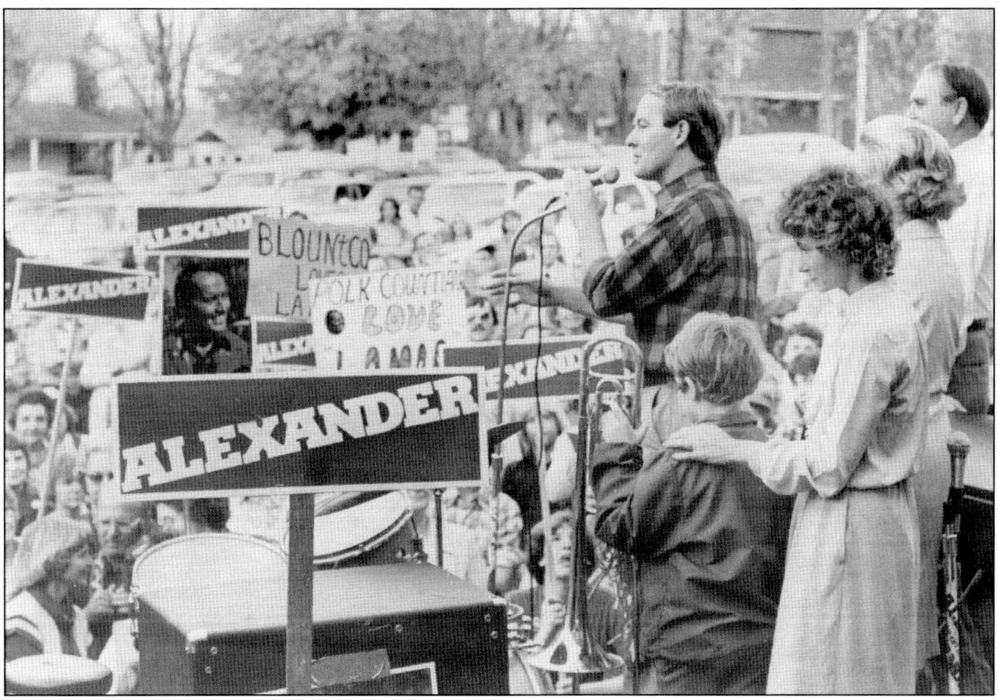

CIRCULAR.

TO THE VOTERS OF THE SIXTH SENATORIAL DISTRICT:

"A constant drop will wear a hole in a rock." That is an old and quaint saying, which has a truth and significance easily understood.

Several weeks ago, a meeting was held in Maryville, composed of men of different political affiliations, but all very anxious to know that the future legislation of this State should be a forward movement in curtailing the evils of the liquor traffic. I was chose to preside over that meeting, and as chairman was directed to ask of our legislative candidates what their course would be on this subject, if elected to the Legislature, and that their answers be published for the benefit of all temperance people.

I wrote to Mr. Nelson, who had been nominated for the Senate, as I did also to Mr. Hale, the candidate for Representative of Blount County, and asked the question as directed.

Mr. Hale replied that he would be up in a few days, "and see me in person about that matter." Mr. Nelson gave me quite an extended history of his private life, temperate habits, his support of the Amendment last fall, his refusal to have blackberry wine in the house, &c., but carefully avoided answering the question asked him. In compliance with my instructions, I had these letters published in the *Maryville Times*, and commented on them. From this, quite a lively controversy grew up between Mr. Nelson and myself, until finally he absolutely refused to answer the question. During the controversy, letters began coming to me, and also friends of temperance came, urging that I become a candidate for the Senate against Mr. Nelson. I had no more thought of doing so than I had of flying, but the more I tried to evade the matter, the more pressing came the calls, until it began to appear as something of a duty. My professional duties are pressing me, so that I have no time to canvass the district, but this has not proved a sufficient excuse with those urging me to make the race.

I learn that Mr. Nelson has made a special study of the tariff, and from what I am informed as to his position on that subject, I agree with his views in the main; but we are reminded that the legislature has little to do with the tariff—that is a great question for Congress to settle. But the question which effects our State the most, the question that goes into our homes, that places skeletons in the closet of almost every household, that brings misery and woe and suffering to the hearthstones of our own Tennessee, is a question on which Mr. Nelson refuses to commit himself. He claims that his own very exemplary life is a sufficient guaranty as to what his course as a legislator will be. This is a singular position. He proudly points to his *private* life, of which the public has no right to enquire except so far as the same may affect his public acts; and he refuses to declare his position on a *public* question of which the public has a right to demand and know.

I can point to more than one whose private lives have been that of sobriety and abstinance from intoxicating drinks, but whose public career have been opposite in the extreme.

In cities and towns it is said that this trick is sometimes resorted to: Starting a fire, and raising the alarm; while the citizens gather around the devouring element to stop its ravages, forgetful of their homes in their efforts to save their neighbors, thieves go in and help themselves to what is most valuable in the open houses. It is greatly feared that this is the case with Mr. Nelson. He raises the cry of "tariff! tariff!! tariff!!!" in order to attract and draw our attention away from our homes; and while as a member of the legislature he can do absolutely nothing on the tariff question, the thief that has brought ruin into so many homes can come in and take the most precious boys of Tennessee from tender mothers' arms, blasting the fondest hopes of loving parents. And yet, Mr. Nelson refuses to place himself under obligations to so much as raise his finger against the ravaging thief, and will not promise that he will do so. He reminds one of a deacon who charged his new minister not to preach on card playing, dancing, dram-drinking and the like, because there were influential members of his church who followed all these practices, but he could give blizzards to the Mormons—there was not one of them there. So, Mr. Nelson refuses to declare his position on the great evil which affects our homes, brings sorrow and death into our families, converts the young men into criminals, crowds our dockets with litigation and heaps costs upon the tax-payers, to be paid by a direct tax levied upon the little homestead and forced out of the earnings of the hard working citizens over the State; and instead he raises the cry of the tariff and protection of our American industries—*because the legislature cannot act on them.*

Taking all these things together, and looking with alarm at the bold approach and solid advancing columns of the liquor dealers, under cover of this cry of protective tariff, I have very reluctantly consented to become a candidate for the Senate in this district.

Mr. Nelson has said that I could not consistently run against him, because I was in a convention that helped to nominate him. In this he is mistaken. I was in a convention at Maryville, just before the Senatorial matter was taken up, but was not there when they sat upon Mr. Nelson's case. If I had been, and if I had by my own exertions secured his nomination, and then he had refused to declare his position on the questions of leading importance, I would feel under no obligations to support him. In addition to this, I was credibly informed that when the committee on delegates retired to select names to represent Blount County in the Senatorial Convention, my name was suggested and urged, but a gentleman for whom I have the highest respect, who was a chief fugleman for Mr. Nelson, very persistently refused to allow it. If I am not worthy to sit in a convention, then I am under no obligations to support the actions of that convention.

I have no charges to make against Mr. Nelson personally. I have a very high regard for him, and will say that if he should be elected, this district will be ably and *well represented on the tariff;* but I can not say what he will do on subjects which immediately concern the people of Tennessee, over which the legislature has exclusive control.

It is said that the friends of the liquor traffic are taking advantage of this attempted exclusive discussion of the government tariff, are perfecting their organizations and strengthening themselves for aggressive action in their trade. If this is true, and Congress should repeal the internal tax on distillers and liquor dealers, and our legislature should repeal the four mile law and other restrictive measures on our statute books, then, like the Israelites by the rivers of Babylon, our people could weep and wail to be delivered from cruel bondage—the bondage of strong drink—and reflect on their own acts as bringing the terrible curse upon them.

In conclusion, allow me to urge the voters of this district to look well to the interest of the State. Whatever will curtail evil, suppress vice, elevate the right, build up the interests of the State and add to our peace and prosperity as a people, let *that* be supported and maintained in a spirit of patriotism and devotion to our commonwealth. If casting your votes for me and the principles I have here indicated will be in this line, I shall deem it a very great honor and feel profoundly thankful. If, on the other hand, you believe that in voting for Mr. Nelson and the principles he has enunciated is advancing in that direction, it is your duty to do so, and none can bow more gracefully to the result than

Your humble servant,

WILL A. McTEER.

MARYVILLE, TENN.
Sept. 24, 1888.

In 1888, Will A. McTeer, a Union officer in the Civil War and prominent local leader after the war, issued this circular to voters in the sixth senatorial district in his campaign for state senate. The primary point of this flier was temperance, and he warned the voters that if government continued to promote liquor traffic, "then, like the Israelites by the rivers of Babylon, our people could weep and wail to be delivered from cruel bondage—the bondage of strong drink ." (Courtesy of the City of Maryville.)

Six

Maryvillians

To name all the individuals and families who have populated Maryville through the years would be impossible. Each person left a mark upon the history of the town, and even if their names have been obscured by the passage of more than two centuries, we can see the results of their efforts in government, business, education, the faith community, and the fabric of our society as a whole.

A small sampling of the people of Maryville is included in this chapter. Photographs of individuals, family gatherings, and children at play will give a glimpse of the lives of Maryvillians from the mid-1800s to the mid-20th century. The names may be different, but the common history they share is the same.

Take a look back at the Blount County Fair, once held near the courthouse and then at Five Points, where Harper Street, Old Knoxville Highway, and Everett Avenue converge. Maryville's first Boy Scout troop, the men of Co. B, 117th Infantry preparing to leave for World War I service in 1918, elegant ladies' teas, and picnics. These scenes from Maryville's past will evoke memories of its residents' past and, hopefully, encourage everyone to be a bit more careful about preserving local heritage for future generations.

The Blount County Historical Museum, located at 1006 East Lamar Alexander Parkway, Maryville, has a number of exhibits—photographs and relics from the past—that tell the story of Maryville and Blount County as a whole. The private, nonprofit historical museum is open from 10 a.m. until 3 p.m. Tuesday through Saturday and is closed on Sunday, Monday, and major holidays. No admission is charged, but donations are appreciated. For information, call 865-454-4256.

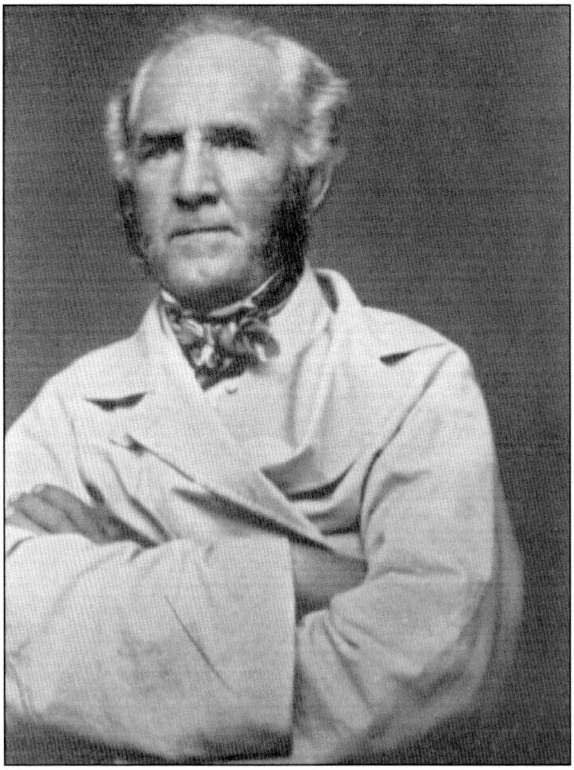

Sam Houston "took a dollar from the drum" on Maryville's Main Street and enlisted in the US Army on March 24, 1813. Houston was later a governor and US congressman for Tennessee, general of the Army of the Republic of Texas, president of the Republic of Texas, and governor and US senator for the State of Texas. The schoolhouse where he taught at age 19 in 1812 is a Tennessee state historic site. It was listed in the National Register of Historic Places in 1972. (Courtesy of the City of Maryville.)

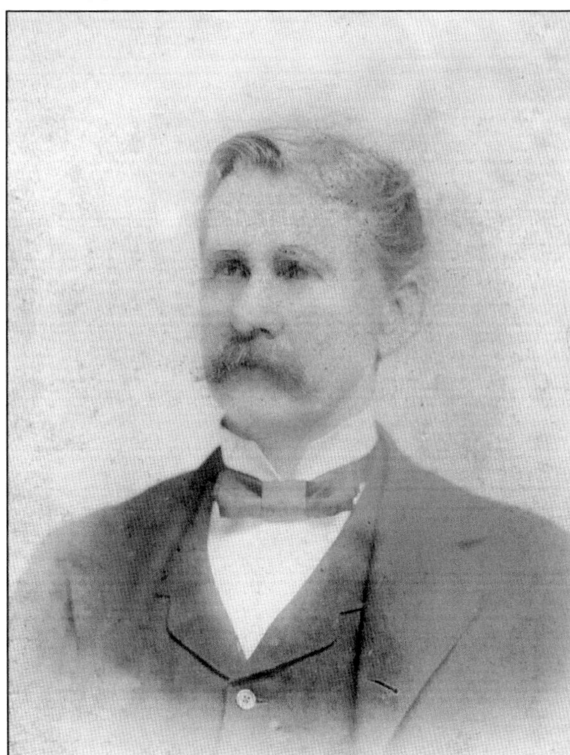

Samuel Preston Rowan, born in 1838 in Blount County, was a Maryville College graduate. He read law from 1860 until 1862 when he entered the federal army and served as captain in the 2nd Tennessee (Union) Cavalry until the spring of 1864, when he resigned due to bad health. He was admitted to the bar in 1865, at Maryville. Rowan was a member of the legislature of 1885–1886 as senator from the Sixth Senatorial District. (Courtesy of Marion Rowan Brink.)

Mary Elizabeth Bicknell Brown (right) and her husband, William Beard Brown, purchased what is now know as the historic Thompson-Brown House in 1867. "Parson Billy" Brown was a Presbyterian clergyman who had ministered to the wounded and dying on both sides in the Civil War, moving to Tennessee from north Georgia in 1865. Brown had attended Maryville College when it was still called Southern and Western Theological Seminary and chose Maryville so his children could be educated at the college. He served rural churches in Blount County until his death in 1879. His widow, Mary, and son John Fielding Brown continued to farm the home place, later operating Cedar Grove Dairy on the site. The property remained in the Brown family until 1934, when it was sold to Maryville College. (Courtesy of Sarah Brown McNiell.)

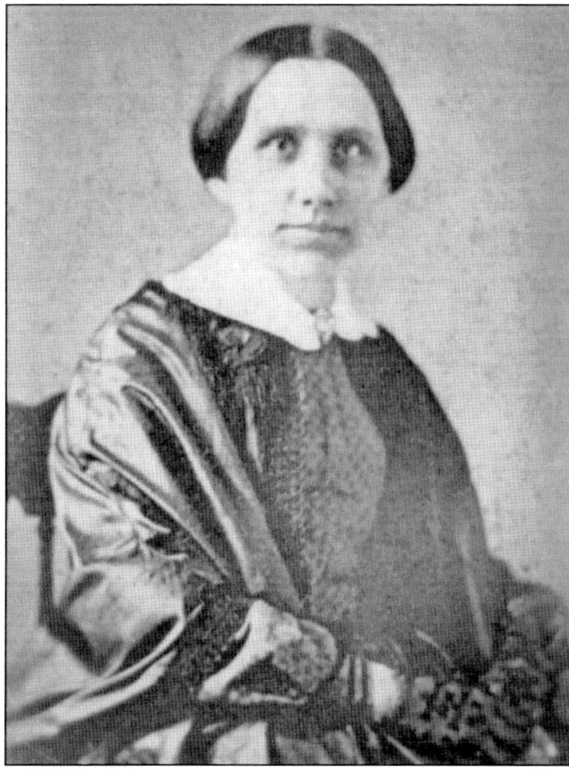

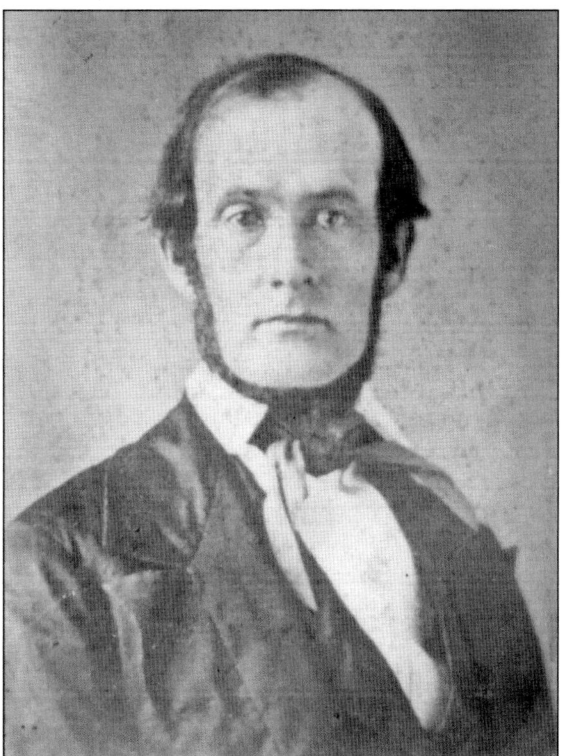

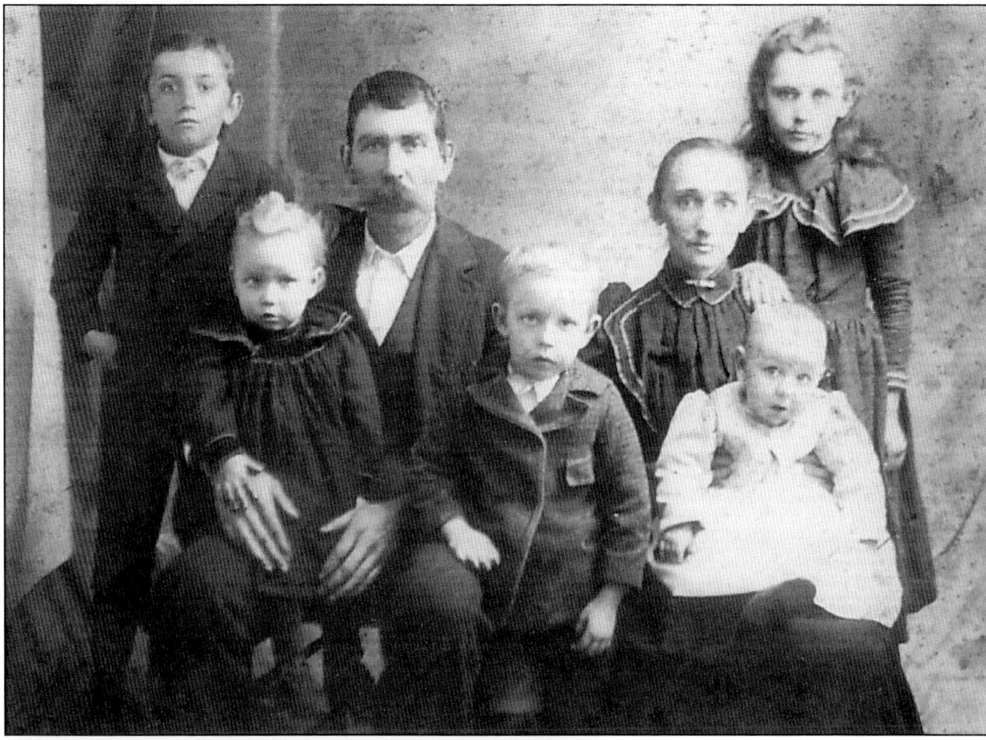

The family of William Bennett "Ben" and Martha Jane Wallace Talbott is pictured above around 1895. From left to right are (first row) Charlie, Rol, and Jim Talbott; (second row) Bill Talbott, William Bennett Talbott, Martha Wallace Talbott, and Grace Eugenia Talbott. (Courtesy of Joe Swann.)

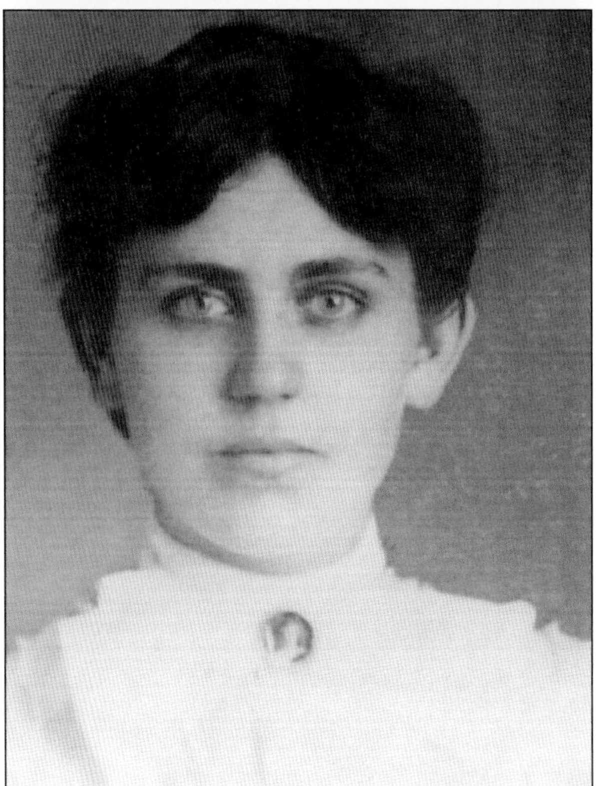

Grace Eugenia Talbott (1888–1991), shown to the left in 1905, married Granville Andrew Morton. They had six children, one of whom was Sue Morton Swann. Sue married Eugene Swann and is the mother of former Maryville mayor Joe Swann and Tennessee state representative Art Swann. (Courtesy of Joe Swann.)

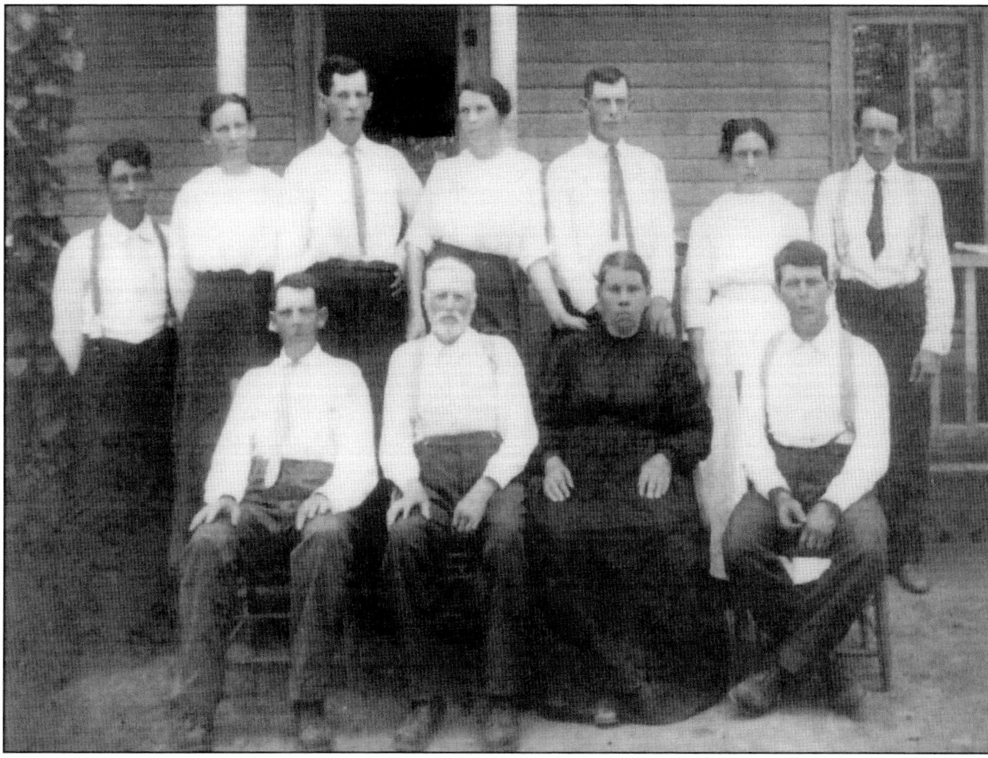

The family of John Davis Morton and Mary Elizabeth Smith Morton is pictured around 1920 and includes, from left to right, (seated) William Wade, John D. and Mary, and Thomas Houston; (standing) Granville Andrew, Celia Ann Morton Simmerly, Alexander McTeer, Hettie R., Roscoe Leroy, Mary Jane, and John Wilson. (Courtesy of Joe Swann.)

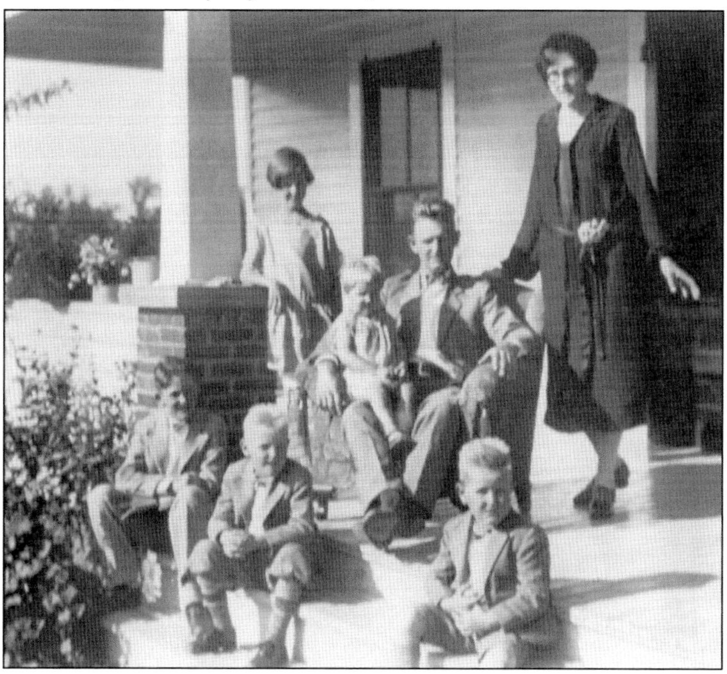

The J.W. "Will" Spradlin family home was located where Home Depot now stands. On the front porch in 1928 are, from left to right, (first row) Herbert, Harry and Ray Spradlin; (second row) Bernice, Will holding Dorothy, and Nora Spradling. (Courtesy of Connie Catron Miller.)

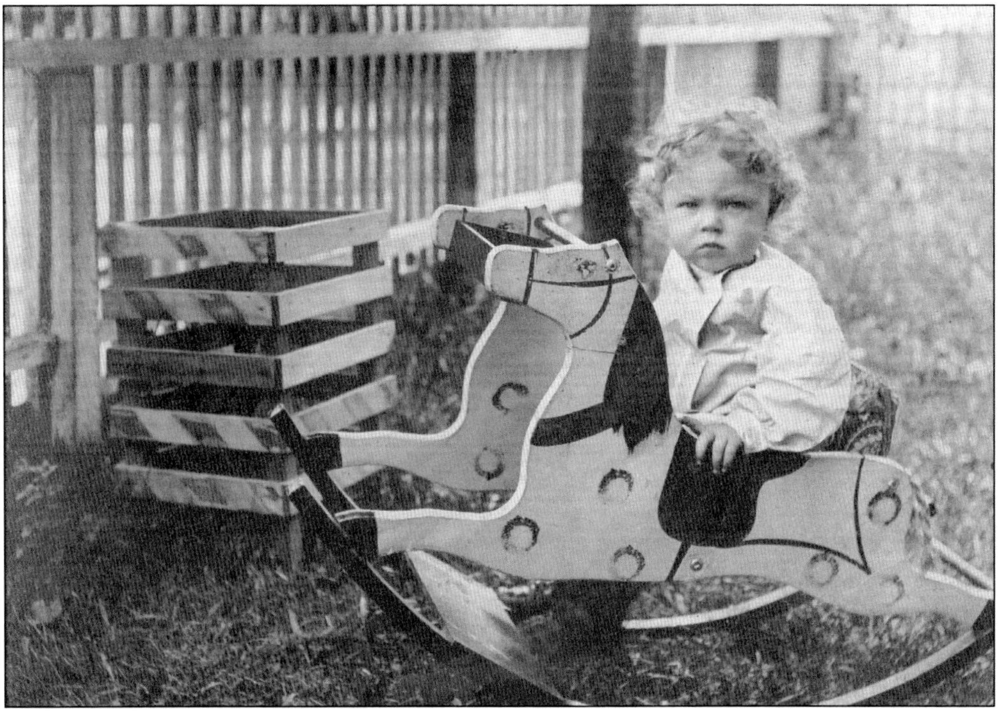

Max McCulloch, son of Dr. and Mrs. J.A. McCulloch, sits in his rocking horse at the family home at the corner of College Street and Ellis Avenue around 1908 in the above photograph. Below, Max is shown as the "mascot" of the Maryville College baseball team around 1907. His uncle, Andrew "Drew" McCulloch, coached the team and is standing at left with the black hat. (Both, courtesy of Kathryn McCulloch Peery.)

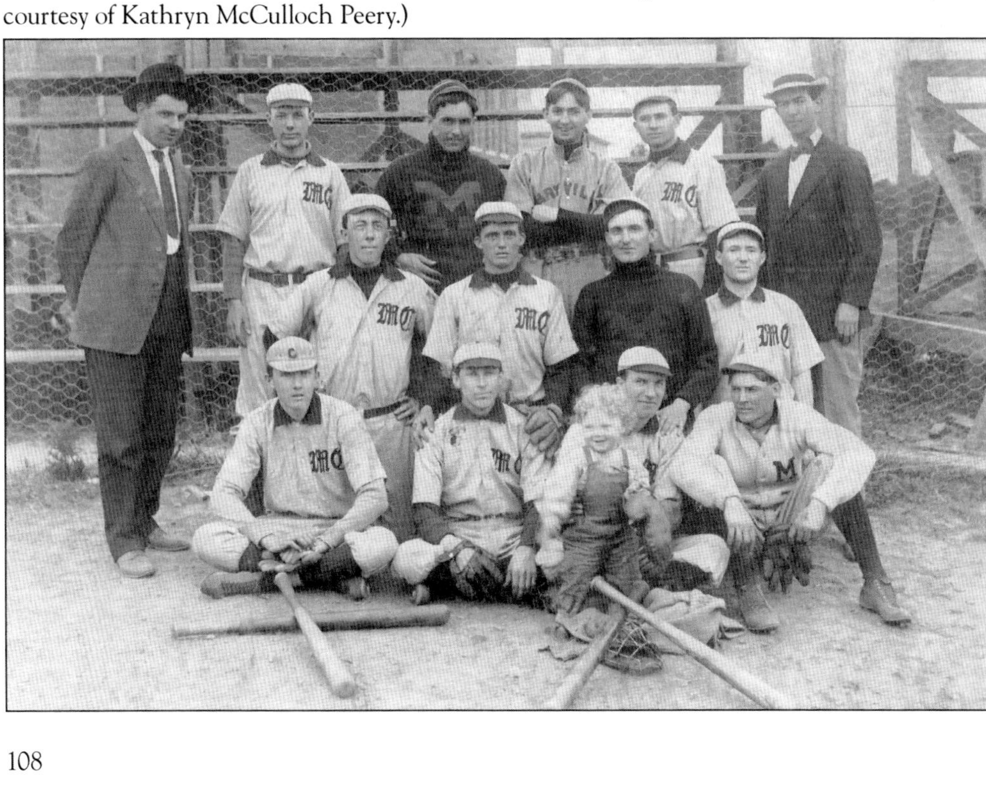

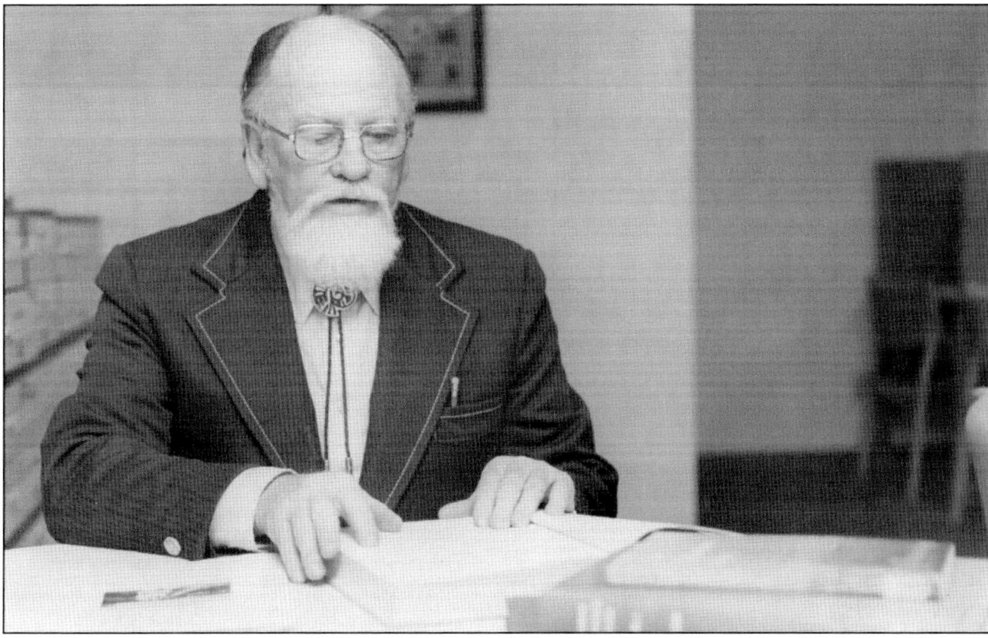

Dr. A. Randolph Shields (1913–1996), shown here around 1974, was head of the biology department at Maryville College. He was born in Cades Cove, graduated from Walland High School in 1930 and Maryville College in 1934, and received a master of science degree in 1939 and doctor of philosophy degree in 1962 from the University of Tennessee. In 2012, Shields was inducted into the Educators Hall of Honor at the University of Tennessee. (Courtesy of the *Daily Times.*)

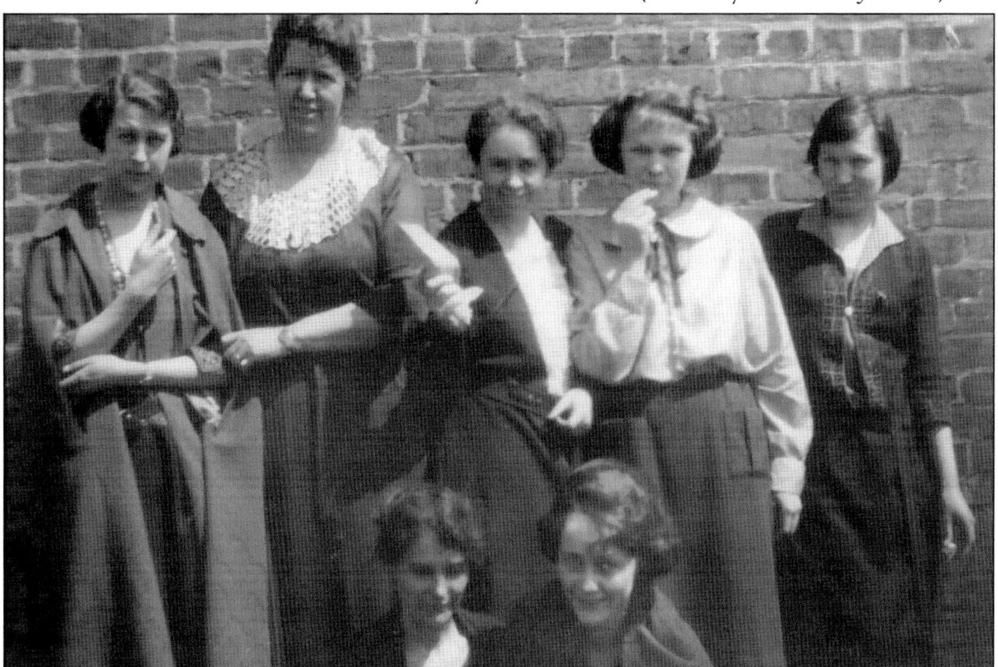

Teachers at West Side Elementary School are shown in 1922–1923. Emma Beals Allen is standing second from left. The others are unidentified. (Courtesy of Ann Talley Hitch.)

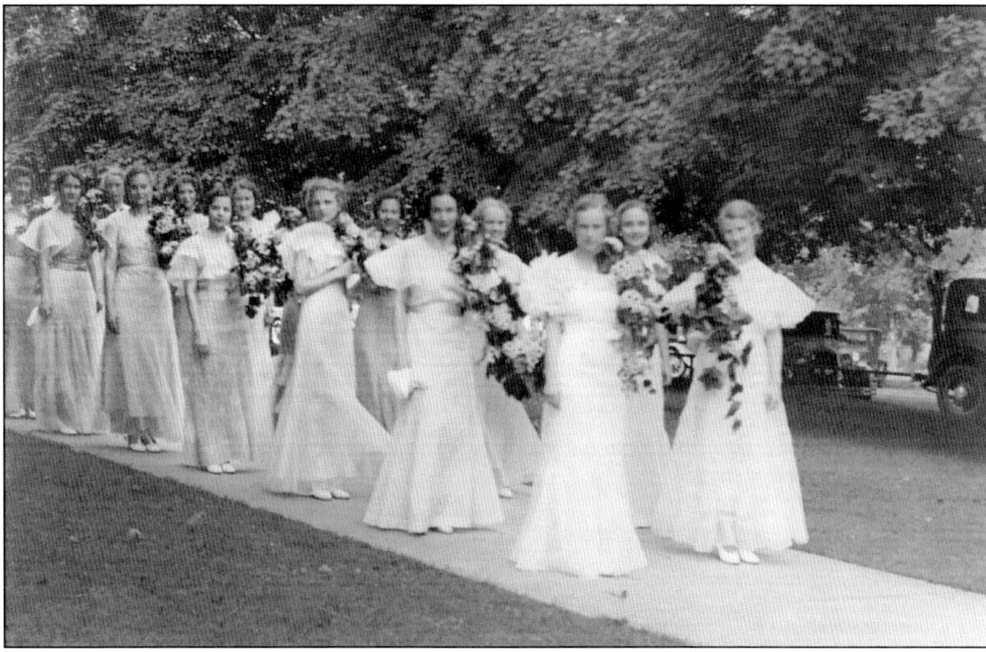

Among this group of Maryville College students from the 1930s carrying the traditional daisy chain are Grace Proffitt MacArthur and Adeline Murphy. Fourteen girls from the junior class formed the chain, through which the graduation procession passed. (Courtesy of Louise Crawford Berry.)

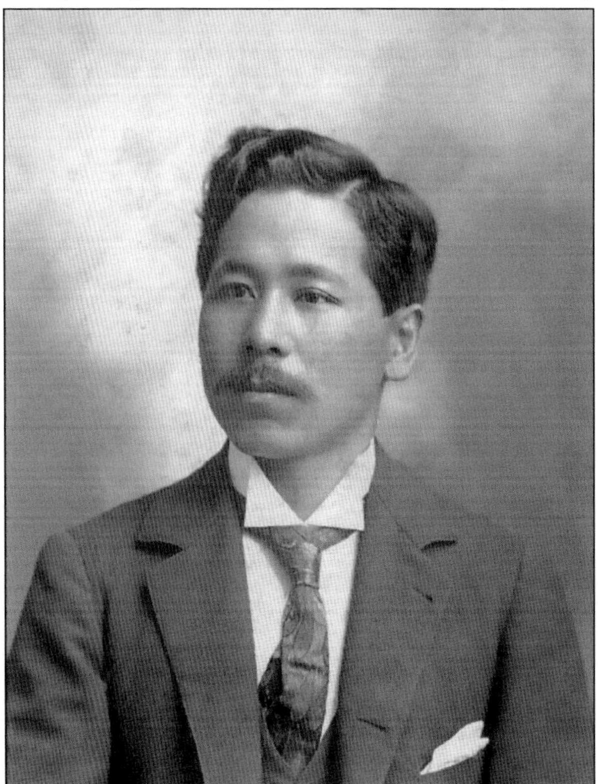

Kin Takahashi, pictured here in 1896, came to Maryville College in 1888 after learning of the college's commitment to aid financially strapped young students who wanted a college education. In his short time as an undergraduate, he started the first football team, organized a self-help project for financially strapped students, and spearheaded the building of Bartlett Hall. He died in 1902 at the age of 36. (Courtesy of Maryville College.)

Harwell Webb Proffitt (1918–2000), left, and John Woodfin "Jack" Proffitt (1919–2004) are sons of David Wilson "D.W." and Lillian Gray Webb Proffitt. For 70 years, Harwell worked for Proffitt's Department Store, a business founded by his father in 1919 in Maryville. Both Harwell and Jack as well as Harwell's son Fred Ortman Proffitt headed the business at different times before it was sold in 1984 to a group of investors. (Courtesy of Louise Crawford Berry.)

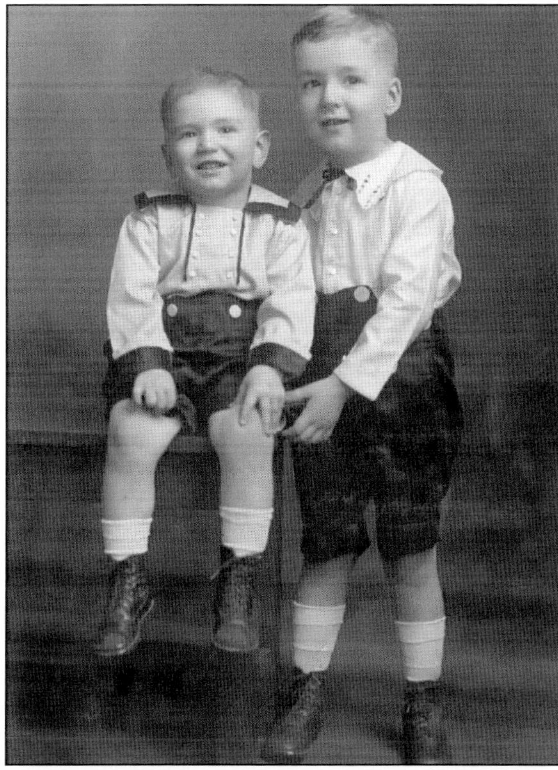

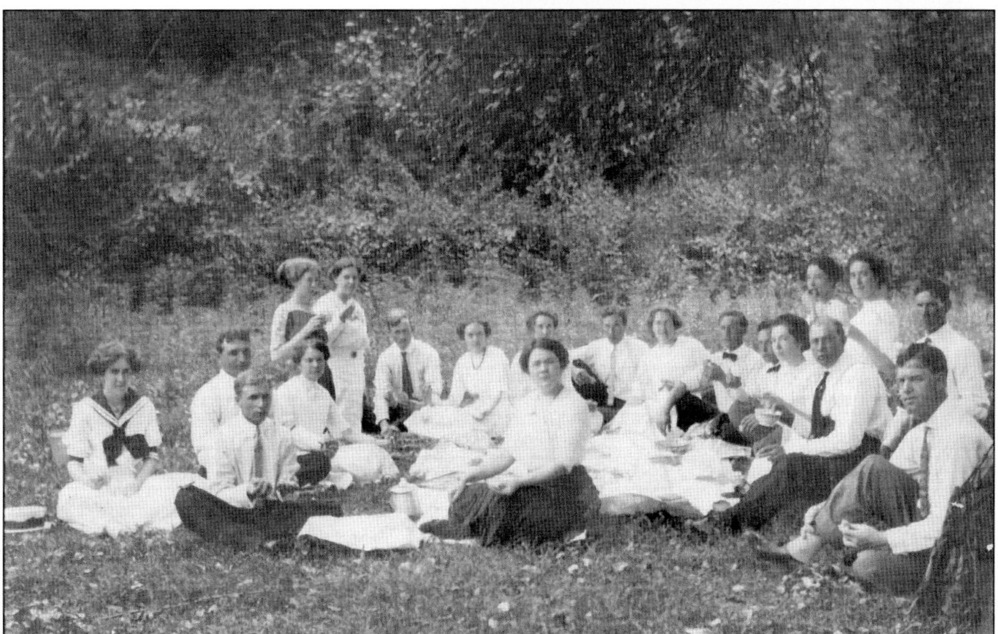

The Badgett family of Maryville enjoyed a picnic at Kinzel Springs, Townsend, around 1910. From left to right are Hazel B., Oscar C., Gertrude B., ? G., Ora B., Nita B., James F., Belle F., Madge B., Beaut S., Bob P., Pleas W., Margaret G., Dr. K., Ada B., Grace S., Bob G., and Clark and Guy Badgett. (Courtesy of A.B. Goddard.)

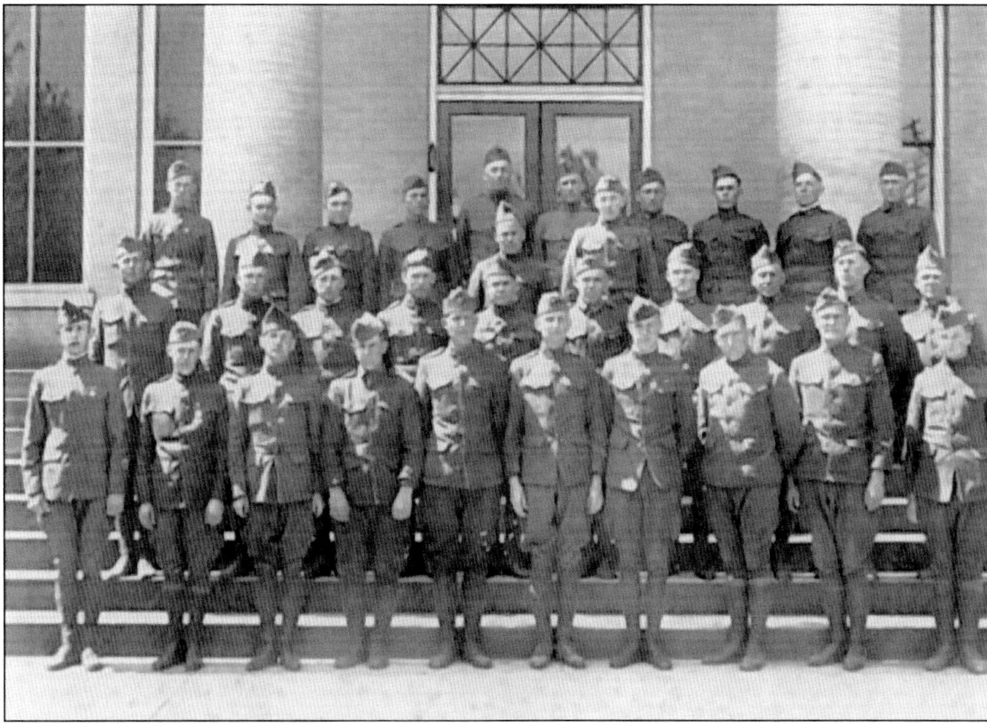

Maryville men of Company B, 117th Infantry are pictured on the steps of Maryville Methodist Church "after the Great War, 1918," according to the caption written on the photograph. (Courtesy of the City of Maryville.)

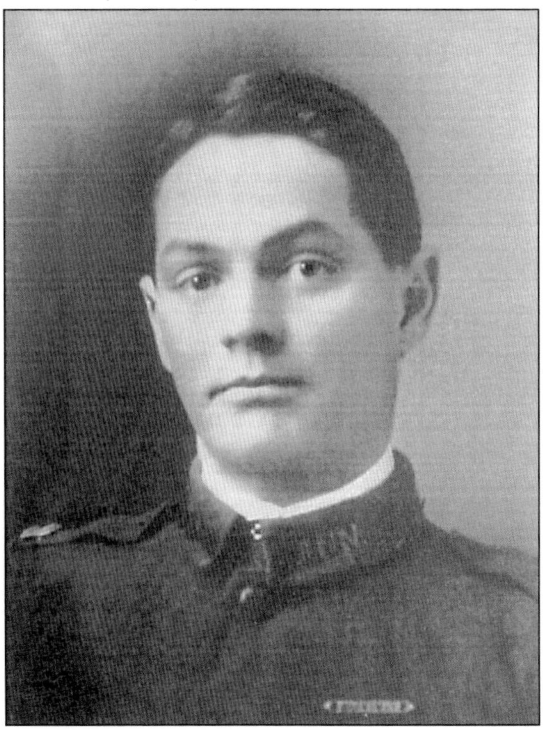

Capt. Emerson J. Lones, born in 1883, was the highest-ranking Blount County man killed in World War I. He led Company B, a group of volunteers who answered the call for service against Germany, drilling in Maryville for several weeks before being called to Camp Sevier and then sailing to Europe from New York City on May 10, 1918. When Company B returned to Maryville, Lones was not with them. He was killed in action during the Somme Offensive on September 29, 1918, less than a month before the war came to an end. (Courtesy of City of Maryville.)

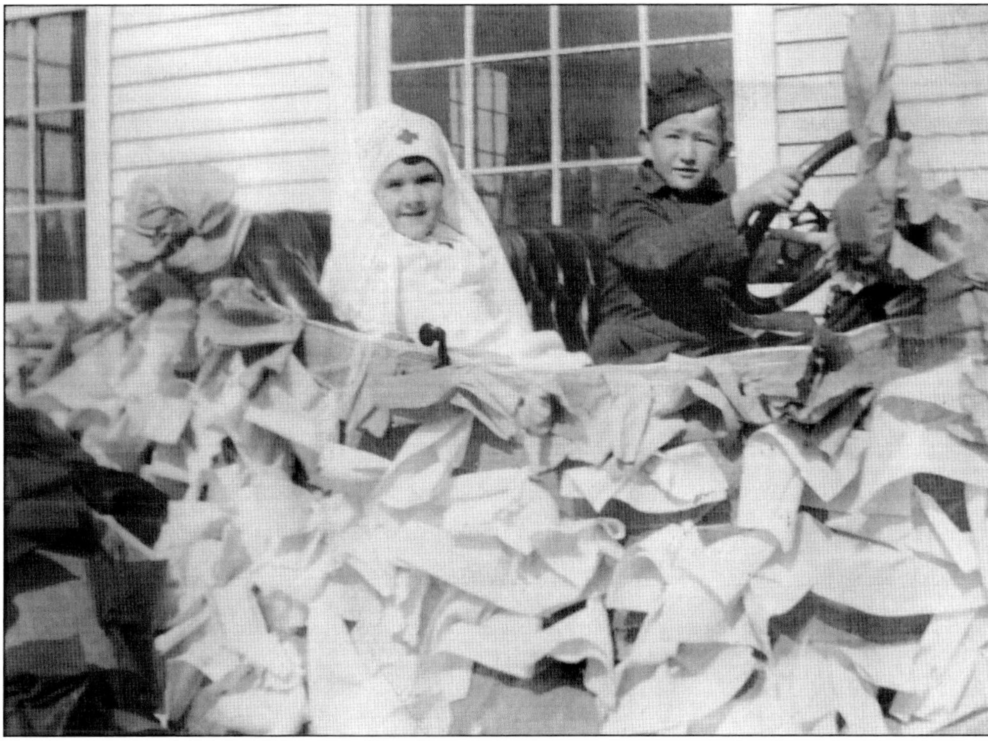

Lillian Crawford (1916–2005), left, and Ray Sullinger portray a Red Cross nurse and World War I soldier in this photograph taken around 1919. Lillian was the daughter of Hugh Rankin Crawford and Nora Crawford. (Courtesy of Louise Crawford Berry.)

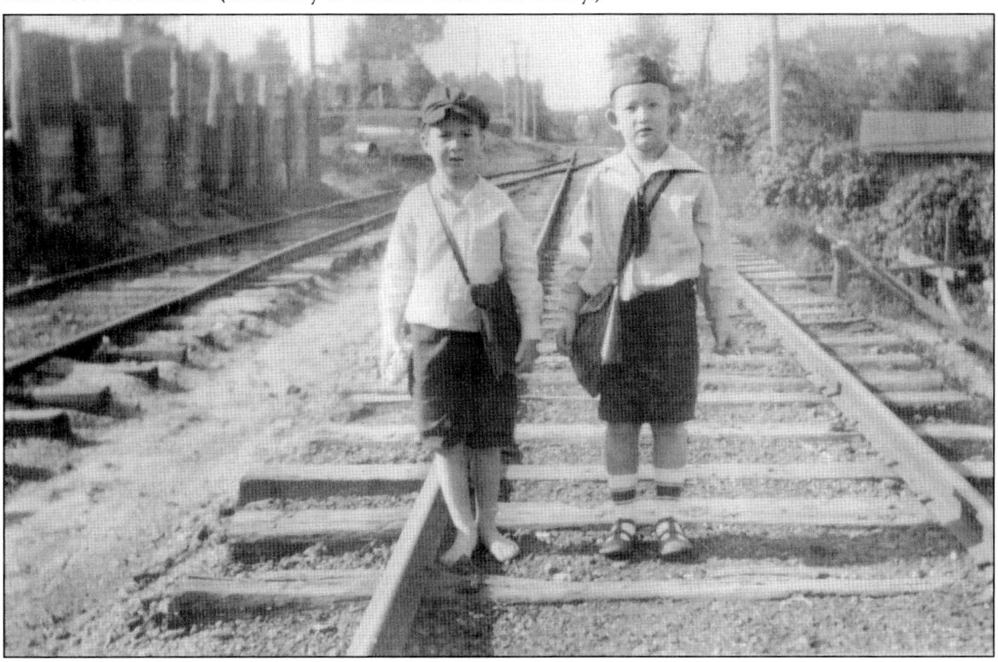

Hugh Crawford Jr. (1913–1986) and neighbor Ray Sullinger walk the railroad tracks from their homes on Court Street in Maryville to school around 1919. (Courtesy of Louise Crawford Berry.)

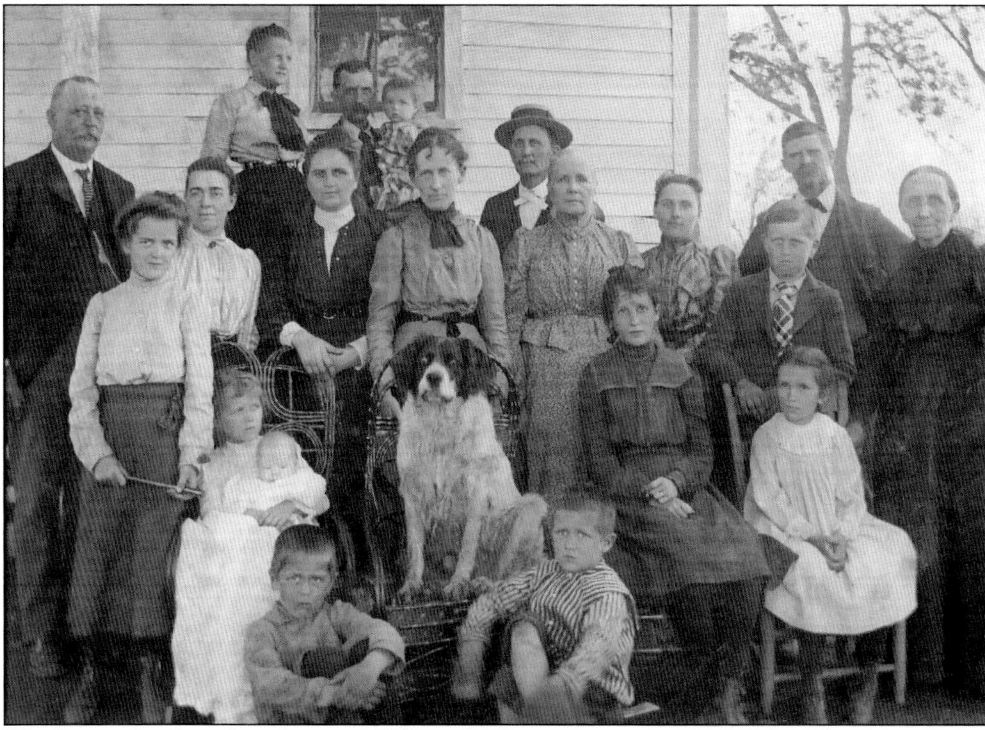

The Brown family gathered around 1901 at the Brown home, now called the Thompson-Brown House. From left to right are (seated, first row) T.N. Brown and Elmer Brown; (seated, second row) Margaret Brown holding Mary Brown, James Brown's dog, Eve Alexander, and Christine Alexander; (standing, third row) Dr. James Brown, Olivia Brown, Louella (Mrs. Thomas) Brown, Sarah McIlvaine Brown, Ethel Brown, Thomas Brown, Mary Alexander McIlvaine, Hattie McIlvaine, Ernest Brown, Joe McIlvaine, and Mary Elizabeth Bicknell Brown; (standing on porch) Margaret (Mrs. James) Brown and John Fielding Brown holding son James Brown. (Courtesy of Sarah Brown McNiell.)

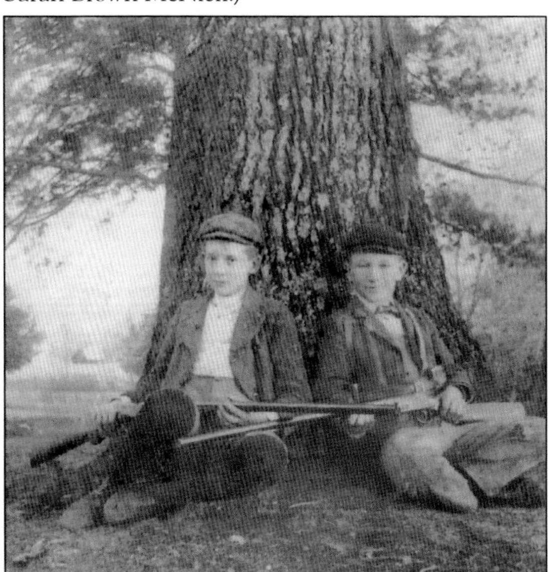

Squirrel hunting pals Charles "Snake" Blankenship, left, and Carl Burger are pictured in 1898. (Courtesy of Becky Blankenship Darrell.)

The McCulloch Family, pictured in the summer of 1915, includes, from left to right, (first row) Dorothy McCulloch Brown, Mrs. J.A. (Grace Badgett) McCulloch, Max McCulloch, Stella McCulloch Mitchell holding Caroline Mitchell, Hettie McTeer McCulloch, Stuart Caldwell, Cora McCulloch Caldwell, Lloyd McCulloch, Albert McCulloch (in front of Lloyd), and Freddie Goddard McCulloch; (second row) Dr. J.A. McCulloch, John Mitchell, Annie McCulloch, Joe Caldwell, and Drew McCulloch. (Courtesy of Kathryn McCulloch Peery.)

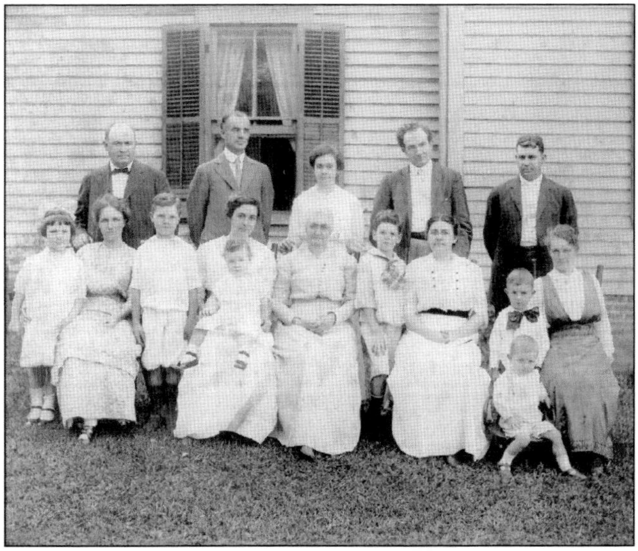

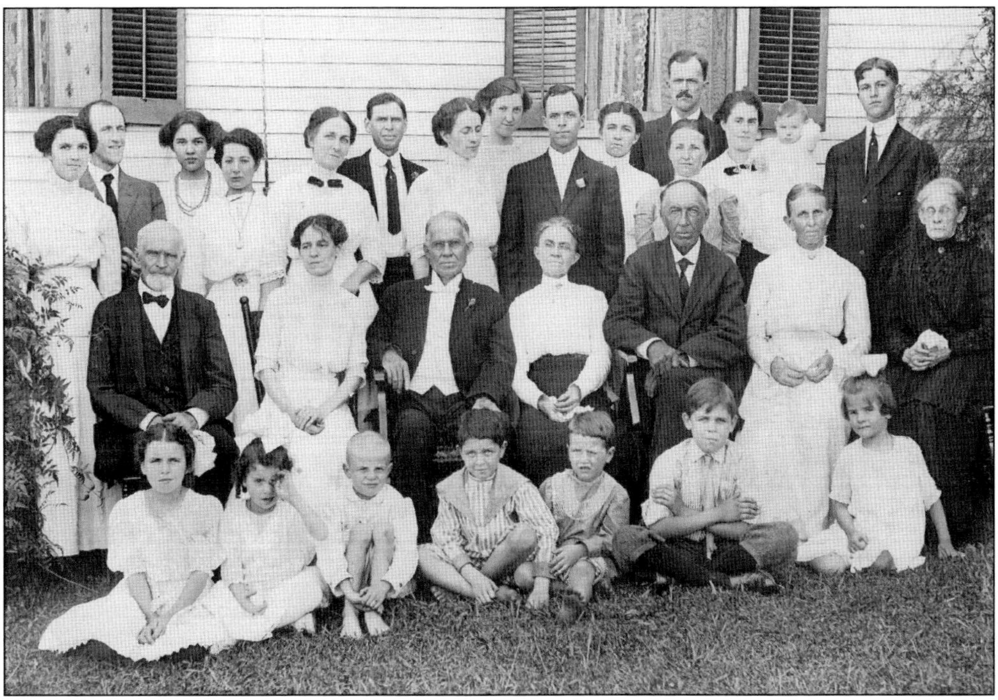

This photograph was taken at the Crawford home place on the Maryville College campus at the time of the wedding of Hugh Crawford and Adeline Murphy on August 27, 1912. From left to right are (first row) Jennie Montgomery (Thomas), Myrtle Rollings, Calvin Duncan Jr., John Crawford Jr., George Crawford, John Montgomery, and Katherine Duncan; (second row) ? Montgomery, Mrs. C.A. (Eleanor) Duncan, Rev. Calvin A. Duncan, M.E.J. Crawford, John Duncan, Mrs. John (Ellen) Duncan, and ? Montgomery; (third row) Jeanie F. Crawford, Dennis Crawford, Fidelia Duncan, unidentified, Mrs. John Webb, Ed Montgomery, Mrs. Hugh (Addie) Crawford, Gray Webb (Mrs. D.W.) Proffitt, Hugh Crawford, Stella Montgomery, Mr. and Mrs. John (Maude) Crawford, Mrs. E.O. (Effie) Rollings, (probably) Ernest Rollings Jr., and Earle Crawford. (Courtesy of Louise Crawford Berry.)

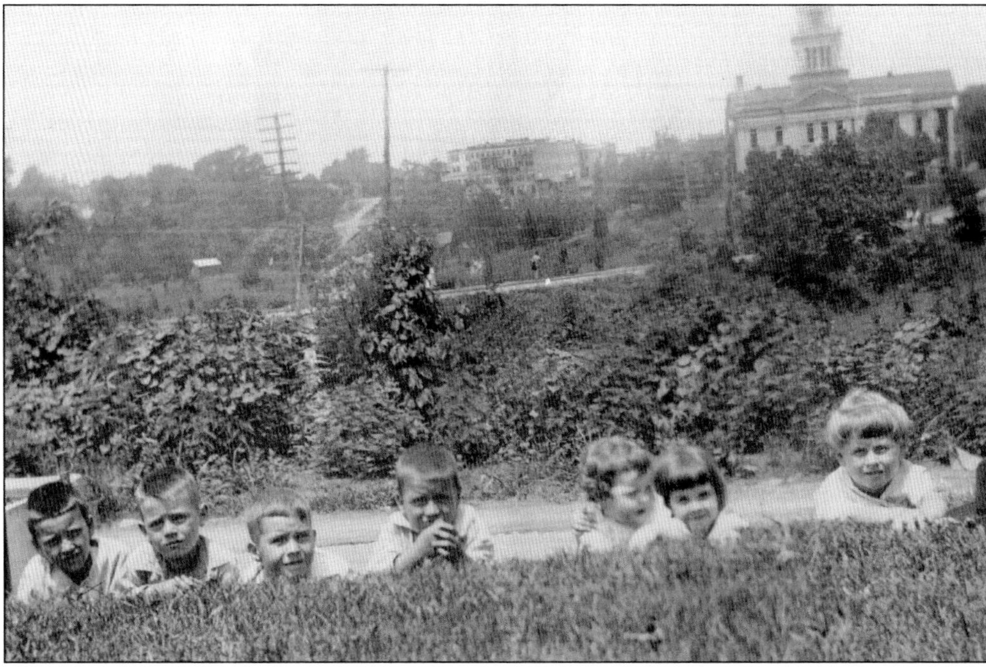

Court Street neighbors are playing together in this scene captured around 1919. They include, from left to right, Evan Ames, Earle Crawford, Hugh Crawford, Lynn Crawford, Ruth Crawford, Lillian Crawford, and Louise Goddard. Note the Blount County Courthouse in the background. (Courtesy of Louise Crawford Berry.)

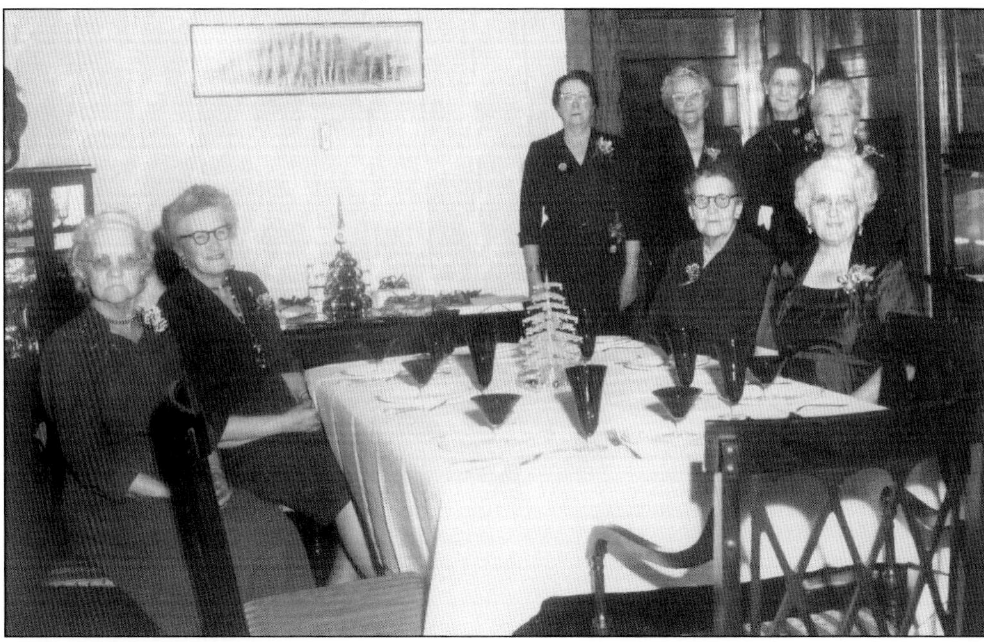

Ladies gathered together for a Christmas tea around 1950 include, from left to right, (seated) Mrs. W.B. Townsend, Myrtis Maynor, Mrs. Earl Hunter, and Hazel Badgett; (standing) Mrs. Ada Waters, Mrs. Homer Goddard, Stella Blankenship, and Kathleen Montgomery. (Courtesy of Becky Blankenship Darrell.)

Harry Edmondson is holding Harry Blankenship, who was born July 6, 1906, in Maryville. Blankenship died on May 7, 1972, and is buried at Grandview Cemetery, Maryville. (Courtesy of Becky Blankenship Darrell.)

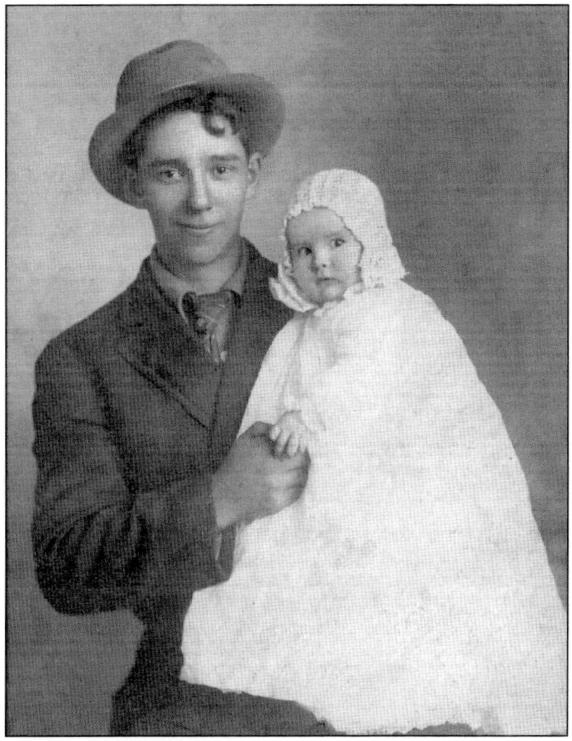

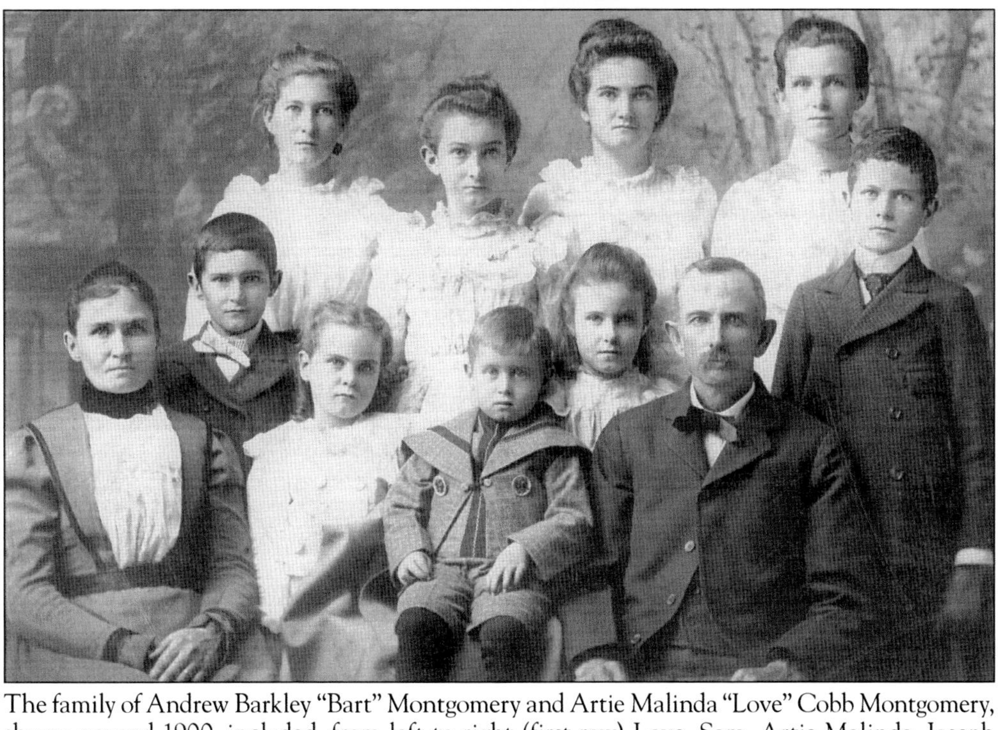

The family of Andrew Barkley "Bart" Montgomery and Artie Malinda "Love" Cobb Montgomery, shown around 1900, included, from left to right (first row) Love, Sam, Artie Malinda, Joseph Barkley, Myrtis, Bart, and Frank; (second row) Sarah Stella, Annie, Lula Etta, and Jonnie Pearl. (Courtesy of Becky Blankenship Darrell.)

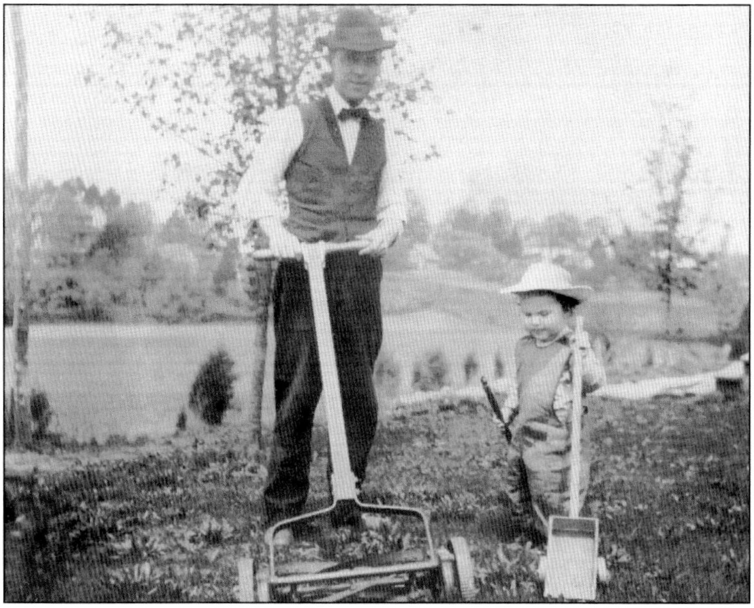

Hugh Crawford Sr. (left) mows the lawn at the Crawford home in Maryville as Hugh Crawford Jr. helps. The photograph was taken around 1914. (Courtesy of Louise Crawford Berry.)

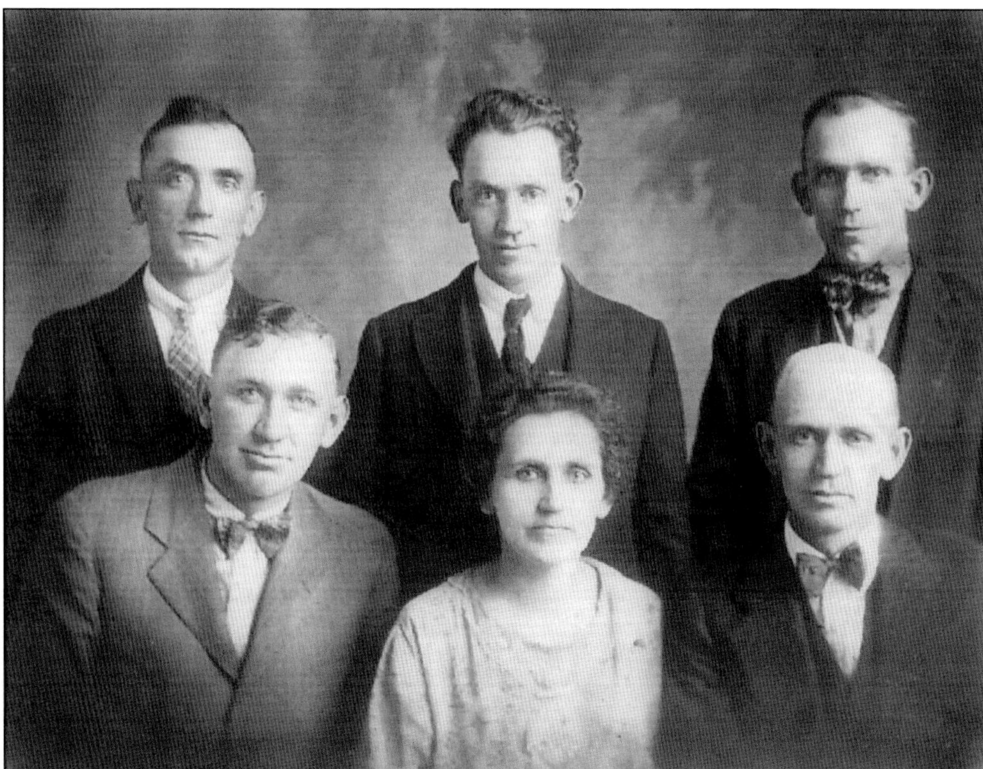

The Talbott siblings in 1926 included, from left to right, (first row) Jim Talbott, Grace Talbott Morton, and Rol Talbott; (second row) Bill Talbott, Ben Talbott, and Charles Talbott. (Courtesy of Joe Swann.)

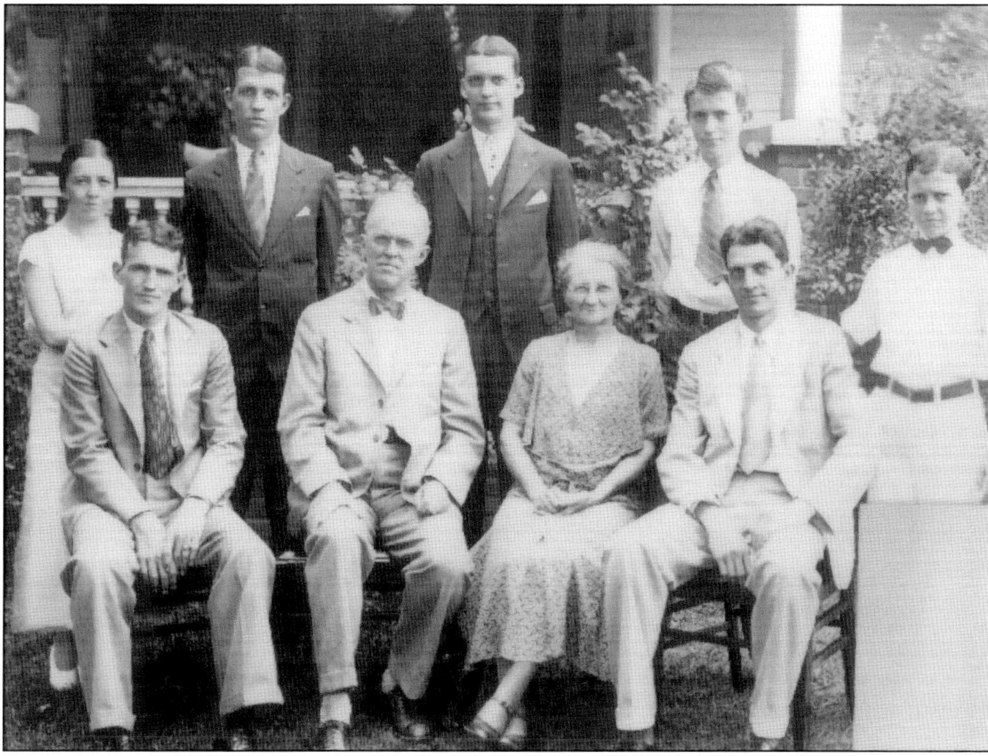

John and Maude Crawford are pictured with their six sons and a daughter-in-law at their home on Crawford Street about 1931. From left to right are (first row) George, John and Maude, and John Jr.; (second row) Mary (Mrs. George), Lynn, Earle, Ernest, and Roy. (Courtesy of Duncan Crawford.)

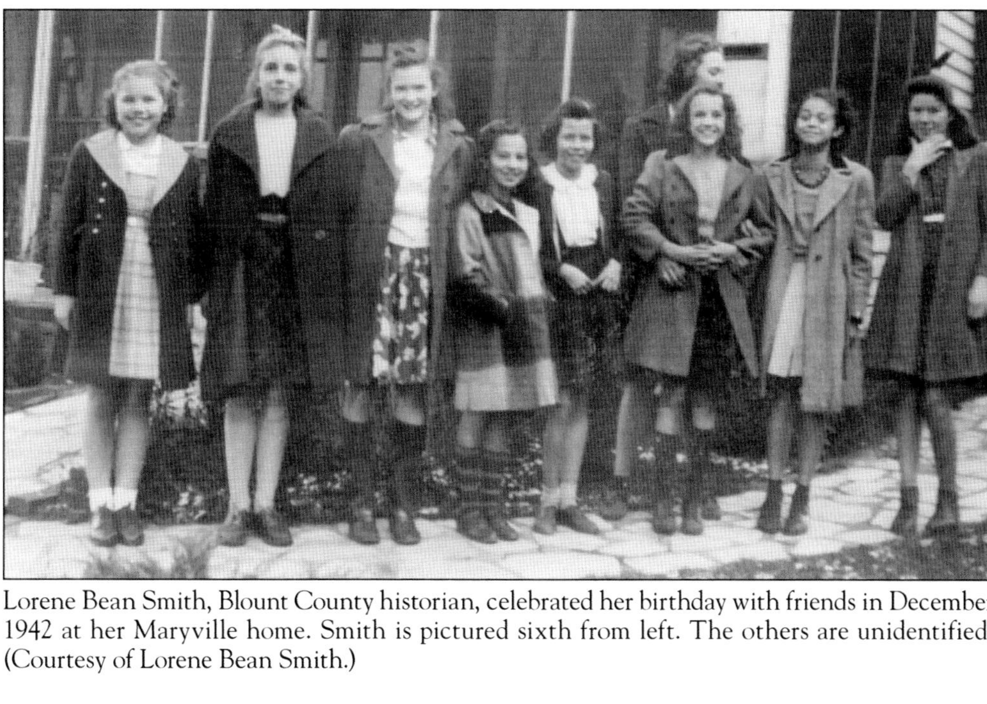

Lorene Bean Smith, Blount County historian, celebrated her birthday with friends in December 1942 at her Maryville home. Smith is pictured sixth from left. The others are unidentified. (Courtesy of Lorene Bean Smith.)

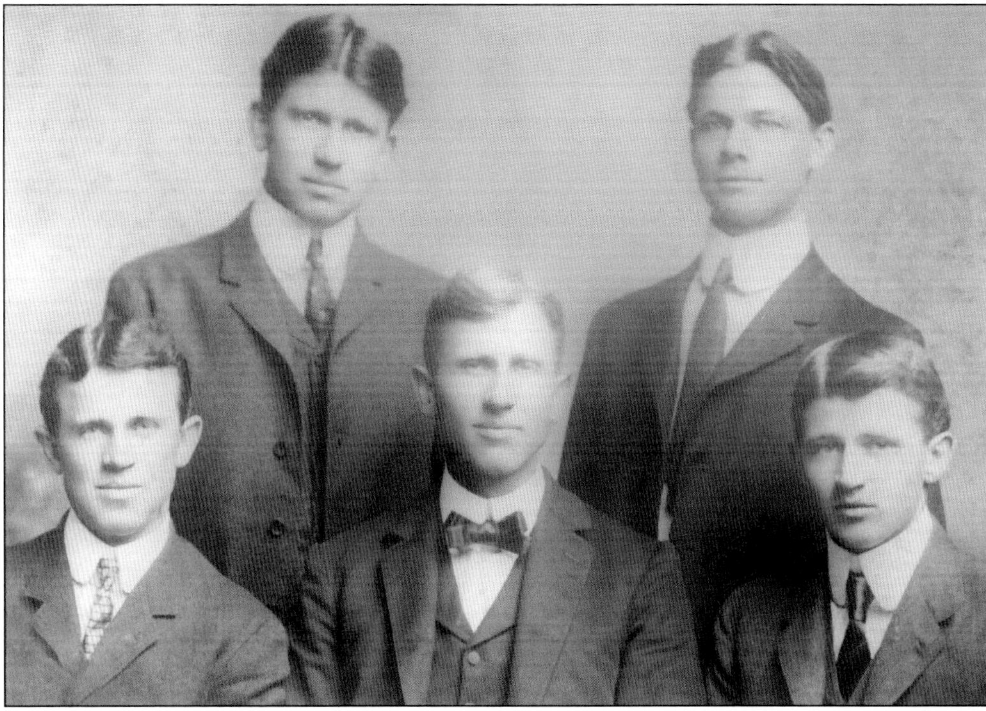

The Houston brothers, sons of Robert Lockhart and Margaret Nimon Houston, include, from left to right, (first row) Robert Lockhart Jr., Samuel O'Grady, and Joseph Oscar; (second row) William Edgar and Carl Thomas. Samuel O. Houston entered Maryville College in the fall of 1890, graduated with a bachelor of arts degree in 1898, served as chairman of the board at the college from 1932 to 1953, and received an honorary doctor of laws degree in 1938. Robert L. Jr. was a member of the class of 1905. Carl. T attended the college from 1890 to 1892. W. Edgar also attended. (Courtesy of the Blount County Genealogical and Historical Society.)

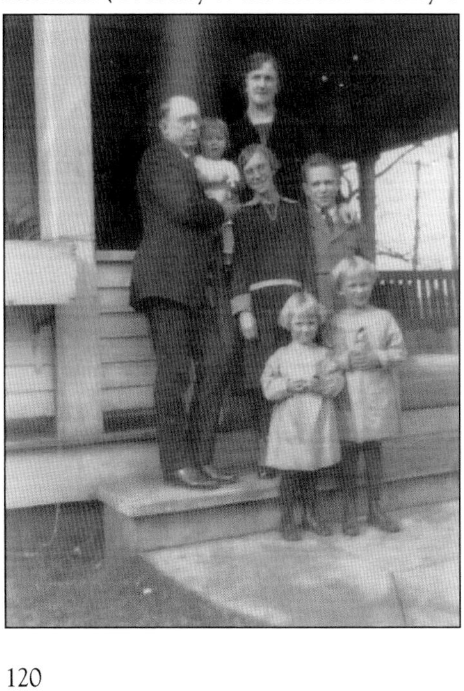

Walker and Gussie Lee Johnson stand with their children on the steps of their home on High Street in Maryville in the early 1920s. From left to right are (first row) Evelyn Johnson and Helen Johnson; (second row) Walker Johnson holding Sara Lou Johnson, Gussie Lee Johnson behind Ruby Lee Johnson, and Charles Walker Johnson. (Courtesy of Walker Johnson.)

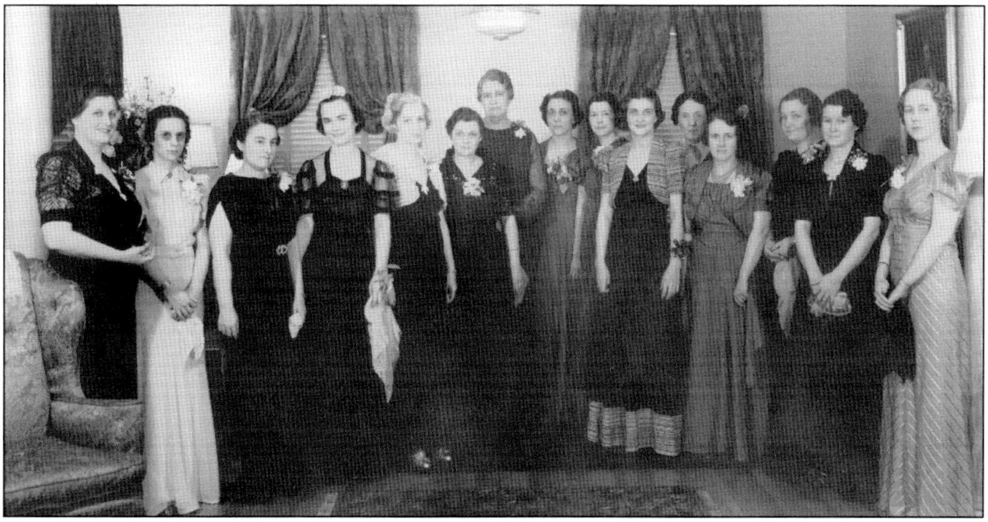

A group of ladies are pictured at a social event around 1938. They include, from left to right, Mrs. Elizabeth Ruble, Mrs. Holmes Sempken, Mrs. Carl Birchfiel, Mrs. Knaffl Walker, Mrs. Robert Hatfield, Mrs. Joe Montgomery Sr., Mrs. Joe Allen, Mrs. George Burchfield, Mrs. Jack Culp, Mrs. H.E. Blankenship, Mrs. Edward Caldwell, Mrs. George Buford, Mrs. Monroe Wells, Mrs. Merle Hall, and Mrs. Joseph Hoyt. Mrs. Knaffl Walker may be best known as Mary Starr, who hosted a successful cooking show on a Knoxville television station for many years. (Courtesy of Becky Blankenship Darrell.)

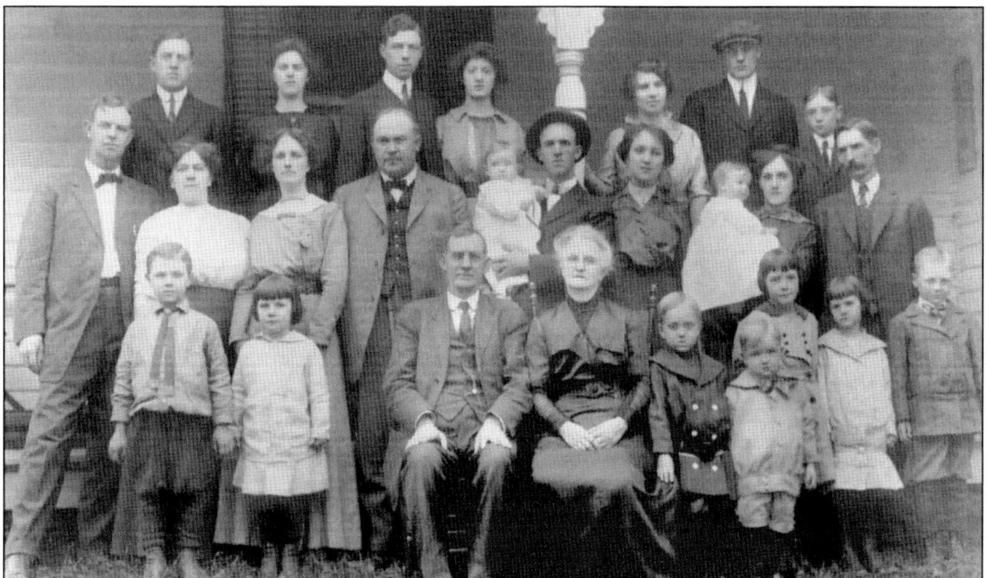

The family of James Newman Badgett and Lucinda McBath Badgett, shown around 1915, includes, from left to right (first row) Max and Dorothy McCulloch, J.N. and Lucinda McBath Badgett, Charles and Douglas Badgett, Aileen, Margaret, and Ray Rowan; (second row) Guy Badgett and wife Clark, Grace Badgett McCulloch and husband Dr. John A. McCulloch, Katherine Badgett with Charles and Millie Badgett, Sam Rowan with mother Nora Badgett Rowan and father Ed Rowan; (third row) John Badgett, Nita Badgett, Rosco Smith and wife Lucille Badgett Smith, Frankie and Lon Badgett, and Victor Rowan. (Courtesy of Kathryn McCulloch Peery.)

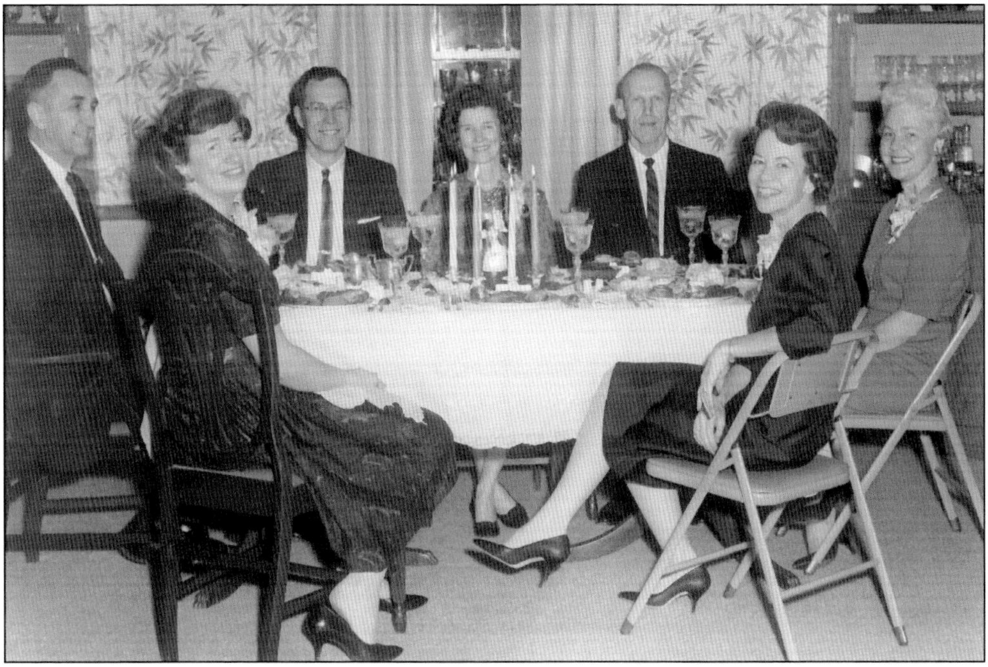

An anniversary party was held for Hugh and Dottie Crawford around 1955. Those attending are, from left to right, Howard Lamon, Margaret Sherer, Hugh and Dottie Crawford, Leslie and Ruth Webb, and Mrs. Howard Lamon. (Courtesy of the Blount County Genealogical and Historical Society, Ned T. Sherer photograph.)

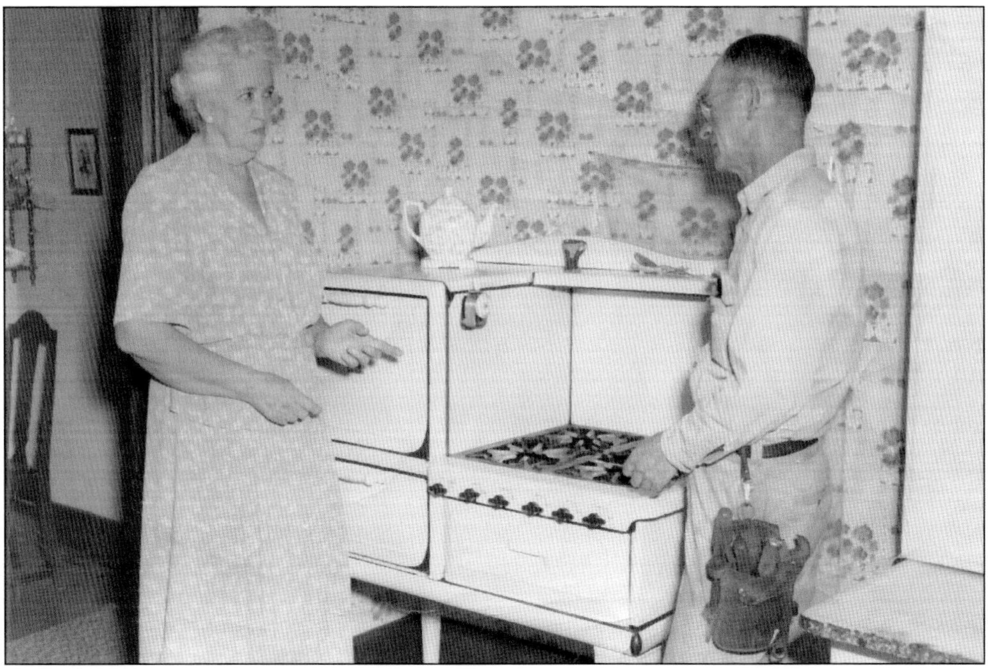

Mrs. Samuel Joseph (Emma) Allen admires her brand-new gas stove installed at the Allen home at 203 Goddard Street with ? Everett around 1940. One of the Maryville newspapers included an article about the stove, reputed to be the first gas stove in Maryville. (Courtesy of Ann Talley Hitch.)

Dr. Granville Dexter LeQuire, a prominent Maryville physician, is pictured with his wife, Eleanor, and their children around 1925. (Courtesy of John and Karen Kenst.)

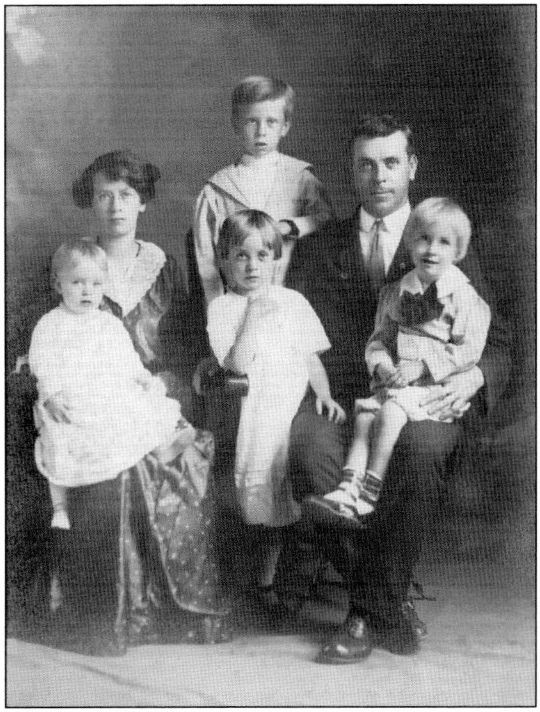

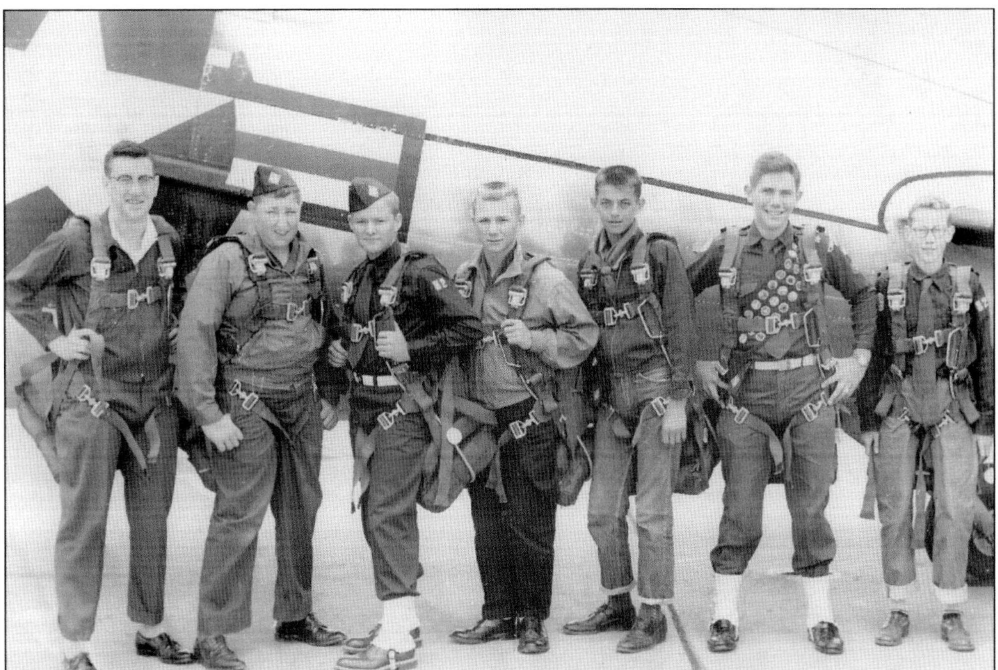

Explorer Post 82 at Broadway United Methodist Church sold the most tickets to a Boy Scout exposition at the Jacobs Building in Knoxville in the mid-1950s. The scoutmaster, Eugene "Vandy" Vanderhyden, a World War II veteran, arranged for the post's first-prize flight on an Air Force C-47. Pictured are, from left to right, Ken Black, Buddy Stinnett, Lowell Ridings, Jerry West, Bob Mull, Ray Henderson, and Richard Lindsey. (Courtesy of Ray Henderson.)

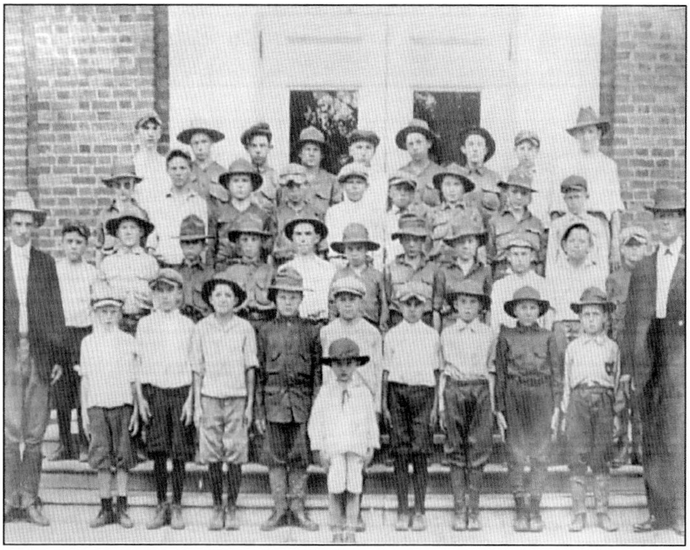

The first Boy Scout troop in Blount County, shown here, was formed at First United Methodist Church. The church continues to sponsor Boy Scout Troop 81 and Cub Scout Pack 81, both members of the Great Smoky Mountain Council of the Boy Scouts of America. Originally chartered in 1916, Troop 81 is the first and oldest Boy Scout troop in Blount County. (Courtesy of the City of Maryville.)

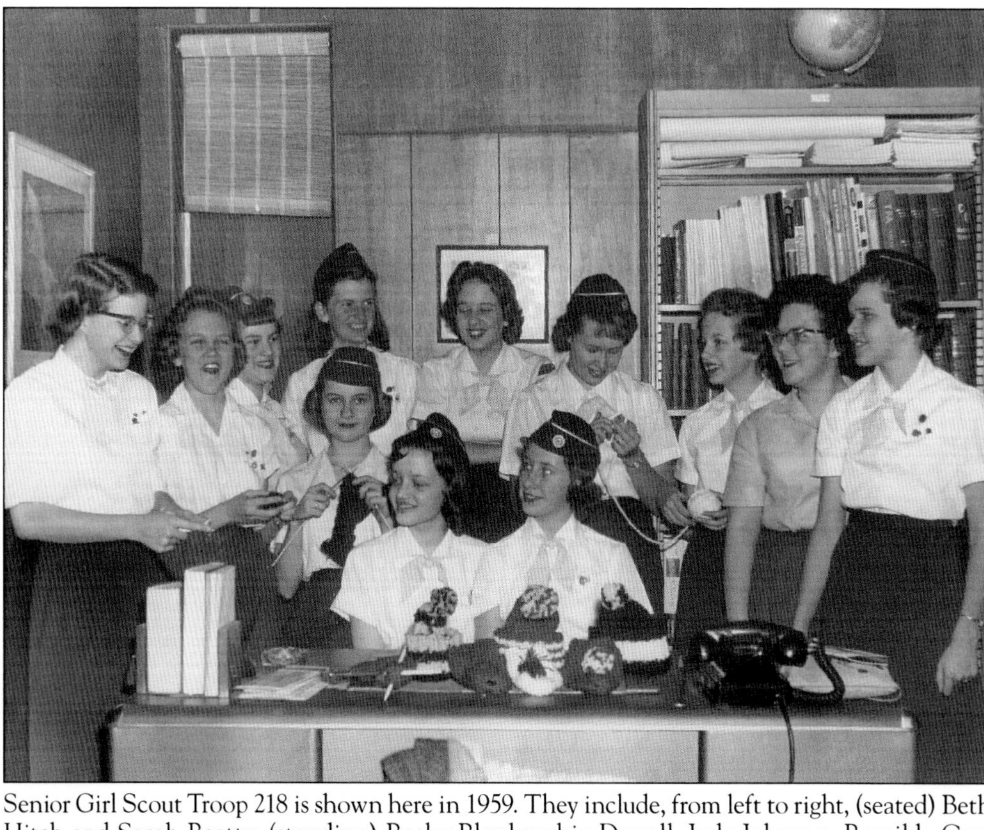

Senior Girl Scout Troop 218 is shown here in 1959. They include, from left to right, (seated) Beth Hitch and Sarah Beatty, (standing) Becky Blankenship Darrell, Judy Johnson, Romilda Cox, Catherine Callaway, Sandy Long, Mary Carroll, Verla Bridgers, Mary Knoll, and Ruth Carroll. (Courtesy of Becky Blankenship Darrell.)

Earlene Baumgardner Duggan, the coauthor's mother, sits inside the office of Earl Blazer Insurance Agency, located in the Bank of Maryville building on the corner of Broadway and Cusick Streets, in 1956. Note the Coca-Cola bottles with the long straws, a favorite refreshment at the time. (Courtesy of David R. Duggan.)

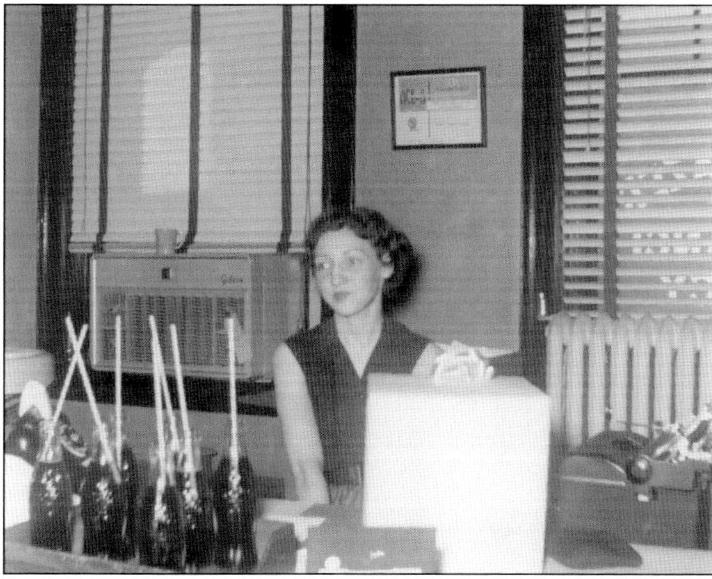

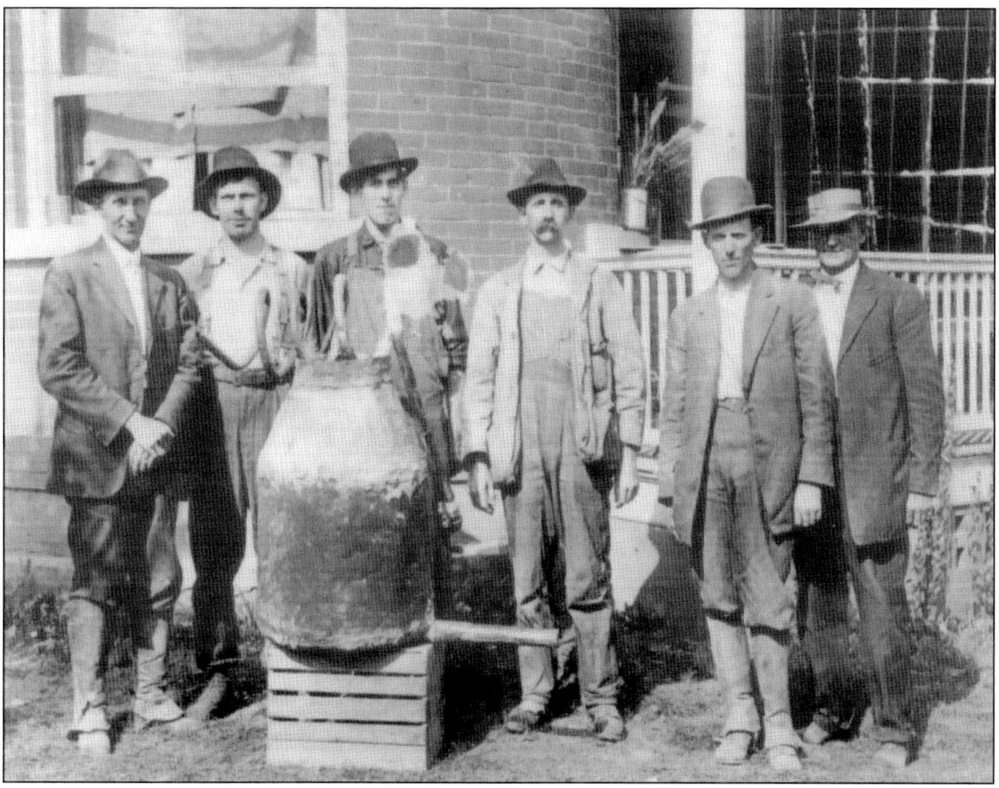

A moonshine still confiscated from Jake Garland is displayed in 1914 in front of the old Blount County Jail in Maryville. From left to right are Bill Dunlap, Jake Garland, Jim Garland, and three unidentified. The Garlands were being held in the jail at the time. (Courtesy of Jimmy Garland.)

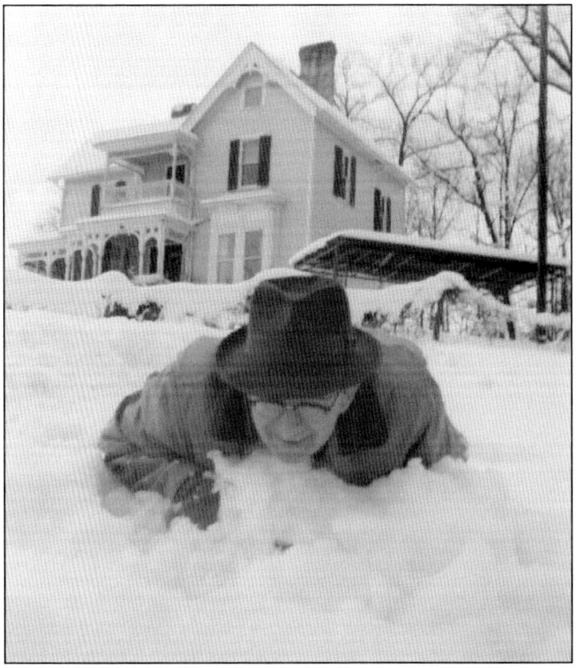

Harry Blankenship, father of Becky Blankenship Darrell, enjoys sliding down snowy Pflanze's Hill in Maryville in 1958. The Pflanze home is pictured in the background. (Courtesy of Becky Blankenship Darrell.)

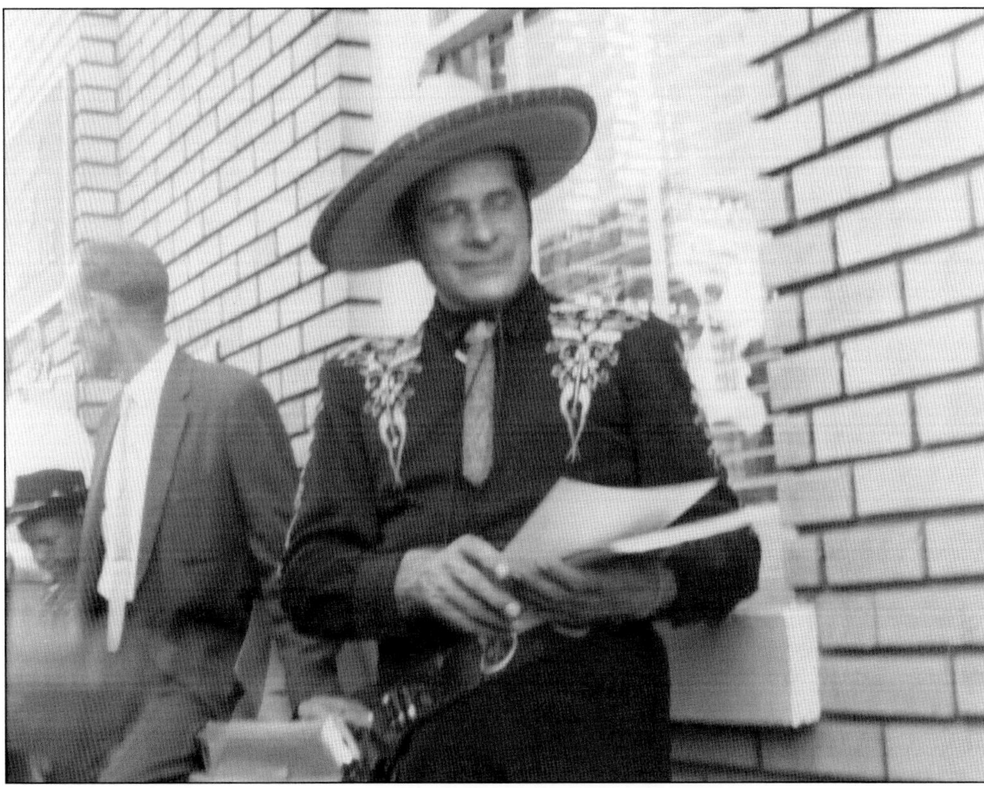

The Cisco Kid was a popular television show that ran from 1950 to 1956 starring Duncan Renaldo in the title role. Renaldo is shown here after riding in the Maryville parade around 1959. (Courtesy of Becky Blankenship Darrell.)

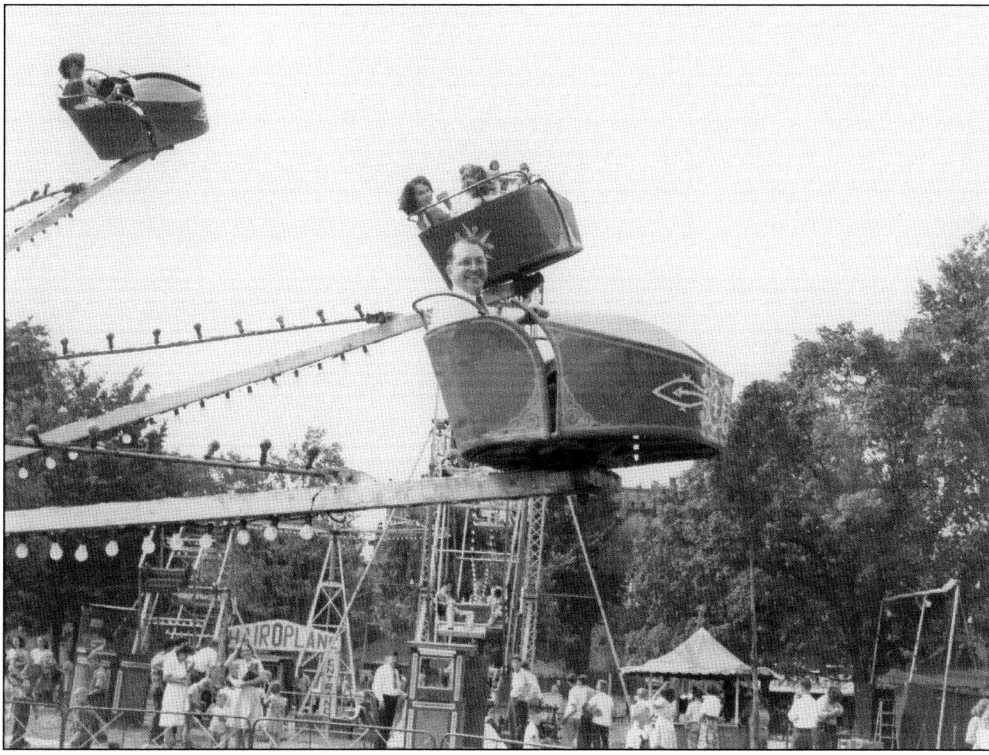

The Blount County Fair, shown above, was held below the Blount County Courthouse in Maryville until land was set aside for that purpose at Five Points. The postcard photograph below shows the midway at the Blount County Fair sponsored by Emerson J. Lones American Legion Post 13 of Maryville. Post 13 purchased and modernized the property for the fairgrounds. That property is now occupied by several businesses and United Way of Blount County. (Above, courtesy of the Blount County Genealogical and Historical Society; below, courtesy of B. Kenneth Cornett.)

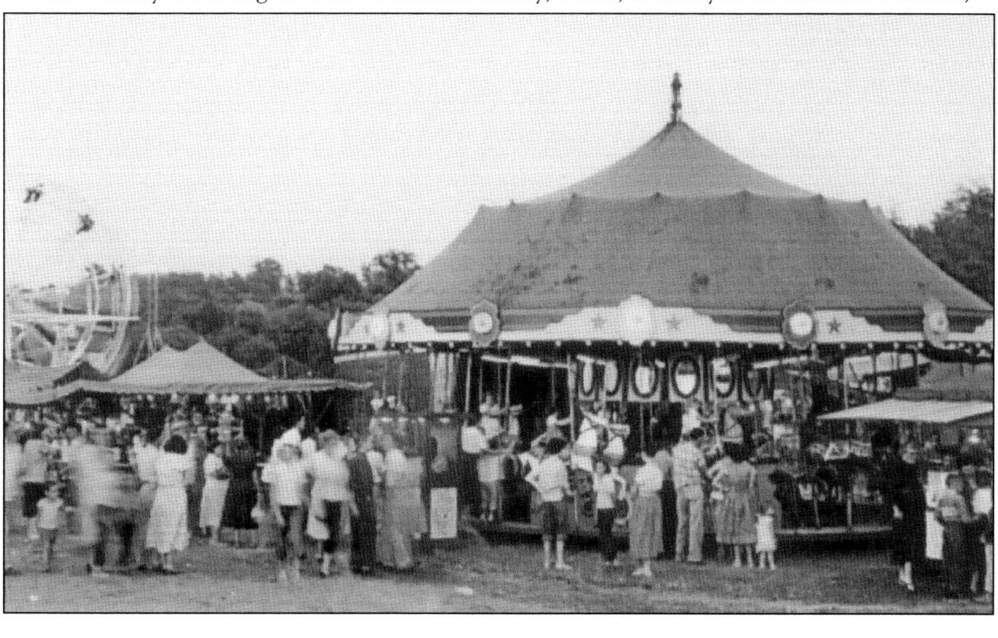

Consistent with our mission to preserve history on a local level, this book was printed in South Carolina on American-made paper and manufactured entirely in the United States. Products carrying the accredited Forest Stewardship Council (FSC) label are printed on 100 percent FSC-certified paper.

MADE IN THE USA